HAIM NAHUM

JUDAIC STUDIES SERIES

Leon J. Weinberger, General Editor

HAIM NAHUM
A Sephardic Chief Rabbi in Politics, 1892–1923

Edited with an Introduction by
Esther Benbassa

Translated from the French by
Miriam Kochan

The University of Alabama Press
Tuscaloosa and London

Translated into English from *Un Grand Rabbin Sépharade en Politique, 1892–1923,* copyright 1990, by Les Presses du Centre National de la Recherche Scientifique (CNRS), Paris, France. Translation rights obtained from the publisher.

English translation copyright © 1995
The University of Alabama Press
Tuscaloosa, Alabama 35487-0380
Manufactured in the United States of America

designed by zig zeigler

∞

The paper on which this book is printed meets the minimum requirements of American National Standard for Information Science-Permanence of Paper for Printed Library Materials, ANSI Z39.48-1984.

The translation was made possible by a grant from the French Ministry of Culture.

Library of Congress Cataloging-in-Publication Data

Nahoum, Haïm, 1872–1960.
   [Grand rabbin sépharade en politique, 1892–1923. English]
   Haim Nahum : a Sephardic chief rabbi in politics, 1892–1923 / edited with an introduction by Esther Benbassa ; translated from the French by Miriam Kochan.
      p.   cm.—(Judaic studies series)
   Includes bibliographical references and index.
   ISBN 0-8173-0729-X
   1. Nahoum, Haïm, 1872–1960—Correspondence. 2. Rabbis—Turkey—Correspondence. 3. Jews—Turkey—History—20th century. 4. Turkey—Politics and government—1909–1918. 5. Jews—Ethiopia—History—20th century.
6. Alliance israélite universelle. 7. Turkey—Ethnic relations. 8. Ethiopia—Ethnic relations. I. Benbassa, Esther. II. Title. III. Title: Sephardic chief rabbi in politics, 1892–1923. IV. Series: Judaic studies series (Unnumbered)
   BM755.N26A4 1995
   296'.092—dc20
   [B]   94-25824

British Library Cataloguing-in-Publication Data available

for J. C.

Do not seek to approach power.
PIRKE AVOT, I, 10

CONTENTS

PREFACE

THIS BOOK WAS COMPLETED at the Department of Jewish History at the Hebrew University of Jerusalem, where I was a Lady Davis postdoctoral fellow and a Yad Hanadiv/Barecha Foundation Fellow in Jewish studies for the academic year 1988–1989. It owes a great deal to the stimulating atmosphere in which I pursued my work and to the discussions I had with several of my Israeli and American colleagues, particularly Michel Abitbol, Israel Bartal, and Joseph Hacker of the Hebrew University and Yaron Tsur of the Open University, Tel Aviv.

Particular mention must also be made of Jean-Christophe Attias of the Centre National de la Recherche Scientifique (CNRS) in Paris and Aron Rodrigue of Stanford University, who both spent the same sabbatical year in Jerusalem and were always available, critical, and even intransigent.

Last, it is a pleasure for me to thank Louis Bazin of the University of Paris III, who has encouraged and supported my projects over a long period.

The first part of this book is based on rich and varied sources. Unfortunately, I cannot acknowledge by name everyone who made it possible for me to gain access to these sources. I hope that they will accept my expression of gratitude to them collectively.

The letters presented in the second part are preserved in manuscript form in the archives of the Alliance Israélite Universelle in Paris. Their use and publication would not have been possible without the help and cooperation of the curator, Georges Weill, as well as that of the librarians, Yvonne and Rose Lévyne.

I thank my editor for the technical support he has so kindly given me and Nicole Mitchell of The University of Alabama Press, who has been extremely kind and helpful. Last but not least, I thank my translator, Miriam Kochan.

I was guided in my choice of letters by a desire to collect the documents that best represented their author's career and the communal context in which Haim Nahum evolved.

The spellings of names and places in the body of the book and in the documents do not strictly follow Haim Nahum's usage; the spellings were slightly adapted to the English usage. The Hebrew and Turkish have been transcribed with the intent to give as clear as possible a phonetic reconstruction for the English reader.

ESTHER BENBASSA

CHRONOLOGY

1835	Creation of the office of chief rabbi of the empire.
1839	Imperial Rescript of Gülhane.
1840	Ritual murder libel at Damascus.
1856	Reform Decree definitively abolishing the *dhimma*.
1858	Mortara affair.
1860	Foundation of the Alliance Israélite Universelle in Paris.
1865	Organic statute granted to the Jewish community.
1873	Birth of Haim Nahum in Magnesia.
1876	Reign of Abdülhamid II begins and constitution promulgated. The constitutional period lasted for less than a year and was replaced by an autocratic regime.
1878	Treaty of Berlin. After its defeat by Russia, the Ottoman Empire was saved by the other European powers but was much reduced.
1882	Restrictions on Jewish immigration into Palestine introduced by the Ottoman authorities.
1893–1897	Nahum studies in Paris.
1897	Foundation of the Zionist Organization. Nahum begins work as a teacher for the Alliance.
1897–1907	Nahum climbs the ladder of communal organization.
1898	Nahum runs as candidate for the position of chief rabbi of Bulgaria.
1899	Nahum marries Sultana Danon.
1900–1904	Nahum teaches at the École Supérieure du Génie et de l'Artillerie.
1901	Foundation of the Hilfsverein der deutschen Juden.
1902	Nahum runs for the post of chief rabbi of Rome.
1903	Kishinev pogroms.
1905	Fresh pogroms in Russia.
1907–1908	Nahum's mission to Ethiopia.
1908	Young Turk revolution and reestablishment of the 1876 constitution (23–24 July). Nahum's election to the position of acting chief rabbi (August). Establishment of a Zionist agency in Istanbul.
1909	Nahum's election to the position of chief rabbi of the Empire

(24 January). Failed counterrevolution in Istanbul (13 April). Sultan Abdülhamid II deposed.

1910   Nahum's pastoral journey to the major Jewish centers in the Empire (from April to July).

1910–1911   Organization of the first communal elections since 1865 with universal suffrage.

1911   Debates against Zionism in the Chamber of Deputies (March and May). Italian troops invade Tripolitania (October). B'nai B'rith lodges set up in Istanbul.

1912–1913   Balkan wars.

1913   Coup d'état by Committee of Union and Progress (January). Abolition of the Red Passport (September).

1914   Outbreak of First World War.

1915   Plan for a separate peace between the Ottoman government and France and England. Nahum serves as intermediary.

1916   Sykes-Picot agreements (May).

1917   Expulsion of Jews from Jaffa. Cambon Declaration (June 4). Balfour Declaration (November 2). The Bolsheviks seize power in Russia. The British occupy Jerusalem.

1918   Nahum's first mission to Europe for the Ottoman government (July). Second mission to Europe, this time for the grand vizier, Izzet pasha (October). Signature of the armistice of Mudros (30 October). Flight of the principal leaders of the Committee of Union and Progress. Zionist coup; establishment of the Jewish National Council (November). Allies enter Istanbul (November). A resistance movement, led by Mustafa Kemal, is organized in Anatolia.

1919   Peace conference opens in Paris (January). Establishment of the Zionist Federation of the East. Nahum's return to Istanbul and the dissolution of the Jewish National Council (March). Treaty of Versailles signed (28 June). Nahum's unofficial mission to France for Mustafa Kemal (end September to beginning December). Communal elections begin.

1920   Official occupation of Istanbul by the Allies. Nahum resigns (30 March). San Remo conference (April). Mandate over Palestine granted to Great Britain. Treaty of Sèvres signed (August).

1921   Nahum goes on two missions for the Alliance to the United States (January and October). London conference opens.

1922   Official ratification of the British mandate over Palestine (July). Nahum goes on another mission to France for the provisional government in Ankara (autumn). Lausanne conference opens (November). Nahum is adviser to the Turkish delegation.

1923   Treaty of Lausanne signed (July). The Allies evacuate Istanbul. Turkish Republic proclaimed. Mustafa Kemal becomes its president (October).

1925   Nahum becomes chief rabbi of Egypt and the Sudan.

1948   Establishment of the State of Israel.

1952   Coup d'état by the clandestine organization of "free officers" led by Nasser. End of the reign of Faruk and the beginning of Nasserite Egypt.

1953   Proclamation of the Egyptian Republic.

1956   Suez campaign. Mass exodus of Jews from Egypt.

1960   Nahum dies in Cairo.

ABBREVIATIONS

AAA	Auswärtiges Amt Akten (Bonn)
AAIU	Archives de l'Alliance Israélite Universelle (Paris)
BAIU	*Bulletin Semestriel de l'Alliance Israélite Universelle* (Paris)
CZA	Central Zionist Archives (Jerusalem)
MAE	Archives du Ministère des Affaires Étrangères (Paris)
PRO	Public Record Office (London)

HAIM NAHUM

INTRODUCTION

IN JANUARY 1892 a young Jew sent a letter in halting French to the Alliance Israélite Universelle in Paris.[1] He was asking the Alliance for a grant that would enable him to study law, diplomacy, and theology in Paris. Haim Nahum, as he was called, had been born into a Sephardi family (that is, into a family of Jews who had originated in Spain) in the Ottoman Empire.[2] He was just eighteen years old when he wrote the letter.[3]

Born in Magnesia, near Smyrna, Haim Nahum had lived in the most abject poverty. As a child, he had been taken by his grandfather to Tiberias in Palestine, where he had learned Arabic and had been introduced to the Talmud at a religious school, or yeshiva. On his return, he attended various institutions, in the process learning French and Turkish.[4] Later on, the governor of his native town financed his studies at the imperial lycée in Smyrna. His sole assets were the certificate granted by the rabbis of Tiberias and the *baccalauréat ès sciences* and *ès lettres* earned at the lycée. He went to Istanbul to study Muslim law and diplomacy but lacked the financial means to pursue his studies, hence his letter to the Alliance. This early letter already contains the germ of the unwritten moral contract that was to link the Alliance, the jewel of emancipated French Jewry, with this unknown but promising young man from Asia Minor. "I will be indebted to you for my material and moral life," he wrote in the first letter reproduced below. He would also owe the Alliance many of the difficulties that he was later to encounter.

West and East

Large numbers of Sephardi Jews settled in the Near East after their expulsion from Spain in 1492. Marranos, or crypto-Jews, also from the Iberian peninsula, swelled the ranks of this Sephardi Jewry in their attempt to escape the Spanish Inquisition. From the end of the seventeenth century, the Italian Jews, or Francos, also of Spanish origin, opted for the lands under Ottoman suzerainty, where they obtained the commercial facilities attached to the system of *capitulations*. Through these, the Ottoman rulers, like other Muslim leaders, granted the nationals of Christian states the right to trade freely while still enjoying the fiscal exemptions and the protection of the diplomatic mission to which they belonged.[5]

For both economic and political reasons, the Ottomans, masters of the Near East, did not oppose the settlement of these European immigrants. Their knowledge, their know-how, and the techniques that they imported from the West contributed to the development of the host cities. The Ottoman Empire thus became a second homeland for these Europeans. In the course of time, towns like Istanbul, Smyrna, Adrianople, Salonika, and Philippopoli came to have large Jewish centers in which Spanish was spoken—a Spanish that would henceforth be studded with words borrowed from the local languages. The Sephardim found native Jews of Byzantine—or Romaniot—origin already settled there, and these were gradually assimilated into the dominant group.

The Ottoman territories continued to be a center of Jewish immigration in the nineteenth and twentieth centuries, when Jews from Eastern Europe, escaping the pogroms and anti-Jewish discrimination, found temporary or permanent refuge there. To this amalgam of Jewish populations were added Aramaic-speaking Kurdish Jews, Arabic-speaking Jews, Ashkenazim, and Karaites (a heterodox Jewish community not recognizing the authority of the oral law). When Haim Nahum was born at the end of the nineteenth century, the Jewish population of the Empire had risen to about 200,000.[6]

The Near Eastern Sephardi communities did not follow the same course as their Western counterparts. Their own history and local circumstances determined otherwise; so that, over the centuries, they became strangers to the West from which they had come. Although the period when they had settled had been marked by an economic and cultural effervescence, the golden age on Muslim soil soon passed. In the nineteenth century, Sephardi Jewry was at the opposite pole from the predominant model then being furnished by Western Jewry, well on the way to achieving its emancipation. The Alliance would be one preeminent means by which Western Jewry imposed its canons on its Eastern brethren. As a result of its work, Sephardi Jewry became the receptacle for those ideologies imported from the Jewish West.

On Islamic territory, Jews, like Christians, were subject to the *dhimma,* an agreement governing relationships between dominant groups, or Muslims, and dominated groups, or non-Muslims.[7] Under this system, which was basically discriminatory, in return for payment of the capitation tax (*jizye*), non-Muslims enjoyed the protection of the authorities and some degree of freedom in everything concerning their internal affairs. This arrangement gave them relative autonomy as an organization, including the choice of leaders, with the blessings of the Muslim authorities.

Despite the autonomy, discrimination was real. It was primarily social in nature. Non-Muslims were differentiated from Muslim society by their dress, hairstyle, choice of name, height of dwelling, and a whole series of other restrictions. These changed with the whim of the regime, and interested parties introduced compromises. But they still remained tolerated groups: a non-Muslim, or *dhimmi,* was regarded as an inferior being, and his relationships with the Muslim environment were marked by inequality. This system also prevailed in the Ottoman Empire, and the Jews there were subject to it.

Nahum was born into this Empire, which had been slowly opening its doors to the West from the end of the eighteenth century. Europe, its presence increasingly felt, was putting pressure on the "sick man" to institute reforms.[8] Economic colonization was accompanied by a program of voluntary westernization, which encompassed an improvement in the status of Christians.[9] The Empire in the nineteenth century thus experienced an important reform movement, the *Tanzimat* (reorganization), aimed at westernization, administrative centralization, modernization of the state machinery, and secularization. The Imperial Rescript of Gülhane (Hatt-i-sherif of Gülhane), promulgated on 3 November 1839, marked its starting point.

On 18 February 1856, the dhimma was definitively abolished. The Reform Decree (Islahat Fermani) promulgated that year introduced equality between Muslims and non-Muslims—at least on paper.[10] In addition it proclaimed the creation of mixed courts (religious and secular) and the admission of all subjects of the Empire, without distinction as to religion, to public offices and to the civil and military schools. It also called on the non-Muslim communities to undertake reforms, including the institution of mixed councils, composed of religious leaders and laymen, to administer secular affairs. Secular forces were actually already present, recruited from among notables holding economic power, who were sometimes in close contact with the Ottoman authorities. These forces now officially entered communal institutions. This institutionalization of the role of laymen became a determining factor in the new political career of these religious groups, institutionally isolated from the central power, particularly in the era of nationalism in the Near East. The Jews profited from the new situation even if the structures advocated were not really operational. Their coreligionists in Western Europe interpreted this change of course in the light of their own experience, as inaugurating the era of the emancipation of the Ottoman Jews. They were anticipating by a great deal.

In 1840, the Damascus affair[11] had already brought Eastern Jewry to European Jewry's attention. Initially it was only a ritual murder libel directed against the Jews. Ritual murder was a frequent accusation at the time when European powers manipulated the different religious groups for political purposes by setting them against one another. Echoes of this affair soon reached Europe, producing a wave of solidarity in the Western Jewish world. Western Jews were shocked to find that the vestiges of a past that had disappeared, as far as they were concerned, before emancipation, continued to exist in the East.[12]

Articles on Ottoman Jewry that appeared in the West stressed its precarious situation. In fact, its image was confused with that of the Muslim East, and the discussion was far from being objective.[13] Condescending in the extreme, the Western viewpoint reflected the perception European Jewry had of its own superiority and that of the West generally, a sense of superiority bolstered by triumphant imperialism in the East. The negative image of Eastern Jewry made it a source of embarrassment, and Jewish philanthropists decided to concern themselves with its fate.[14] Moreover, the Jews of Western Europe, in the process of acculturation, held the same attitude toward the Jews of Eastern Europe, who were no less a source of embarrassment and who also had a negative image.[15]

From now on the Jewish East looked to outstretched Western hands for support. Suffering from endemic unemployment and poverty, it no longer had the necessary dynamism, and the state, at the height of its disintegration, could scarcely come to its aid. The local Jewish bourgeoisie, which also needed support from outside the Empire in order to consolidate its political and economic position, lacked adequate infrastructures to remedy the situation: apart from the classic charitable work, its means of action were limited. Everyone hoped and waited for salvation from the West.[16] The same was true of Haim Nahum.

Circumstances in the late nineteenth century were therefore particularly favorable for the spread of Western culture and practice. The westernization process would have many vicissitudes, both in the Empire and within its Jewish communities.

The foundation of the Alliance in Paris in 1860 institutionalized solidarity in the Jewish world on an international scale. It was connected with the repercussions of the Damascus affair and then, in 1858, with the Mortara affair in Italy, which involved the secret baptism of a Jewish child and the Church's refusal to return him to his parents. Other Jewish organizations of the same type were created in its wake. The Alliance, established by liberals nourished on the ideas of the French Revolution, undertook to defend the rights of persecuted Jews and to work for their emancipation.[17] It naturally took the idealized emancipation of French Jewry (1790–91) as its model and adopted the speeches of its protagonists in the century of the Enlightenment, which it applied to Jewry in Muslim countries. Because the idea of "regeneration," which opened the door to emancipation, presupposed schooling and education, the Alliance covered the Mediterranean basin with a sizable network of schools for boys and girls, including apprenticeship schemes and agricultural schools. The Ottoman Empire was the favorite area for its activities, especially as the weakened state gave this campaign free rein.[18] The Alliance's educational outposts were dedicated to the education of the poor and, in principle, applied the program of French primary schools plus instruction in Jewish subjects and local languages.

At the end of the nineteenth century, the Alliance thus set Sephardi Jewry on the road to westernization, or rather Frenchification. The Alliance contributed to the formation of a French-speaking middle bourgeoisie that promoted new values and forced Ottoman Jewry to make up lost ground in an economic market dominated by Greeks and Armenians. "Productiviza-tion" through apprenticeship to modern trades also figured in the program of "regeneration."[19] Through these attempts—which were the only ones aimed at creating favorable conditions for realizing its plans—the Alliance in a way appropriated some of the prerogatives of the modern European na-tion-state and simultaneously those of the anemic communal organizations. Its ambition matched French Jewry's high opinion of itself and confidence in its chances of "victory."

If the success of the Alliance was noteworthy, it was not unqualified. The Alliance could not achieve its gains without a struggle, because conservative groups placed no shortage of obstacles in its way. It relied primarily on its ability to mobilize men for its cause and negotiated above all with local notables, who furnished part of the communal funds and guaranteed the institution locally. Those among the locals who were the most open to progressive ideas became the architects of this modernization from the top, which was synonymous in the event with westernization. In the field, the teachers, mostly born in the Jewish East, which the Alliance wanted to "regenerate," but educated in the West in its own institutions, were in their turn transformed into emissaries of its ideology.[20]

When he appealed to the Alliance, Haim Nahum did not yet know that he was going to join the battalions of the French "civilizing mission" and that he would in the end become its key man in the East and its favorite inter-mediary. A typical representative of a new generation of Jews who had grown up in a transition period for Ottoman Jewry, caught between prevail-ing tradition and a faltering modernity, he was the product of the era of reforms that enabled Jews to gain access to governmental schools. Even if he was not educated in the Alliance schools, as were a fair number of contem-poraries in his circumstances, Nahum corresponded to the model of the "regenerated" Ottoman Jew glorified by the Alliance.

A Splendid Rise to Power

Between 1893 and 1897, Haim Nahum pursued his studies at the rabbinical seminary of Paris. This institution was one of a line of seminaries founded by Western Jewry in the era of emancipation, in defiance of opposition from Jewish orthodoxy. These establishments set out to dispense both secular and religious teaching with the aim of creating a new type of rabbi open to the progress that was taking place around him. Haim Nahum did receive a financial grant from the Alliance. The latter subsidized the studies of a number of young people from Turkey and Tunisia at the Paris seminary. When they returned, they were bound to serve as rabbis in their native communities. The plan was gradually to substitute progressive rabbis for conservative scholars, insofar as the former could in time support the work of the Alliance locally in its struggle against the old guard, which opposed the introduction of a European, and therefore secular, type of educational network, competing with the traditional schools.

In 1895, two years before he was ordained as a rabbi,[21] Nahum obtained the diploma of the religious sciences section of the École Pratique des Hautes Études and then, the following year, the diploma of the École Spéciale des Langues Orientales Vivantes, in written Arabic and Persian.[22] At the Collège de France, he attended courses given by the great orientalist scholars and at one time even thought of writing a thesis. This cultural indoctrination, which combined secular and religious knowledge, went far beyond that of an ordinary rabbi, particularly in the East; it was rare to find a rabbi in the East who spoke the language of the country. His stay in Paris, where he mixed in the circles of the Young Turks in exile, also enabled him to build up a fund of relationships that he would be able to use to good advantage when he returned to Istanbul.[23]

For an ambitious young man of modest origins, the Empire at that time offered no great possibilities. At the end of the nineteenth century, one opening for someone who wanted to improve his position and who identified with the values propounded by the West was to become a teacher on behalf of the Alliance. As for the rabbinate, the traditional profession of those who possessed some learning, it hardly permitted a rise in the social scale. When he later returned to Istanbul, Nahum worked as both rabbi and teacher at the same time. The friction between East and West, a characteristic of his native milieu, seemed also evident in Nahum the man. Perhaps in another place he would have chosen other opportunities. After all, he had begun by studying law and diplomacy. At first he settled for temporary solutions. The eventual integration of the Jews into an empire in the process of evolving might open new perspectives. He himself seemed to think so. The provisional boundaries that Nahum initially mapped out for himself demarcated a context that he would later use all his ingenuity to break away from. He neglected no opportunity to do so.

His life in the active service of the Alliance began in 1897. He was engaged by it to assist Abraham Danon—his future father-in-law—at the rabbinical seminary of Istanbul, which the Alliance subsidized and which pursued the same aim as similar institutions in the West. In the view of the Alliance, the modernization of the oriental communities depended on the education of a new generation of rabbis. Who better suited to the task of teaching in such an establishment than Haim Nahum, himself an example of the modern rabbi?

Even while he was supplementing his work at the seminary by teaching in the two Alliance schools, Nahum was barely satisfied with his position; he was aiming higher. From the moment he arrived, he engaged in an intense social activity, using the opportunities afforded by the Alliance and seeking to gain entry to circles that were likely to help him locally. The Alliance, a peripheral force, gathered together notables who were dissatisfied with the communal regime or excluded from it. This progressive sector—progressive at least by comparison with the existing leadership—was waiting for an opportune moment to seize communal power. These circles liked his Western style of preaching and opened to him the doors of the residential districts where it lived.

While working zealously for the Alliance cause, Nahum formed support and propaganda committees in the suburbs of Istanbul on behalf of the rabbinic seminary that could educate the new men that the oriental Jews needed. At the same time he spread the message to the synagogues through his students. He was set on convincing notables open to the Alliance's ideology that the time had come to put an enlightened man at the head of Ottoman Jewry. In fact, promotion of the seminary was mixed up with his own promotion, and through the committees, he made his own allies.

Very early on he had set his heart on the chief rabbinate of the Ottoman Empire, the supreme position in Sephardi Jewry and the greatest promotion possible for a Jew in Islamic lands; he was already mentioning it two years after his arrival in Istanbul.[24] The Alliance, which had every interest in placing one of its own in this position, must have given him assurances in the matter. Would religious responsibilities be enough for someone who had cherished the dream—impossible for an Ottoman Jew—of succeeding in politics or in the state? Having decided to take an indirect route, he came to politics by way of religion.

Meanwhile he tried to solve the Alliance's administrative problems with the Ottoman bureaucracy. Knowing the language of the country and above all its customs, he used every subterfuge to conquer the administration's lethargy. In this way he served his apprenticeship in the role of mediator, which he played throughout his career in the Empire. He gradually became the Alliance's intermediary with the Ottomans and with the community. It was a hard task, given that the Paris Alliance was not in good odor with the conservative community leaders and also given that the Ottomans were suspicious of foreign organizations. In addition, many of the Alliance schools operated without permission and therefore illegally.

Nahum continued to work out carefully the various stages of his ascent. Bachelors were not highly regarded in the circles in which he moved. In 1899, with the Alliance's consent, he married the daughter of the director of the rabbinical seminary, Sultana Danon. His wife, also one of the Alliance's teachers, came from a progressive background. Her father, Abraham Danon, was connected with the Alliance, had also been active in Haskalah (the Jewish Enlightenment) circles in Adrianople, and had achieved distinction as a scholar and orientalist. In 1891 he was involved in founding the rabbinical seminary in Adrianople, later transferred to Istanbul, where Nahum taught. It was a marriage "in the family" and would produce two children.

Even if the Alliance was omnipresent in his life, Haim Nahum did not for that reason disdain contact with the chief rabbinate, which was increasingly coming under fire from the reformist notables. This he did to such good purpose that only a year after his appointment as teacher at the seminary he had found a place in the hierarchy of the chief rabbinate administration. The Alliance was delighted:[25] its protégé had penetrated the inner circle and could advance the Alliance's cause. He manipulated the *kaymakam* (locum tenes, acting chief rabbi) of the day, Moshe Halévi (1873–1908), whom he would have liked to win over, especially as Halévi was well regarded at the palace and could be dangerous if he wanted. But Nahum was already aware of the paralysis and corruption of the communal system, which made effective action impossible.

He was also opening paths beyond Istanbul Jewish society. In 1898, with the full paternal blessing of Jacques Bigart, secretary-general of the Alliance (1892–1934), he ran for the office of chief rabbi of Bulgaria. This position could serve as a springboard to the chief rabbinate of the Empire, which he still coveted. He failed but tried again in 1902, this time for Rome. Unfortunately for Nahum, a rabbi with nationalist leanings succeeded on this occasion. Nor had the report sent by the Istanbul rabbinate been favorable to Nahum. His rise was obviously not in everyone's interest.

On the other hand, Nahum had many assets that would win him admission to Turkish circles. Few Jews spoke Turkish at that time, which greatly limited the possibilities of contact with the surrounding society. The linguistic barrier did not create a total gulf but did segregate the two religious groups.

At the beginning of the century, an influential introduction secured him a position as French teacher at the École Supérieure du Génie et de l'Artillerie. In this seedbed of progressive military men, which contained some of the future architects of the 1908 revolution, he forged useful contacts.[26] When the time came, he would be able to turn them to good account.[27] Possibly he felt close to the Young Turks on the strength of his own inclinations. They were the men who wanted to save their country from decline and to put it on a par with modern nations. The Young Turks were also influenced by trends in Western thought. In fact, after the revolution, the Alliance itself emphasized certain convergences between its own views and those of the new masters of the Empire. Nahum had looked ahead and had not been wrong.

He continued to neglect no opportunity that could contribute to his ascent. In the same period, he tried to obtain a position in the sultan's private library. In the community he sought to make himself acceptable both to progressive circles and to the ruling group. He did the same in Turkish circles and cultivated his contacts with influential foreign personalities. As a result of these efforts he came within a hair's breadth of being appointed deputy to the locum tenens.

Even though he left nothing to chance, Nahum did not manage to avoid the internal quarrels of the community as he became increasingly involved in its affairs. His relationship with the ruling clan deteriorated. The Alliance decided to withdraw him until better times and in 1907 entrusted him with a mission to the Falashas, the Jews of Ethiopia, in order to ascertain their possible adherence to Judaism and the educative action that should be undertaken for their benefit.

His conclusions ran counter to those of a parallel mission investigating the Falashas at the same time and had repercussions.[28] The Zionists exploited the affair in their efforts to thwart the Alliance. For Nahum himself, the mission had unfavorable consequences, especially when his report was published after his accession to power. Identified with the Alliance, he became the favorite target of its opponents in the Jewish world.

The Revolution, the Alliance, and Haim Nahum

The mission to Abyssinia was for Nahum only a temporary diversion from communal activities. The Young Turk revolution propelled him to the forefront of the political scene of the Jewish community.

On 23–24 July 1908, a bloodless coup d'état brought to power the Young Turks, who opposed the despotic regime of Abdülhamid II (he was sultan during the years 1876–1909). Hoping to turn the Empire into a modern, centralized state, they reestablished the constitution of 1876. The men of the former regime, including the sultan, remained in commanding positions. The changeover in the state machine and in the administration occurred only gradually.

From the start, the Jewish press in the Empire hailed the event in exaggerated terms. There was some measure of enthusiasm among the local populations, including the Jews. They were docile, accustomed to adapting themselves to successive regimes. The Jewish community was able to make the most of the clandestine participation by some of its members in the activities of the Young Turks, though the extent of this participation has often been exaggerated.[29]

The reformist Jewish notables, connected with the Alliance, took advantage of the new situation to call for a reorganization of the structure of their communities. Change was in the air. After Istanbul, Jerusalem, Damascus, Saida, and other communities demanded reforms. Most of the chief rabbis in office had compromised themselves with the old regime. Now was the chance to get rid of them and their entourages. The plans of these notables, however, were in no way revolutionary. On the model of the Young Turks (who were themselves no more revolutionary), they asked only that various dormant communal procedures be resumed.

Power had hitherto been concentrated in the hands of a single man and his close entourage. The autocracy of the locum tenens, Moshe Halévi, had some similarity to the absolutist regime in force. The councils that should have supported him in the exercise of his duties were not used. Increasingly vehement criticism had already been spreading from abroad before the revolution.[30] In fact, the communal leader's intimacy with the palace made his prospective local opponents, forced to stay silent, fear the worst. Nahum had been able to get well out of it at the time, fearing to compromise himself with the ruling clique, nicknamed the *banda preta,* the "black band," in Judeo-Spanish. This strategy would have advantages for him after the revolution.

Fortune now favored the Alliance. Some Jews active in the ranks of the Young Turks had attended its schools, as had some of the future Jewish deputies in the constitutional period. In addition, certain Young Turk Muslim leaders had had contact with the Alliance as pupils or as teachers in its schools.[31] For the time being, the new authorities did not regard the Alliance as suspect. They acknowledged the merits of its work and took them into account.[32] The Alliance, for its part, made much of the role it had played in educating a younger generation in gratitude and devotion to the Empire.

The Alliancist notables (those connected with the Alliance Israélite Universelle) now had the opportunity to take the conduct of the community in hand. They thus moved from the periphery to the center of power, taking advantage of the volatile situation of the Jewish population. The dispute between conservatives and reformists was long-standing. The reformists reckoned to profit from the new situation to take revenge. This being so, once they were in power, they would be no less "conservative" than their predecessors. Such a story is not uncommon.

The dismissal and replacement of the current acting chief rabbi were on the agenda. In the end, he would be forced to hand in his resignation, ostensibly because of his great age. The laymen who now held power within the community then intended to proceed with the appointment of the future chief rabbi without delay.

His image as a young, progressive rabbi and man of action more versed in the temporal than the spiritual made Haim Nahum the natural candidate of the great Jewish bourgeoisie. On the morrow of the revolution it needed a leader capable of facing up to the new situation. His connections with the new cadres of the regime also reassured the more affluent classes, which worried about the change and its possible political and economic repercussions. As for the notables who wanted to seize power, they were not experienced politicians. Occupying themselves with communal affairs in their spare time like dilettantes, they could not do without a leader who would be loyal to them. By elevating him to power, they were also buying his loyalty.

Described as small, stocky, and shortsighted, with a slight paunch, Nahum was nonetheless an attractive man, possessed of a vast culture, at the meeting point of East and West.[33] His stay in Europe and his close links with the Alliance had made him familiar with the West, which offered both a model and an unattainable goal of the more affluent classes of Ottoman Jewry. He knew not only the ideal of the Jews in the East, however, but also, and very intimately, the realities of French Jewry. He particularly admired Zadoc Kahn (1839–1905), chief rabbi of France, with whom he had become acquainted in Paris; Kahn was a reference point in that changing Jewish world. But Nahum was not a man who would merely import a strictly European model into Islamic territory. His experience of oriental Jewry kept him from slavish imitation. Although Western influence would to no small extent mark his future choices concerning the community in his charge, he knew the Empire and its leaders well enough. Precisely this knowledge qualified him above anyone else to assume the difficult office of chief rabbi (*haham başi*). He was indisputably the man for the situation.[34] He was in Paris in the summer of 1908, after returning from his mission in Abyssinia, when his friends in the Ottoman capital summoned him. Thus, a week after the revolution, he prepared to return to Istanbul.[35]

The Alliance, however, which had hitherto supported him, drew back and voiced its preference for his father-in-law, Abraham Danon, who was more unobtrusive and had no political affiliations.[36] Its concern about the excesses in the capital were making it more cautious than ever, and it preferred not to expose its protégé to a political about-face, something always to be feared.

Despite the Alliance, Nahum was elected acting chief rabbi in mid-August. Overtaken by local forces, the Alliance bowed to the inevitable.[37] Time would pass, however, before it positioned itself squarely at its protégé's side.[38] In contrast, Nahum quickly received the backing of the Young Turks. In fact the Alliance was not at first able to estimate the extent to which its local sympathizers wanted changes. It may not have understood their resolve to take power and may thereby have made an error of judgment. Distance from the center of events naturally accentuated remoteness from local dynamics.

The reformist notables, like Nahum himself, had associated themselves with the Alliance because it constituted a new, alternative force, with plans that were also their own. It represented the only way forward at that period. Haim Nahum had no choice: what else could he rely on to succeed?

Nahum's definitive election to the position of chief rabbi had still to be secured. Much remained to be done because the conservative camp was mobilizing against him within the community. The conflicts in provincial communities grew sharper. Groups opposed to the Alliance were afraid that it would monopolize communal leadership if its candidate were definitively elected. They joined forces to avert this outcome. Long-standing conflicts focused on the person of Nahum. His image did not suit all the groups.

The success of the Alliance and of Nahum also signified the victory of the French over the German camp. The Hilfsverein der deutschen Juden, founded by German Jews in 1901, was engaged in work paralleling that of the Alliance in the East on a smaller scale. Insofar as the Hilfsverein set out to help expand German influence and trade by spreading German language and culture, it was disturbed by the Alliance's recent breakthrough. The Zionists, for their part, fought the Alliance because of its hostility toward them. For the good of the cause, they therefore aligned themselves with the Hilfsverein and the orthodox Jews. In 1908, Jerusalem became an important pocket of opposition. The dismissal of the local locum tenens, as a result of pressure from the "modernists," fanned the conflicts. The focus of activity then switched to Istanbul, seat of the chief rabbinate, which soon became the center of the struggles between the various pressure groups occupying the forefront of the communal scene. The day after the Young Turk revolution, the Zionists established themselves locally by setting up a branch in Istanbul. They were counting on the new Ottoman leaders to promote the Palestine question. At the same time they also initiated activities inside the communities to reach their objectives. They thus confused the whole political chessboard.

All the opposing groups sought support in Europe. The representatives of the foreign powers in Istanbul also took a hand. Not everyone wanted to see a definitive victory for Nahum and therefore for the Alliance and the French language. Germany intervened by supporting groups that could obstruct the French camp's advance, and a German front came into being.[39] The Germany-Hilfsverein-Zionist coalition, which haunted the Alliance, its representatives, and the Quai d'Orsay for a long time was no myth. It would try to bar Nahum's path.

Supporters of the old communal regime, the rabbis, and the whole movement supported by European orthodox circles, with a long history of hostility to the Alliance, its ideology, and its achievements behind it, rallied to the German camp. In the event, it was a resumption of the war between "old" and "new" in an ultimate struggle for power. From this point of view, Nahum's election and the Alliancists' takeover of control of the communities threatened to mark the end of an era.

The relative political freedom after the Young Turk revolution promoted this confusion. In the Empire, demands were heard from all sides, and the different communal movements took advantage of the situation to settle their scores. Muzzled until then by the strict regime of Abdülhamid II, nicknamed the Red Sultan, individuals and groups swung into action. A period of open politicization now began. At the same time, the preponderance of the political over the religious dimension, which characterized

Nahum's duties and activities throughout his rabbinate, was taking shape. It is true that a chief rabbi could no longer confine himself to spiritual functions in such a context, sheltered from the tumults of a country and a society in process of change. Nevertheless one might ask whether this was the expression of a personal characteristic or the impact of specific circumstances conducive to politicization. Some of his opponents even went so far as to ask to what extent the appointment of a chief rabbi, administrator of Ottoman Jewry, was justified in the new constitutional era, since the Jews were now guaranteed representation in the Chamber, through its deputies.[40] They would have preferred the election of a chief rabbi who would be the trustee of the moral and religious interests of all the Jewish communities in the Empire.

Whatever the case, despite his initial reticence to proclaim his personal preferences, Nahum was the real leader of the local Alliancists, as distinct from the Alliance proper. As such, he belonged to a movement that acted as a real pressure group in this period of unrest. In the struggle for power, in which he was directly involved, Nahum formulated strategy but still lacked experience. The various Jewish pressure groups publicly took up positions supporting their candidates. The Jewish newspapers in the capital and the provinces, the communal notables, and the various associations entered the fray. The European Jewish press joined in.[41] As a sign of protest, some provincial communities, although they were obliged to send their delegates to take part in the elections, refused to comply.

In January 1909, Nahum won the election against his father-in-law and caused a split within his own family. The French Jewish press hailed the event as the victory of a liberalism similar to the liberalism of the French chief rabbinate.[42] The Alliance did likewise.[43] Nahum was now regarded as the champion of French-style liberalism. The Alliance had won. Its sympathizers held the reins of power, had seats on secular and mixed authorities,[44] and, above all, were the masters of the executive. Its protégé had arrived at the center of power. The Alliance counted on his loyalty and knew that he would watch over its work.

Haim Nahum was the first and last chief rabbi of the Empire[45] to be duly elected after the Jewish community had been granted an organic statute (*Hahamhane Nizamnamesi*) in 1865, which officially organized the Jewish minority into a religious group and determined its procedures.[46] This statute, somewhat ambiguously worded, had not really been applied. Nahum's predecessor, for example, had been able to hold office as locum tenens for thirty-five years without holding an election for a titular chief rabbi, although the statute required such an election. Nor had the population been called to the ballot boxes to elect the lay members of the Councils, since the sole elections of this type dated from 1865.

The statute was no less imprecise about the powers of the chief rabbi of the Empire. He was, in principle, the head of all the Jews of the Empire and the executive agent of the Ottoman government.[47] He led the community in conjunction with Councils composed of laymen and rabbis. But in fact, he was dependent on the government, which had to endorse his election as well as that of the lay members of the Councils. This situation was obviously not favorable to large-scale innovating initiatives.

The situation was somewhat chaotic when Nahum attained this supreme position. He was now the head of more than 250,000 Jews,[48] but the victory of the "new" remained precarious, partly because it had been won on ground undermined by past quarrels and present divisiveness and partly because of the political instability of the country. Nahum's position seemed very uncertain.

The Alliance had not been wrong to draw back at the last moment before Nahum's election and to opt for his father-in-law. In fact, the Alliance had hesitated to move into the center of power with all the risks involved in the current context. Moreover it had not foreseen the formidable rise of Zionism in the Empire's communities and had misinterpreted the communal situation by seeing it as no more than the classic dichotomy between conservatives and reformers.

The Rise of Zionism

The Zionist movement, the new active participant, with its logistics (newspapers, associations) and by its strategy as an opposition party, upset the political ideas hitherto accepted in the communities. By the purchase of newspapers, the creation of structures for leisure and social activity, by professional militancy, by the dispatch of senior leaders to the area, by infiltrating communal institutions, it gradually won over the various levels of local Jewish society.

The Alliance's anti-Zionism took its place in the more general framework of the alternatives open to a large part of Western Jewry and its institutions at that period.[49] The society's disappointments in Bulgaria,[50] an important center of Zionist agitation, had only hardened its stand; at the beginning of the century the Zionists had forced most of its schools there to close. The Alliance was afraid that the movement would spread to the large centers of the Empire, its favorite place for pursuing its activities. Nonetheless it had neither the means nor the inclination to disseminate an ideology capable of mobilizing the masses on a large scale. It therefore chose to take up a position above the fray, preferring as usual to deal with the notables and particularly with their legal leader, Haim Nahum.

The only legally permissible political area for the Ottoman Jew was his community. It was a limited area, subject to an oligarchical operation, and offered no great possibilities of access to power. Those who controlled it guarded it jealously. Possession of communal power generally confirmed the social ascent of the Jewish notable. The bitterness of the power struggle inside the communities must be understood in this context. Nor did these notables understand politics in the modern sense. Recruited from merchant or banking circles, from the liberal professions or from among the few Jewish high officials, they had no inclination to be militants. As he owed them his victory, Nahum was obliged to serve their interests and to accustom himself to their incompetence. In reality, this oligarchy had only taken the place of its predecessor by a sort of bloodless coup d'état, comparable to that of the Young Turks. In addition, precisely because of the communal system, it was cut off from the masses.

In this context, Nahum and his friends, devoid of ideological tools, professional militants, or propaganda machine, were incapable of competing with Zionist populism and were doomed to be outflanked by Zionism sooner or later.

The Alliance counted on Nahum to lead a campaign at the highest level to stem the rising tide of Zionism. Through its secretary it suggested bribing Ottoman parliamentarians to provoke an anti-Zionist debate in the Chamber of Deputies.[51] Faced with this dangerous initiative, which could ultimately turn against Ottoman Jewry, Nahum chose to let things drag on. In the early days, he preferred less radical solutions; mobilizing the youth and certain categories of Jews around the Alliance he saw as an alternative to grappling with the Zionists. But his activities in this direction were unsuccessful.

In fact, debates against Zionism did take place in the Chamber in March and May 1911, led by the opponents of the Committee of Union and Progress (the Young Turk party in power) and by Arab deputies. From 1912, they fueled an anti-Jewish campaign in part of the press and the population.[52] The course of these debates did not correspond to the scenario suggested by the secretary of the Alliance, and there is nothing to prove that Nahum had instigated them.

The Zionists took advantage of the internal conflicts that preceded and followed Haim Nahum's election to form themselves into an opposition party to the chief rabbi, the oligarchy, and the Alliance.[53] The Alliance's growing intransigence helped to harden its opponents' attitude both to itself and to Nahum. A year after his election, Nahum had to face a divided community: the Zionists made every initiative or attempt at reform on his part a pretext for a fresh burst of propaganda.

The chief rabbi and his friends succeeded neither in restructuring the institutions nor in achieving the projected reforms. The chief rabbinate's financial difficulties, the opposition's maneuvers, and the absence of logistical support from the Alliance[54] were mainly responsible for this failure. As a result the communal institutions became less and less stable and the activities that depended on them were paralyzed.

At the end of 1910, in an attempt to rid himself of the last conservative lay elements sitting on the general council, the chief rabbi then tried to organize genuine elections on the basis of universal suffrage. To make sure that his Alliancist friends were heavily represented, he provided for a division into electoral constituencies unfavorable to districts of working-class population, increasingly won over to Zionism.[55] This was not enough, however, to prevent Zionist infiltration, and this period became the prelude to a real crisis.

In fact, cohabitation with the Zionists did not enter into the plans of the notables connected with Nahum, particularly as nothing had prepared them to exercise any division of power. They had no experience of democracy, either inside or outside the community. Nor did the organic statute provide for a pluralist leadership, with a chief rabbi and an executive holding different views. Previous chief rabbis were more used to ruling as absolute masters, supported by an entourage sharing the same aims. This time the opposition was organized. To prevent Nahum's election, and acting in conjunction with the Hilfsverein and the rabbis, the Zionists imported the German model into Istanbul, as they had already done in Jerusalem in 1908. The Zionist camp was also strengthened by the lodges of B'nai B'rith (a Jewish organization, structured into lodges and chapters on the model of the Masonic orders, founded in the United States in 1843 and established locally in 1911). Their founders were also German. In addition, the Zionists took advantage of the ethnic divisions between Sephardim and Ashkenazim to form an alliance with the latter, who were excluded from communal institutions.

This, then, was open war, in which the community was sacrificed on the altar of power. Neither the support that Haim Nahum received from the Ottoman authorities nor his threats to resign succeeded in stemming the Zionists' infiltration into the official body of the community, where they sat intermittently until the eve of war.

The local activists were not primarily concerned with the question of the national home in Palestine. Rather they sought to modify, for the benefit of the malcontents, the initial plans of the World Zionist Organization, which aimed to expand local Zionism. Although the boundary between official Zionism and local nationalism intermingled with Zionism became confused, Nahum remained the principal target.

The Zionist leaders were themselves divided and ambivalent on the policy to follow concerning Nahum. On the one hand, he was popular with part of the population and was in no danger of being unseated for a long time; moreover, he could still serve as an intermediary with the Ottoman authorities. On the other hand, he had entrée into high places and could be dangerous if he wished. His position made it impossible to circumvent him and as a result was a genuine obstacle to the local development of the movement. The president of the Zionist Organization therefore tried to curb the zeal of its militants in Istanbul.[56]

Nahum's own position was also ambiguous. Zionist ideology ran counter to his own social plans. His ideas were similar to those of the Alliance and other European Jewish leaders and institutions that resolutely supported integration and the abandonment of Jewish particularism—at least until the Balfour Declaration (1917), in which the British acknowledged the need to establish a Jewish national home in Palestine. Nahum, however, did not go as far in the direction of emancipation and assimilation as his Western models. He was a realist.

Nahum did not believe in the future of Zionism, but he did fear its propagation locally. His hostility was essentially directed against Zionists recruited locally, whom he regarded as personal enemies. He maintained apparently cordial relations with the official leaders of Zionism,[57] seeing them as valuable spokesmen and acting as their intermediary with the Ottoman authorities. Nahum, above all an organization man, preferred to negotiate with institutions or within official bodies rather than with individuals.

In addition, the expansion of Zionism within the communities might displease the authorities and attract their hostility. The Jewish community had hitherto been considered loyal to the central power and enjoyed relative tranquillity, for which it paid by remaining silent and by abstaining from politics. Last, and of prime importance, was the policy of the Young Turks toward the Zionist movement. To this policy Haim Nahum was obliged to yield.

Haim Nahum, the Zionists' Intermediary

Nahum's high-level intervention on behalf of the Zionists essentially concerned the restrictions the Ottoman authorities imposed on Jewish immigration after 1882 and on the purchase of land in Palestine in 1892. The waves of immigration in the last decades of the nineteenth century, following the pogroms, notably in Russia, only strengthened the authorities' determination. Their opposition to Jewish settlement in Palestine was nothing new.[58] Nahum was not the first spiritual leader to serve as intermediary between the Ottoman government and the Zionists. His predecessor had already played this role when Theodor Herzl visited Istanbul in 1902.[59] It is, however, interesting to note that Nahum intervened even when the Zionists were attacking him.

The new regime proved no more kindly disposed to the Zionists than its predecessor,[60] and the pro-Zionist declarations by a few Young Turk leaders at the beginning of the revolution were not pursued.[61] Its hostility to Zionism did not really diminish until between autumn 1913 and summer 1914, when the Young Turks sought financial support, which they thought depended on the Jews of Europe. Approaches were then made to Victor

Jacobson, the official representative of the World Zionist Organization, but when these efforts did not succeed, the climate once again deteriorated.

The Zionist leadership, for its part, modified its separatist policy at the Hamburg congress in 1909, then at the Basle congress in 1911, and provisionally adopted the principle of the integrity of the Ottoman Empire. Nevertheless the leadership did not lose sight of the immigration question and the creation of a Jewish national home in Palestine that would form an integral part of the Empire.[62] The Zionists focused their efforts on the removal of restrictions, an indispensable condition for the realization of their plans. When they failed, they appealed to Nahum to negotiate, knowing that the Ottoman authorities regarded him as a neutral spokesman, above political and national quarrels. Moreover, the Young Turks knew his opinion of Zionism, which made him even more acceptable.

It might at first seem surprising that Haim Nahum should have agreed to play the role of intermediary and to take a whole series of steps to secure the abolition of the restrictions. But he wanted to be chief rabbi of the whole of Ottoman Jewry and wished to prevent the Palestine question from becoming the Zionists' preserve. By taking this tack he could strengthen his position beyond Istanbul. His office required that he convey the grievances of the Jews of the whole Empire, those of Palestine as well as those of the Yemen.[63] Nahum favored centralization. Because there was no ecclesiastical hierarchy among the Jews, the supreme head of Ottoman Jewry did not directly appoint the chief rabbis of the provinces, although he could exercise influence over their election and particularly over its ratification in high places. This absence of centralization had always been a source of conflict. The provincial communities needed a leader whose personal authority and brilliance could reflect on Ottoman Jewry as a whole.[64] Consequently, Nahum, wishing to become a powerful chief rabbi, master of all the Jewish communities of the Empire, set off on a four-month pastoral journey in 1910 that took him to Adrianople, Salonika, Alexandria, Cairo, Palestine, Damascus, Beirut, and, finally, Smyrna.

He also wanted to gain the sympathy of the Zionists in order to settle or diminish the conflicts between them and his supporters, a strategy capable of shielding him to some extent from attack. By intervening on their behalf, he did not put the Ottoman Jewish community in any danger, because the restrictions in question were in principle aimed at Jews of foreign nationality. After all, he was chief rabbi not of foreign Jews but only of Ottoman Jews, a legal device that allowed him to protect himself.[65]

On the night of 12/13 April 1909, opponents of the Committee of Union and Progress mobilized troops and religious factions to destroy it. There were a few violent scenes when soldiers of the First Army Corps stationed at Istanbul mutinied. This attempted coup d'état, known as the "31 March incident," provoked a serious political crisis. The sultan was deposed and was exiled to Salonika. Within a few months, the Unionists (members of the Committee of Union and Progress), Nahum's friends, had consolidated their power. The chief rabbi then entered into negotiations with influential members of the government to obtain the abolition of the "red passport," a residency restriction on foreign Jews in Palestine.[66] The Zionist leaders put pressure on him to persevere.[67] The red passport was not finally canceled until September 1913[68]—Nahum having taken advantage of the temporary state of grace that the Zionists were then enjoying with the Young Turks to have it eliminated, an achievement that in fact remained theoretical.

Nahum continued to intercede on behalf of the World Zionist Organization until the First World War. He did this not in his own name but in that of the chief rabbinate. Although he never openly denounced Zionism, even at the most crucial moments, he did ensure that the anti-Zionist booklet by his ally, the journalist David Fresco, circulated in governmental and press circles while he was taking these steps for the abolition of restrictions.[69] This booklet would show its readers to what extent the Ottoman Jews rejected Zionism. It was a profession of faith coming from inside the community. The author was an Alliancist, someone who had contributed to Haim Nahum's victory, and editor of the popular Judeo-Spanish language newspaper *El Tiempo*. By his actions, the chief rabbi was hoping to provoke the authorities into taking a public stand capable of tempering the zeal of the Zionists and particularly the local Zionists. After the debates against Zionism in the Chamber of Deputies in 1911, the communities of Salonika and Smyrna did publicly break away from the Zionists,[70] hoping to protect themselves from possible repercussions. Despite pressure, the Istanbul community did not follow their example. A move made by a provincial community only involved itself; a move by Istanbul ran the risk of involving Ottoman Jewry as a whole. Nahum, aware that he was playing a weighty role, preferred to remain aloof. Moreover, he was not a man with clear-cut intentions; some people even thought him vacillating. A pragmatist, he adopted policies dictated by circumstances.

On the eve of the First World War, he interceded with the authorities in order to facilitate procedures for the adoption of Ottoman nationality by immigrant Jews in Palestine.[71] Naturalization on a large scale would in effect have prevented the expulsion of Jews originating from enemy states[72] and the dismantling of settlements. Despite his increasingly pressing interventions, the plan did not succeed.

The Great War

Haim Nahum's ambiguous attitude to Zionism, observed in the preceding years, continued during the war. Zionism was no longer a problem inside the community. A temporary consensus was established to guard against the difficulties engendered by the conflict. The various communal partners joined forces to engage in welfare work and to help war victims. In this period of respite, Nahum used all the advantages at his disposal to comfort his flock and put all his savoir-faire at the service of his community. During the Balkan wars (1912–1913), he had already tried to unite the efforts of the various local Jewish organizations, who were often at loggerheads. Even before the outbreak of hostilities, his personal political policy led him to do his utmost to maintain relations, varying in intensity, of course, with the leaders of each of these organizations—despite warnings by the Alliance, which jealously sought to keep him exclusively in its grip.

Nahum therefore took the risk of increasing the number of participants in the communal scene and succeeded in mobilizing them at this critical period. The Alliance was out of the game at that juncture: the Empire, allied with the Central Powers, was cut off from the countries of the Entente, which included France, the Alliance's seat. The Alliance's absence in itself was a calming factor. What is more, if Nahum had relied solely on the support of the Alliance, there would have been the risk that the deprived sectors of the population might have suffered more as a result. He organized a system of genuine relief with the various partners and drew on the aid of American Jewry through the American Jewish Joint Distribution Committee,[73] which played a primary role. Nahum at that time was indisputably the man for the situation.

The European powers took a close interest in Palestine during this period. They were concerned about the future of the Near East; Zionism threatened to become an international political issue. Haim Nahum mistrusted the Ottoman leaders. He adjusted his position according to circumstances and depending on the person with whom he was speaking.

In conversation with the German ambassador in Istanbul in February 1917, he expressed views that were not particularly favorable to Zionism. He stressed the need for the integration of the Jews and for their identification with the surrounding society,[74] an all-purpose theme that he borrowed from the emancipation of Western Jewry. He emphasized that it was in the Ottoman Jews' interest to keep their distance from Zionism in order to preserve their good relations with the authorities. During discussions with the Ottoman minister of public affairs at almost the same period, however, he declared that the Zionist movement could not harm the Empire's interests and that it aimed only to establish a cultural home for the Jews in Palestine.[75] He made other statements of the same nature later.

It seems that Nahum made a distinction between the attitude to Zionism to be adopted by Ottoman Jews, on the one hand, and the Palestine question, on the other. The official representative of the Zionist Organization was aware of this, since he even went so far as to suggest that the chief rabbi prepare a report on Zionism for the government. At the same period,

Nahum took steps to bring the Zionist leader, Richard Lichtheim, back to the capital.[76] Cut off from the Alliance and France by the war, Nahum needed an efficient collaborator in contact with Europe in these difficult times. In addition, the presence of a Zionist leader in the capital would make it possible to control the local militants and their excesses.

As a result of the war, Cemal pasha, appointed supreme commander of the Fourth Ottoman Army, became the real master of Syria and Palestine. There were continual anti-Zionist campaigns and anti-Zionist measures there during 1915–1916. These were not directly ordered by the Porte and affected Ottoman and non-Ottoman Zionists alike.

At the time of the expulsions from Jaffa, Nahum again held the center of the stage. Following the British defeat on the Gaza front in April 1917, 7,000 to 9,000 Jews from Jaffa were driven back northward. Although the expulsion did not involve only Jews, they were widely affected. Western Jewry was alarmed. Cemal pasha forced a few religious dignitaries and Zionist leaders to deny what happened at Jaffa.[77] Nahum let himself be taken in,[78] thus providing his critics, notably the British, with an opportunity to accuse him of colluding with Cemal and in particular, of having himself wrung the famous denial from its authors.[79] Even the World Zionist Organization, however, knew the full details of this denial only a month later.[80]

After the war, the chief rabbi claimed that he had intervened with his Ottoman political friends in Istanbul in order to end the 1917–1918 deportations[81] and maintained that he had spared the Jews from massacres similar to those that had beset the Armenians and the Greeks.[82]

In fact, he had shown judgment in order to prevent the worst from happening to the Jews of Palestine and had behaved like the chief rabbi of all the Jews of the Empire at the time of that affair.[83] This would be his attitude to Zionism and to Palestine until the end of the war.

Later on, he had to adapt himself to new issues because a new situation developed with the eviction of the Young Turks from power. The members of the Triumvirate—Talât, Cemal, and Enver—left the dismembered Empire at the beginning of November 1918. They were blamed for the debacle and were held up to public obloquy; the witch hunt had begun. Haim Nahum's relations with the old regime pushed him into the front line. Hitherto he had drawn most of his authority from his governmental support. Now he was alone in facing the Zionists, whose claims became more pressing and who enjoyed the support of the British, one of the forces occupying the capital. The Balfour Declaration was already explicit evidence of their aims vis-à-vis Palestine.

The struggles between the various pressure groups resumed with renewed vigor. Locally, the Allies supported whichever camp suited their own interests. With the connivance of the local Zionists, joined by Nahum's personal enemies, the British instigated hostile propaganda campaigns against him. They were afraid that the Francophile chief rabbi would champion French interests and would lead the community in that direction.[84] Jewish public opinion could in fact influence the appointment of the future Palestine mandatory power. The Cambon Declaration of 4 June 1917, expressing France's sympathy for the Zionist cause and the possibility of a subsidy for the creation of a Jewish national home in Palestine under the Allies' protection, had already preceded and to some extent precipitated the Balfour Declaration. It might have been an answer to Zionist aspirations, because it proved that France continued to be interested in Palestine; the Sykes-Picot agreements (May 1916) had allotted part of Palestine to France. Moreover, the Balfour Declaration was not a legal document, and it remained to be ratified by peace treaties. Therefore nothing had yet been officially set in motion.

Nahum did not conceal his preference for France,[85] which paid homage to his loyalty.[86] France counted on safeguarding its influence in the Near East. The Alliance schools and the local Jews could serve its cause. The French embassy in Istanbul asked the Alliance to adjust to the new context and to place more emphasis on Hebrew while still handling the Zionists with kid gloves to prevent them from having these schools closed.[87] In fact the chief rabbi enjoyed French protection after the capital had been occupied by the Allies.

In comparison with the Greek and Armenian patriarchs, however, the chief rabbi did not represent much of a force for the Allies to reckon with, as the British themselves realized.[88] Even so, the prevalent political uncertainty bred mistrust, including mistrust of a communal leader with limited power. What really interested the British was the Jewish community itself. But Nahum could turn this community in a direction favorable to other members of the Entente, thus thwarting their plans and jeopardizing the work the Zionists had accomplished on their behalf.

The Zionist Blow

Nahum was on a mission in Europe at the request of the Ottoman authorities in October 1918 when the armistice of Mudros was signed, setting the seal on the Ottoman debacle. The subsequent occupation of Istanbul by the Allies aroused new hopes among minorities, determined to make their national claims succeed in this favorable context. The official bodies of the Jewish community and its notables, many of whom were close to Nahum, succumbed to panic in the absence of their leader. A collective position capable of meeting the new situation and its threatening repercussions was essential. People in responsible positions in the communities joined together to create the Jewish National Council, in actuality a Zionist initiative to replace the chief rabbinate. Haim Nahum's friends dared not forfeit their position and followed the tide. The Zionists hoped that this authoritarian seizure of power would rid them of the chief rabbi. They held the reins of the community in a sort of sacred union that was to their advantage. Nahum's overseas mission was disclaimed.

March 1919: It caused a sensation when the chief rabbi returned to Istanbul. A virulent power struggle began. Even though his authority was weakened, he still had cards to play. Some notables were afraid of the anarchy that a two-headed leadership would create. They were joined by others who had grown rich on the opportunities the war had offered and who wanted a stability that would be propitious to their commercial interests. They felt that the chief rabbinate was worth more than a Jewish National Council lacking any official recognition, and they were prepared to support the man who was its leader.[89] Nahum, however, was shaken and thought seriously of giving up his position. The notables, his friends of old, put pressure on him to stay.[90] Strengthened by this support, the chief rabbi dissolved the Jewish National Council, the real counterpower. The Zionists, with the blessing of the vox populi, responded by voting for his dismissal.

The prewar Zionist agitation vigorously resumed and took the form of open demonstrations within the population. Now it was the Zionists' turn to reap the benefits of support from outside the community, which Nahum himself had enjoyed before the war. Helped by the political situation in the country, fortified by British promises on Palestine, the Zionists were openly active and formed more and more associations. In 1919, local Zionists founded the Zionist Federation of the East, with the purpose of supervising Zionist activity in the country. Propaganda was carried on, on the ground and through the press.

The World Zionist Organization began to withdraw from the scene,[91] because Istanbul no longer had the same importance since the Balfour Declaration. The center of negotiations had moved to London. These negotiations no longer involved the Ottoman authorities. The organization was now waiting for the word from England. Its new representative in the Ottoman capital was not entirely up to the difficult task that fell to him, and he did not succeed in stemming the excesses. The local Zionists, who wanted more than anything else to deal a mortal blow to the chief rabbinate, intensified their demonstrations, with Haim Nahum more than ever their favorite target, especially as the conflict was exacerbated by personal enmities.

Istanbul Zionism recruited the bulk of its membership from working-class districts and from among the youth. The anarchy that pervaded its activities increased the World Zionist Organization's mistrust of it. In fact, it eluded all control.

As the agitation increased, the notables closed ranks, prepared to pay the high price to save Nahum's position and thereby their own. Zionism was in the air, not that it mattered. To suit the occasion, these notables became dyed-in-the-wool nationalists. They set up associations likely to draw away Zionist membership and borrowed their opponents' speeches. But they did not succeed in reversing the tide. The demonstrations against Nahum and the oligarchy were in full swing, and violence increased. Nor did the British embassy in Istanbul spare its efforts to secure the resignation of the chief rabbi. The British wanted to replace him with the former chief rabbi of the Sephardi community of Great Britain, Moses Gaster, an eminent figure in Zionism. The Foreign Office appealed to its men to show more caution and discretion.[92] Nahum's resignation was only a matter of days. The Zionists and the Zionist press were dead set against him. The chief rabbi did in effect resign. Then, under pressure from the notables, he went back on his decision, although he had desperately tried to rid himself of the office.

The day after the war, the various communal organizations were in an unconstitutional position, not having had the time to hold proper elections. More urgent matters had had to be attended to first. The atmosphere in Istanbul in 1919 was such that it was not prudent to embark on elections to renew the official bodies of the community, especially as the Zionists had every chance of winning them.

Nahum gave in to his opponents' demands, however, and decided to proceed with elections. Even the French and British high commissioners thought this course of action precipitous: it would have been better to wait for the signing of the peace treaty.[93] By embarking on this course, Haim Nahum was surrendering to Zionist pressure.

The electoral campaign that, in principle, concerned only Ottoman Jews proceeded in anything but a calm atmosphere. The Zionists counted on the votes of Jews of foreign nationality, particularly those of the Russian community, increasingly numerous in Istanbul, and demanded that they be allowed to participate in the elections. The government was opposed and showed its disapproval, but it did not obtain the support of the chief rabbi, who, curiously enough, sided with his opponents on this point. Despite pressure from the authorities, he did not withdraw from his position and resigned in March 1920, using his health as a pretext. After providing for the interim until his resignation was ratified at the end of April, he left immediately for France, where his family awaited him.

His resignation did not meet with silence. Even his most bitter opponents, among whom the Zionists were most prominent, paid homage to this chief rabbi who had bowed to the wishes of his community and had gone so far as to infringe government orders because he knew where his duty lay as a man and as a Jew.[94] All things considered, Nahum had made an honorable exit. That being so, those who knew him well were well aware that he had intended to resign for some time.[95]

The results of communal by-elections had underlined the Zionists' indisputable advance, even in the wealthy districts. The movement was spreading to the whole town, and an uncontrollable dynamic was seizing the people. Nahum could have settled his dispute with the Ottoman leaders opposed to the participation of foreigners in elections, but against the Zionists he could do nothing. Hitherto he had depended on support outside the community to stand up to them, but the weakness of the government made it no longer possible to regain control of a community plunged into complete institutional anarchy in a dismembered Empire with an uncertain future.

Moreover, the Empire, reduced to a shrunken skin after the war, was of less and less interest to him.[96] Mustafa Kemal's troops—forces of resistance to the foreign occupation—were advancing in Anatolia. Knowing the political situation in Turkey, Nahum decided to secure a position elsewhere that would be more in keeping with his ambitions.[97] He did not deceive himself. In the future republican Turkey, the office of chief rabbi would have far less luster and would have to accommodate itself to the demands of a new secular nation-state. Insofar as he was more a politician than anything else, Nahum could not be satisfied with an honorific role.

The Man of the Embassies

Throughout his Ottoman career, Nahum gave new stature to his position, which distinguished him from his predecessors. In particular, he was able to make himself indispensable to the representatives of the Western powers who called on him. Prior to his election these representatives had rarely come into contact with the head of the Jewish community.[98] They valued his knowledge of the country and its politicians, his affable nature, and sought his company. Nahum established his ability as a statesman. Helped by his knowledge of foreign languages, he skillfully cultivated his diplomatic contacts and used them to enhance his position.

Between 1908 and 1914, for example, he tightened the links he had maintained with the French diplomatic corps since before his election, in the hope of protecting his community at critical junctures.[99] Nor did he hesitate to use these relationships to safeguard his own power, particularly when it was seriously challenged by the Zionists.[100] As a French-speaking Francophile, a champion of the Alliance's educational work, he was a favorite spokesman in the pursuance of the French plan to develop and spread the French language and culture in the Levant.

The French embassy in Istanbul even went so far as to regret Nahum's resignation in 1920.[101] In him it had lost one of its allies and not the least loyal. To be sure France, under British pressure, refused him an entry visa in 1918 when he was in Europe on a mission. But the international situation at the time made Nahum persona non grata. Two years later, on the other hand, he obtained the Legion d'Honneur for services rendered during the war.[102]

He had in fact fought so that the Alliance schools would remain open when the Empire, allied with the Central Powers, was closing establishments founded by the countries of the Entente. Moreover, throughout his term of office, he intervened on behalf of the Alliance to cope with the new arrangements made by the Young Turks, which threatened to shake its fragile structure: the adoption of Turkish as the language of instruction in 1909 or the requirement for teachers in non-Muslim schools to be of Ottoman nationality in 1910. It should be noted that the preferred language of instruction in Alliance schools was French, and few teachers were Ottoman subjects. Despite constant attacks from the Zionists, it was during this period that its schools operated in the greatest security, benefiting from the chief rabbi's full support. For Nahum, France and the Alliance were inseparable.

But the chief rabbi, who liked playing on several boards, did not limit his contacts to one power. In this fragile empire, a diversification of relationships was protection against possible repercussions. This point was proved when the interplay of alliances during the Great War lost Nahum the protection of the French diplomatic corps: his link with the American representatives then became very useful.

Between 1909 and 1917, successive appointments by the United States of three Jewish ambassadors facilitated the establishment of sustained,[103] even amicable, relations. Thanks to his contacts in American diplomatic circles, the chief rabbi came to the aid of his community when it was seriously affected by the Balkan wars (1912–1913) and the First World War. These contacts did in fact mobilize American public opinion and brought in the necessary funds. Because of these privileged relations, on several occasions there was even some talk of Nahum's possible appointment as Turkish ambassador to the United States, an unusual office for a Jew.

These connections were as useful to him in governmental circles as in Jewish circles. After his resignation, for example, he made two journeys to the United States in January and October 1921 on behalf of the Alliance but supported by the Quai d'Orsay.[104] His mission was to make the Alliance's work known in America and to collect funds for its schools. His American friends, notably the former ambassadors to the Empire, helped him with introductions to local dignitaries. But American Jewish philanthropy was not particularly interested in the work of the Alliance, especially as the economic situation was difficult. Moreover, Zionist influence was also making itself felt in the same circles. The Alliance was criticized for being anti-Zionist. When he was in the United States, Zionists leaders were likewise scouring the country to collect money for their own cause. The Jewish press ran a campaign against Nahum's activities. Yet again, the Zionists stood in his way. But when the American press announced his forthcoming appointment as ambassador to Washington,[105] the news caused some change in attitude in philanthropic circles and enabled Nahum despite everything to bring about a partial mobilization of opinion in favor of the Alliance schools, particularly among oriental Jews. Still, the purely financial gains remained sparse. American Jewry was now looking in other directions.

Nahum refused the position of ambassador on the grounds that he did not want to embark on a diplomatic career, which required a lot of relocation. Turkey's political instability, the advance in Anatolia of the troops of Mustafa Kemal—nationalist leader and future head of the Turkish nation-state—were not such as to encourage him.

Nor did the chief rabbi neglect the representatives of the other powers. During the war Germany was also looking in the direction of Palestine: he took pains to deal tactfully with the Germans, who were disturbed by his preference for France. A rumor even circulated in Zionist circles that the German ambassador, Count Johann Heinrich Bernstorff, met with Haim Nahum more frequently than with Arthur Ruppin, then the representative of the World Zionist Organization at Istanbul.[106] At the beginning of the war, however, following an intervention by the ambassador, he was accused of Germanophobia and reprimanded by Talât, the strong man of the government, who instructed him to improve his relations with the Germans.[107] As his influence and his ability became more widely recognized,[108] his words and deeds were all the more closely watched by the German authorities.

This diversity of contacts also harmed him. The objectives pursued by the powers and their aims in the region governed their assessment of his political role. Nonetheless his contacts helped to earn him the aura of a diplomat with the Ottoman leaders. He was therefore in demand as an intermediary with the various successive governments in the Empire whenever there was a delicate question of international policy. This reputation for diplomacy did not fail to strengthen his position with the various governments and thereby his authority within the community.

The Man of the Palace

Haim Nahum was a man for all governments. How did he manage to move smoothly and unscathed from each of the different regimes to the next? He was unaffected when each successive lord of the land began by settling old scores. He was in turn the Young Turks' man, the man of the ephemeral government of Izzet pasha in 1918, and the man of Mustafa Kemal in 1919. He was needed, not only to keep firm control of the community, but also to negotiate. He was a useful intermediary because he did not directly involve the government that employed him, since he was not part of it. Although he rejoiced in an official status as chief rabbi, he always remained an unofficial intermediary.

Haim Nahum owed his rise in governmental circles to the Committee of Union and Progress. In point of fact, it was only after the counterrevolution of 1909, when this party really took over the reins of power, that the committee provided Nahum with a palliative to the weakness of his authority in the community. The tribulations the committee experienced between 1909 and 1918 naturally affected the chief rabbi's position and power.

He was unquestionably welcome in Ottoman ruling circles.[109] On this point at least, his entourage and his opponents were in agreement. People trusted Haim Nahum. As early as 1908, he put great effort into ensuring the victory of candidates supported by the Committee of Union and Progress. He did the same again in 1912. It must also be noted that all the Jewish deputies elected to the Chamber belonged to the Unionist party. In Istanbul, the community gave this party massive support. Nahum saw to that. In the provinces on the other hand, the support was conditional. Nevertheless the Jewish community as a whole continued to opt for this party, if only because of the philo-Semitism of its early days. There was also a convergence of interests between some classes of Jewish society and the Committee of Union and Progress. What is more, the party represented order in the face of anarchy. The communal leaders generally preferred to protect their constituents from adventures without a future.

The positions that the Ottoman power offered Nahum are further evidence of the nature and range of his relationship with it. At the end of 1910 and the beginning of 1911 he was on the verge of being appointed senator. Jewish notables then intervened with the government to make it alter its decision, because it was not possible to combine the two positions, and they had no replacement in mind for the post of chief rabbi.[110] In view of the situation in his community, however, Nahum would have preferred a governmental position to that of chief rabbi—particularly as the authorities let it be understood that in time they expected to entrust to him the ministry of public education.[111] In the end he remained at the head of the community.

On the eve of the war there was again talk of his appointment as senator,[112] but the rumors came to nought, and Nahum never officially occupied an office of state. On the other hand, his role as the favorite unofficial intermediary between the successive governments and the Western powers made him the only chief rabbi ever invested with such a broad political role.

The first call on his services came in 1915 in the context of a plan for a separate peace between the Ottoman government, on the one hand, and England and France, on the other.[113] In pursuit of this plan, he met the British representative at Dedeağaç, but nothing concrete was achieved. The failure of these negotiations would be interpreted in various ways. It is true that they took place in an atmosphere of tension at a time when the Allied fleet was bombarding the Dardanelles. The conditions on both sides were excessive,[114] and in addition, the East was not favorably placed for negotiating an end to the war.[115]

In July 1918 Nahum was entrusted with a second mission. The official pretext for the trip to Europe was a health cure. High government dignitaries were present at his departure, however, and ministers and high officials greeted his return. He reached the Hague, then went to Stockholm, passing through Germany.[116] The chief rabbi had in fact been approached to bring about a reversal of opinion among Western Jews in favor of the Ottoman state.[117] During his stay he was closely watched by the French and German secret services.[118] Then came the Zionists' turn to be intrigued by this mission, though they never succeeded in uncovering its secret. Nahum met important Jewish personalities, including the Zionist leaders. He was also hoping to win over the neutral countries to the Turkish cause.

The failure of the chief rabbi's mission should probably be compared with the failure of the special mission that the president of the United States entrusted to Henry Morgenthau in 1917. That mission also aimed to induce the Ottoman state to conclude a separate peace with the Allies. It miscarried after the intervention of the Zionist leader Chaim Weizmann, who intercepted Morgenthau at Gibraltar in order to dissuade him from embarking on this course.[119] Weizmann had already acted in this cause with Balfour, the British foreign secretary. Thus, in November 1917, Balfour signed the declaration that bears his name.

The Ottoman government, cut off from the Allies, was not aware of the results of the Morgenthau mission. It could still cherish the hope of breaking the impasse by a separate peace. But Nahum returned to Istanbul empty-handed. The Zionists and Great Britain, now more than ever interested in Palestine, had caused the failure of the attempt at a separate peace, which risked leaving that region in Ottoman hands. The chief rabbi had served as intermediary for a cause that was already lost.

When the Young Turk government fell in 1918, the grand vizier Izzet pasha instructed Nahum to put the Ottoman government into contact with the Entente powers.[120] The United States had broken off relations with the Empire when it entered the war (1917). But the Ottomans counted on the United States to serve as their intermediary. His trans-Atlantic friendships would allow Nahum to prepare the ground informally and bring about the return of Abraham Elkus as United States ambassador to the Empire (he had already held this position before his country entered the war).

Because of the secret nature of this third mission, Nahum gave health as the reason for his departure and did not even inform the official bodies of the community. On 25 October 1918 he hurriedly climbed aboard a private yacht headed for Constantza in Rumania. But the plan for a separate peace no longer had any chance of succeeding. Once again, Nahum was emissary of a lost cause. The Empire was played out, particularly at the international level. It emerged from the war defeated, and more than Nahum would be needed to extricate it from the impasse.

Nahum's final destination was to be the United States. But before that, he expected to stay in Holland long enough to obtain authorization from the Americans and British to continue his journey. He also wanted to go to Paris, where he hoped to approach the Allied political authorities and Western Jewish leaders so that his mission would stand the greatest chance of success.

The Zionists were disturbed about such an enterprise and spread a rumor among the Allies that Nahum was trying to reach the States so that he could promote keeping Palestine under Turkish domination and so that he could cheat France of Syria.[121] Thereupon the French minister of foreign affairs, Stephen Pichon, ordered his embassies in the Hague, London, and Washington to refuse Nahum a visa.[122] The French criticized the chief rabbi for his wartime support of the Young Turks' pro-German policy.

It was equally in British interests that the mission should fail, and they too asked the French not to grant him a visa. They had always been hostile to the Committee of Union and Progress, and they feared its return to power. This time, they cited Haim Nahum's relationship with Talât, former leader of the Young Turks, who had been a refugee in Berlin since the end of the war. Nahum went to Berlin twice during the course of this same trip. He wanted, so it was said, to be appointed ambassador to the United States. But Talât was in no position to appoint anyone ambassador. Moreover, the British were afraid that the chief rabbi, with his entrée to the Quai d'Orsay, had the power to sow discord between France and Britain on the Palestine question.[123] As far as they were concerned, Palestine must not remain Ottoman, and they were prepared to do anything to prevent Nahum from going to the United States, since he might promote Ottoman interests with the former ambassadors, his friends Elkus and Morgenthau. Perhaps through them he might even succeed in convincing President Wilson.[124]

In this atmosphere of suspicion and paranoia the European imperial powers were to divide the Empire among themselves. They combined to prevent Nahum from acting. This solidarity did not last long.

Nahum was even accused of bringing a considerable sum of gold with him on this mission, on board the yacht that took him to Constantza, as well as highly important documents belonging to the Committee of Union and Progress.[125] These are the historic funds, no trace of which has ever been found. It is known, however, that they were transferred to Swiss banks by various routes and by various people, including a Jewish banker who belonged to Nahum's entourage; Nahum was in Istanbul at the time.[126]

In the end, the chief rabbi was stuck in the Hague. Meanwhile, government succeeded government in Istanbul. He stayed in Europe for four months, unable to return to the Ottoman capital and resume control of his community. He was thus cut off from local events, and the leaders of the community were afraid of the repercussions of his past allegiances. The new leaders welcomed him with open arms, however, when he returned to Istanbul in March 1919. He had probably not returned without obtaining guarantees from the new lords of the land. His welcome by the current regime gave his supporters new hope and confidence.

On the Side of the Victors

A new mission in autumn 1919 took the chief rabbi back to Europe. This time the reason was a meeting with Henry Morgenthau, former United States ambassador to the Empire, on questions concerning oriental Jewry.[127] In fact, Morgenthau had invited Nahum to Paris to discuss not only the Jewish question but also the future of Turkey. The British and the Zionists again mobilized: had the chief rabbi asked for American support for retaining Arab provinces within Turkey?

At the same time, the members of the Entente were disturbed by the successes that the Turkish national movement led by Mustafa Kemal was scoring in Anatolia. Kemal then proclaimed that the national frontiers were sacrosanct. The Turkish nationalists' claims therefore conflicted on a number of points with the Entente's plans for the Ottoman territories it occupied. In addition, some Kemalists preferred an American mandate on Turkey. Perhaps Nahum's trip was to promote this plan?

In any case, the chief rabbi's talks with representatives of the Entente whom he met in Paris did not fail to refer to certain points in the manifestos of the Anatolian resistance movement.[128] He had come to present the situation in Turkey, but he seemed fully informed on developments in resistance circles. He was aware that the ghost government of Istanbul would not last long.

He had probably been entrusted with an unofficial mission by the Kemalists, independent of the discussions on oriental Jewry that he was to have with Morgenthau. He met several people of importance and made statements to the French press in favor of the Turkish national cause. He probably did not plunge into such propaganda activities on his own initiative, but once again he camouflaged the real motives for his trip. True, the situation required discretion.

Nahum did his best to rectify the unflattering image that the Western press painted of the Kemalists and conducted a veritable campaign to explain the policy of the movement and its leaders. Various articles appeared in the *Journal des Débats* in Paris, inspired by his statements.[129] He himself granted an interview to the Parisian paper *Le Matin* on 9 November 1919, in which he reassured French public opinion: the Kemalists were not adventurers; Mustafa Kemal was not a fanatic. He stressed the semiofficial status of the nationalist movement, which he depicted as a potential participant in later negotiations on the future of Turkey. Last, he appealed to the Turkish nationalists and the Entente to find a modus vivendi. He also spoke of a possible alliance between France and the Turkish nationalist movement.

The possibility that Nahum might cross the Atlantic was mentioned again during this visit. Did he expect to pursue his campaign there? The plan did not materialize. In 1922, however, well after his resignation, on the eve of the proclamation of the Turkish republic, he was sent on a mission by the provisional government[130] and resumed his pro-Kemalist propaganda activities in order to prepare the ground for the signature of the future peace treaty. *Le Matin* again welcomed him to its columns, where this time he emphasized Turkey's desire to be at peace with the Great Powers and made constant reference to Franco-Turkish friendship.[131] He openly spoke in the name of Turkey. He had become Ankara's man.

Now that he was no longer chief rabbi, Nahum was able to act openly alongside the Turkish leaders, but he did not become the official representative of the future masters of the country. The tradition endured, and Nahum worked behind the scenes as in Ottoman times. It was thus that he was given the task of promoting Turkey's interests at the Lausanne conference.[132] He accompanied the various Turkish delegations (November 1922, April 1923) as adviser, under Ismet pasha,[133] a leading figure in the resistance movement and a former pupil of Nahum's at the École du Génie et de l'Artillerie in the 1900s. As before, however, he did not figure in the official lists.

He was particularly noticed for his efforts, especially in Paris, to prevent the breakdown of negotiations. The Turkish press stressed Nahum's work on Turkey's behalf. As for the Jewish press in Paris, it placed his role in an ancient Sephardic diplomatic tradition and compared him with his illustrious predecessors, such as Hisdai ibn Shaprut[134] and General Valensi.[135]

And yet an anti-Semitic lampoon that appeared in 1965, forty years after his mission to Lausanne and, more important, five years after his death, described him purely and simply as a traitor and an enemy of Turkey.[136] It was a very unfair judgment of a Jew who wanted to be seen as a child of his country like its other citizens and who showed a great desire to serve the "homeland."[137]

Nahum had in fact drawn closer to the Turkish nationalist movement as early as 1919, when he could, as was the custom among local Jews, have followed the policy of the Istanbul government, some members of which collaborated with the occupation. He had probably anticipated the development of Turkish policy better than anyone in the Jewish community, in order to serve the future masters of the country, just as he had served their predecessors.

He was no longer chief rabbi, of course, but his activities on the Kemalists' behalf did not fail to reflect positively on the Jewish community at a time when an anti-Semitic campaign was developing in the Turkish press (1922).[138]

In 1925 Haim Nahum found another position as chief rabbi, this time in Egypt,[139] where he lived through the vicissitudes of European Jewry and the birth of the modern Jewish state. The situation there was not the most tranquil; Egyptian Jewry was directly involved in the evolution of Jewish-Arab relations in the Near East. Even after he had become blind, he led his community under successive regimes, including Nasserian nationalism. He remained in the service of Egyptian Jewry until its dispersion began in the 1950s, when the atmosphere deteriorated following the establishment of the state of Israel. The Suez campaign in 1956 sounded the knell of that old Jewish community. Senator, founding member of the Académie Royale de Langue Arabe, writer, and translator, Nahum was no ordinary chief rabbi in Cairo either. At first a witness of the flourishing years of Egyptian Jewry, then more than ever politician and diplomat in difficult times, he died in 1960 and was buried in Cairo, in the Orient to which he was so closely attached.

Nahum now is part of the Jewish-Egyptian legend that the exiles still bring with them to their adoptive countries.

Court Jew, State Jew, or Levantine Intercessor?

Right through this itinerary, the public figure takes precedence over Nahum the individual. The vicissitudes of his career did not fail to take their toll on his family life, which nonetheless showed itself peaceful. What emerges is the portrait of a self-willed but vacillating man. Easily discouraged, of delicate health, worried about the material future of his family, externally, however, he presented the image of someone who was both elusive and forceful. He was a man of paradoxes even at an everyday level.

How can we describe Nahum's Ottoman career, so closely bound up with the history of his community and the Empire? Was he no more than a court Jew?

Historically, the image and function of a court Jew were the product of absolutism and the beginnings of capitalism in Europe.[140] The court Jews of the seventeenth century and the beginning of the eighteenth[141] were recruited from among the rich merchants, bankers, state purveyors, and army contractors. They were indispensable, supplying their sovereigns with funds. In the Europe of that period, where the Jew was still confined to the ghetto, the court Jew enjoyed a precarious but privileged status. As such, he could use his relationships for the good of his community. Rulers sometimes entrusted him with responsibility for various missions concerning the immediate interests of the state.[142] The Ottoman Empire also had its famous state Jews, such as the duke of Naxos in the seventeenth century or the banker, Abraham Camondo, in the nineteenth.

Wealth played no part in Nahum's involvement with ruling circles. All he had in common with the court Jew was the privilege of being in contact with power and remaining inseparably bound to the Jewish world, the community. He was indisputably the Ottoman rulers' man. Very early, even before he became chief rabbi, he tried to approach the Ottoman court, aware of the importance of the support he might find there. Although there is no proof that he owed his leading position to the Young Turks, he remained close to them. Their support furnished the essential elements of his power. And because he was closely connected to Ottoman power he was feared and challenged inside the community. But the Ottoman rulers valued him just as highly for the relationships that he was able to cultivate outside his community, even at an international level. From one point of view Nahum's savoir-faire and network of relationships compensated for the wealth he lacked.

The chief rabbinate of the Empire represented the top of the social and political ladder for a man with no wealth. The Empire was very far from the model of the Western type of nation-state. Equality between Muslim and non-Muslim citizens, proclaimed in 1856, remained theoretical. Non-Muslims had access to positions of high responsibility in the state apparatus relatively rarely except in cases of conversion to Islam. Jews in the civil service were few and far between. After the Young Turk revolution, there was a slight increase in their number. When this increase became known, the Jewish press gave it wide publicity, regarding it as the first sign of the Jews' integration. It reacted in the same way when compulsory military service was introduced for non-Muslims in 1909. Nevertheless, religious particularism still took priority over state control. In fact organization according to religious groups lay at the very foundations of Islam and the Empire, where a person belonged to a religion before he was even a citizen of the country. Failure dogged attempts at "Ottomanization," the ideal means of unifying religious and ethnic groups under the Ottoman banner, revived by the Young Turks in the hope of extinguishing awakening nationalism. The Empire had neither the means nor the structures capable of assuring the success of this ideal imported from the West. The continued existence of small "states" within the large—itself in a weakened condition—could not fail to impede the integration of non-Muslims, including Jews.[143] For this reason, the Jews remained tied to their particularism.

The priority given to Islam over other religions, and restrictions concerning the place of non-Muslims in Islamic society, made access by non-Muslims to positions of responsibility and command inconceivable. There were, of course, exceptions, but the Ottoman Empire remained a theocratic state, and the state religion, Islam. Its very foundations precluded the possibility that a class of state Jews might emerge, as it had, for example, in nineteenth-century France. Such a class could emerge only in a strong state that proclaimed its secularism and confined religious particularism to the private domain. Nor would the future Turkish nation-state, secular from 1928,[144] succeed in erasing the influence of centuries of dhimma. Non-Muslims would never occupy important positions in the state apparatus.

Nahum, who had the stature and ambition of a state Jew, was the symbol of the Jew's impossible ascent, even if he just failed to achieve it. He belonged to that small breed of men, educated in the European tradition but speaking Turkish, who aspired to integration and were anxious to serve an Empire that they regarded as their homeland.[145] Emmanuel Carasso, an influential figure in the Committee of Union and Progress, who was instructed to depose the sultan in 1909, never succeeded in raising himself to a key position in the Young Turk government; he remained a behind-the-scenes operator. The same is true of Nissim Rousso and other Jews in the party, who were already active before it came to power. Only David, the *dönme* (convert),[146] succeeded and became minister of finance.

Haim Nahum could survive the successive regimes because he was not directly and officially involved in the system of Ottoman power. His function as intercessor made him untouchable, even amid the political instability that characterized the Empire.

Can Nahum be likened to the *shtadlanim*[147] of Central and Eastern Europe? It is a well-known fact that the absolutist regimes strove to limit the autonomy of the Jewish communities from the end of the seventeenth century. At that time the state used the shtadlan to enforce its authority over these communities.[148] The role was generally taken by rich and influential court Jews. The shtadlan's role and status varied, depending on the period. He might be a paid and elected member of the community, appointed for a limited period to serve as intercessor between the community and the authorities. On the other hand, he might hold his position on an honorary basis simply because of his prestige. Whatever the case, the shtadlan fulfilled the functions of a diplomat, mediator, and protector of his community's rights.

The chief rabbi of the Ottoman Empire, as leader of all the Empire's Jews and as executive agent of the imperial government's orders, was by definition the official intermediary between the government and the community. He was guarantor of the loyalty of the community with which the Ottoman rulers identified him.

The chief rabbi of the Empire, elected and paid by the community, was not really any different from the European shtadlan even when his appointment had in fact to be ratified by the state and even if Nahum liked to describe himself as an Ottoman higher civil servant.

In fact, dual allegiance was the actual basis of his role. This in itself contained contradictions. How to serve both state and community at the same time, particularly when the community was politically plural and when some of its internal forces conflicted with the interests of the state? Zionism was in fact perceived as one of these forces. Could Haim Nahum have espoused it with impunity? His anti-Zionism was to a large extent also the price he paid for his office.

Nahum was undoubtedly cut out to be a shtadlan. Even before he took office as chief rabbi, the Alliance was using him unofficially to conduct its affairs with the state. When he became chief rabbi he continued to pursue this course and acted in the same way vis-à-vis the Zionists to circumvent them and remain the sole intermediary between the Jews, the Jewish pressure groups imported from the West, and the state.

Nahum was no ordinary chief rabbi. He certainly did not distinguish himself by his contribution to the spiritual realm. Nor did he write anything that might have made him a rabbinical authority. He was in fact the key figure in a period of intense politicization. And if he was the product of communal politicization, he was also its victim.

The Ottoman Empire was at that time in the process of modernization. It was semicolonized, open to new ideas, at the height of transformation, torn apart by the agitation of nationalism. The Jewish community could not remain cut off from its environment. The relative autonomy that it enjoyed did not mean total isolation. The vicissitudes of Haim Nahum's rabbinate showed, moreover, how precarious was this autonomy. Ottoman Jewry also felt the repercussions from national and international tension. In fact Nahum had no alternative but to be a chief rabbi who was also a diplomat and politician.

He emerges as a statesman, the leader of a small state within the large one on which it depended. Centralization, reorganization, restructuring—these were the major axes of Nahum's internal policy. He also acted as the head of the pressure group that had brought him to power. Above all, he was the agent of the Alliancist Jewish upper middle class, in principle the source of communal funds. He tried to adapt the French model of chief rabbinate to local conditions but he did not really succeed. The communal regime remained oligarchical. Its structures were no different from those of the traditional Jewish community in general. The notables who supported it, despite the wish for change that they had demonstrated before taking power, proved no less conservative once they had achieved their ends. In addition, they were far from being professional administrators. Nor did the community's dependence on the state make it easy to implement reforms. Ottoman bureaucracy, the touchiness of the authorities, the sensitivity of the Jewish upper middle class to the mood in ruling circles—all posed obstacles.

Chief Rabbi Nahum's communal career was colored by an inescapable

Zionist presence. At first the Zionists saw him as the Alliance's man, even though he moved away from the Alliance a few years after he took office and formulated new tactics, an attitude that the war later intensified. True, he himself envisaged no other goals for the community than those proposed by the Alliance. In another connection, his elitism harmed him with the masses who were turning toward Zionism. Nor did he exercise the sort of moral authority as a spiritual leader that could win him their respect, at least temporarily, and could prevent them from enrolling in the Zionists' ranks. Well informed on Turkish politics, Nahum was much less so on Jewish politics. For a time, he let the secretary-general of the Alliance, Jacques Bigart, manipulate him, but Bigart did not always understand the internal life of the oriental communities. It was, of course, difficult to assess the local situation from Paris.

But the conflicts that Nahum had to face went far beyond the framework of his community. It was the outside authorities of the warring pressure groups that directly intervened in 1911 to end local agitation.[149] The correspondence between the president of the World Zionist Organization, David Wolffsohn, and the president of the Alliance is very significant from this point of view. It reveals that both organizations had used the chief rabbi's abilities as an intermediary. Nahum, having himself become the focus of the hostilities, bore the cost of the confrontation between these imported ideologies.

Tradition no longer carried the same weight. In Nahum's day, the chief rabbi was less and less able to impose his authority. The threat of the famous *herem* (excommunication), which in the past had brought recalcitrants back to the fold, was no longer effective. The Ottoman Jew now conceived viable areas other than the community, even if there was no question yet of dispensing with it entirely. People on the margins of power relied on external opposition forces to seize it, as Nahum and his friends had done with the Alliance in the past. Those who followed did likewise; for them, Zionism furnished the springboard.

When Zionism became a factor at the beginning of the twentieth century, it threw into disarray the strategies of the Jewish community, whose politicization was an index of its advance into the modern age. This politicization now went beyond the strictly communal framework and brought internal and external forces face to face. Such a situation could not be handled by men with experience of past power and could not be handled within the traditional structures. The need for restructuring, a regular item on the agenda, required reforms to be set in motion, but the situation made reform impossible, since every attempt at change inevitably generated new conflicts. The Zionists themselves then became the victims of this perverse dynamic. When they came to power, they too had to face a now unmanageable community and, despite their plans for democratization and change, were reduced to acting like their opponents. They were no longer able to govern with a chief rabbi who belonged to an opposing faction. Nahum himself was confronted with a similar impossibility when the Zionists sat on the councils. In practice, the impasse was the consequence of political pluralism that required democratic structures to find positive expression. The oligarchical system in force definitively obstructed its operation. Finally, the division of power was not possible in such a circumscribed political space.

Nahum thus found himself at the head of an ungovernable community and could live only on a day-to-day basis. His image and his activities created a dynamic, even an incitement to conflict, however, that woke Ottoman Jewry from its lethargy. The anti-Zionism of Nahum and his Alliancist entourage also contributed indirectly to advancing the Zionist cause among the masses, because Zionism succeeded through this confrontation.

The chief rabbi primarily aimed, if not at emancipation, at least at the integration of the Jews in the postrevolutionary Empire. In fact in the beginning he did not understand the significance of Zionism as a national movement; various other brands of nationalism were developing in the Near East at the same time. In this respect, he remained loyal to the Alliance. But he showed flexibility and did not break off the dialogue with the Zionist leaders. After his resignation in 1923, Chaim Weizmann even suggested that Nahum help to improve relations between Great Britain and Turkey.[150] On the other hand, Nahum did not deny the centrality of Palestine to Jewish life, an attitude that, for such a man, in such a position and in the context of the Empire at that time, did not conflict with his views on Zionism. He continued to pursue this line after his resignation, declaring that the Jews of Turkey would continue to cooperate with the rest of Jewry in the intellectual, economic, and commercial restoration of Palestine.[151] He was thus taking a step forward by acknowledging the importance of the Balfour Declaration in changing the focus of the Jewish people's destiny, but by that time he was no longer chief rabbi and Palestine was no longer Ottoman. The post-Balfour period theoretically marked a new era in Jewry's attitude to Palestine. Nahum was following the trend. As he canvassed for the position of chief rabbi of Cairo, it was in fact more important to deal tactfully with all the tendencies in Cairo Jewry, including the turbulent and increasingly influential Zionist party.

His anti-Zionism allowed the Jewish community to live almost without hindrance through some critical moments in the history of non-Muslims in the Empire. When all is said and done, it was the chief rabbi and not the World Zionist Organization who had to handle the affairs of these Jews. They were far too turbulent for the taste of the Ottoman authorities—themselves supporters of an exclusivist nationalism. Of course, like many others, Nahum did not really believe that the Zionist political plan was viable. On the other hand, he was sufficiently farsighted not to forget that the Jews had long years still to live in a nationalist Turkey little inclined to cherish other brands of nationalism.

Haim Nahum, the last chief rabbi of a declining Empire, neither really a court Jew nor a state Jew, a privileged intercessor of the Jews and the Turks, a Levantine shtadlan, diplomat, and politician, personified Jewry in transition, torn between integration and the call of the West. Haim Nahum was "the most rabbinic of diplomats and the most diplomatic of rabbis."[152]

Notes

1. See the first letter in the correspondence below.

2. Regarding Haim Nahum, see Esther Benbassa, *Haim Nahum effendi, dernier grand rabbin de l'Empire ottoman, 1908–1920: Son rôle politique et diplomatique,* 2 vols. (Thèse de doctorat d'État, University of Paris III, 1987).

3. He was born on 23 December 1873 to Béhor Joseph Nahum and Caden Gracia, born Franco. Itzhak J. Carmin, ed., *World Jewish Register: A Biographical Compendium of Notable Jews in the Arts, Sciences, and Professions* (New York: Monde Publishers, 1955–1956), p. 667.

4. *Die Welt,* 5 February 1909.

5. These privileges were sometimes extended, depending on the period concerned, and a number of native merchants, particularly those belonging to non-Muslim minorities, tried various means to obtain these protective certificates. Only the Treaty of Lausanne in 1923 finally abolished the capitulations.

6. Kemal H. Karpat, *Ottoman Population, 1830–1914* (Madison: University of Wisconsin Press, 1985), p. 149. The figure comes from the census of 1881/1882–1893, which did not include Jews of foreign nationality.

7. For the dhimma, see Antoine Fattal, *Le statut légal des non-Musulmans en pays d'Islam* (Beirut: Imprimerie Catholique, 1958); Bat Ye'Or, *The Dhimmi: Jews and Christians under Islam* (Rutherford, N.J.: Fairleigh Dickinson University Press, 1985); Bernard Lewis, *The Jews of Islam* (Princeton, N.J.: Princeton University Press, 1984).

8. For further details, see, among other works, Ed Engelhardt, *La Turquie et le Tanzimat ou histoire des réformes depuis 1826 jusqu'à nos jours,* 2 vols. (Paris: A. Cotillon, 1882–1884).

9. A. Schopoff, *Les réformes et la protection des Chrétiens en Turquie, 1673–1904* (Paris: Plon, 1904).

10. Roderic H. Davison, "Turkish Attitudes Concerning Christian Muslim Equality in the Nineteenth Century," *American Historical Review* 59 (1954): 844–64.

11. The most recent work on this subject is Jonathan Frankel, "Crisis as a Factor in Modern Jewish Politics, 1840 and 1881–82," in Jehuda Reinharz, ed., *Living with Antisemitism: Modern Jewish Responses* (Hanover, N.H.: University Press of New England, 1987), pp. 42–58.

12. Regarding this solidarity, see Phyllis Cohen Albert, "Ethnicité et solidarité chez les Juifs de France au XIXe siècle," *Pardès* 3 (1986): 41–45.

13. The book by Edward Said, although polemical, emphasizes the role of ideology in the statements by the West about the East; *Orientalism* (New York: Pantheon Books, 1978).

14. See Esther Benbassa, "Israël face à lui-même: Judaïsme occidental et judaïsme ottoman, XIXe–XXe siècles," *Pardès* 7 (1988): 105–29.

15. Paul Mendes Flohr, "*Fin-de-siècle* Orientalism, the *Ostjuden* and the Aesthetics of Jewish Self-Affirmation," in Jonathan Frankel, ed., *Studies in Contemporary Jewry*, vol. 1 (Bloomington: Indiana University Press, 1984), p. 102.

16. For relations between Islam and Europe, see Bernard Lewis, *The Muslim Discovery of Europe* (London: Weidenfeld and Nicolson, 1982).

17. For the status of the Alliance, see André Chouraqui, *Cent ans d'histoire: l'Alliance Israélite Universelle* (Paris: Presses Universitaires de France, 1965); for ideology, see Georges Weill, "Emancipation et humanisme: Le discours idéologique de l'Alliance Israélite Universelle au XIXe siècle," *Nouveaux Cahiers* 52 (1978): 1–20.

18. Aron Rodrigue, "French Jews, Turkish Jews: The Alliance Israélite Universelle in Turkey, 1860–1914" (Ph.D. diss., Harvard University, 1985). See also the published version: *French Jews, Turkish Jews: The Alliance Israélite Universelle and the Politics of Jewish Schooling in Turkey, 1860–1925* (Bloomington: Indiana University Press, 1990).

19. See Esther Benbassa and Aron Rodrigue, "L'artisanat juif en Turquie à la fin du XIXe siècle: L'Alliance Israélite Universelle et ses oeuvres d'apprentissage," *Turcica* 17 (1985): 113–26.

20. The recent book by Aron Rodrigue quotes a selection of the letters written by these teachers: *Images of Sephardi and Eastern Jewries in Transition. The Teachers of the Alliance Israélite Universelle, 1860–1939* (Seattle: University of Washington Press, 1993).

21. J. Bauer, *L'école rabbinique de France, 1830–1930* (Paris: Plon, 1930), p. 187.

22. For a copy of these diplomas, see AAIU, Turkey XXX E, H. Nahum, 29 July 1902.

23. See, for example, the interview Nahum gave to *Osmanischer Lloyd*, reported by *El Tiempo*, 11 June 1909. During his rabbinate, Nahum recalled at leisure his friendships with the Young Turks in Paris, including Ahmed Riza (1859–1930), future deputy and president of the Chamber.

24. See H. Nahum to J. Bigart, 2 February 1899 and 11 January 1900, below.

25. AAIU, Turkey XXX E, J. Bigart, 27 January 1899 (draft of a letter).

26. *El Tiempo*, 19 August 1908; Abraham Elmaleh, "Rabbi Haim Nahoum, sa vie, ses oeuvres," *Le Judaïsme Séphardi* 22 (August 1961): 946.

27. Postwar reflections on these relations, corresponding to the political interests of the European powers in the Near East, were well founded but often excessive: MAE, section Levant, 1918–1929, subsection Palestine/Zionism, vol. 10, Allizer to the Minister of Foreign Affairs, 28 September 1918; PRO, 371/4167/59630, A. Calthorpe to the Foreign Office, 15 April 1919 (there are a number of British sources on this subject).

28. See "The Falasha Adventure," below.

29. Regarding this exaggeration, see Elie Kedourie, "Young Turks, Freemasons, and Jews," *Middle Eastern Studies* 7 (1), (January 1971): 89–104.

30. *La Vara*, 28 July 1905; 11 May 1906; 25 May 1906; 22 June 1906; 18 January 1907.

31. *BAIU* 34 (1909), 93; Tevfik Çavdar, *Talât Pasha: The Biography of a Master of Organization* (Ankara: Dost Kitabevi, 1984), pp. 30–33 (in Turkish).

32. *Jewish World,* 9 October 1908.

33. See the evidence of the United States ambassador to the Ottoman Empire, Oscar Straus, *Univers Israélite* 7 (28 October 1910): 216 (extract from his statement to the *Jewish Chronicle*).

34. *Univers Israélite* 22 (12 February 1909): 697.

35. H. Nahum to J. Bigart, 8 September 1908, below; AAIU, Turkey XXX E, H. Nahum, 18 March 1913.

36. H. Nahum to I. Fernandez, 2 August 1908, below. See also Esther Benbassa, "L'Alliance Israélite Universelle et l'élection de Haim Nahum au grand rabbinat de l'Empire ottoman, 1908–1909," in *Proceedings of the Ninth World Congress of Jewish Studies,* Division B, vol. 3 (Jerusalem: World Union of Jewish Studies, 1986), pp. 83–90.

37. J. Bigart to H. Nahum, 21 August 1908, below.

38. AAIU, Register of Correspondence, S 218, J. Bigart, 29 November 1908.

39. Isaiah Friedman, "The *Hilfsverein,* the German Minister of Foreign Affairs, and the Polemic with the Zionists, 1908–1911," *Cathedra* 20 (Tammuz 5741/July 1981): 101–102 (in Hebrew); *El Tiempo,* 19 November 1908.

40. *El Avenir,* 19 January 1909.

41. See *El Avenir,* 15 January 1909; *El Tiempo,* 22 January 1909.

42. *Univers Israélite* 20 (29 January 1909): 626.

43. J. Bigart to H. Nahum, 25 January 1909, below.

44. The chief rabbi was present at a general council (*meclis-i umumî*) composed of sixty lay members, theoretically elected by the Jews of Istanbul and its suburbs, and twenty religious members chosen from inside the rabbinic corps by the sixty lay members. These eighty people in their turn elected the spiritual council (*meclis-i ruhanî*) composed of seven rabbis, chosen from the religious members of the general council, and the lay council or executive (*meclis-i cismanî*), numbering nine people.

45. This office was created in 1835. When the Ottomans conquered Istanbul in 1453, a temporary office of chief rabbi was introduced, but its jurisdiction did not extend beyond Istanbul.

46. For the original text of this statute: *Konstitusion para la nasion israelita de Turkia* (n.p.: Estamparia del Djornal Israelit, 5625/1865). The Greeks obtained a statute in 1862 and the Armenians the Gregorian rite in 1863.

47. *Konstitusion,* p. 1.

48. Stanford Shaw, "The Ottoman Census System and Population," *International Journal of Middle Eastern Studies* 9 (1978): 337; Karpat, *Ottoman Population,* 169. These data reflect the census of 1906–1907. Statistics produced by the headmasters of Alliance schools, serving in the Empire, show 560,000 Jews in 1909, comprising 70,000 in Istanbul, 90,000 in Salonika, 60,000 in Jerusalem, and 40,000 in Smyrna (*Univers Israélite* 22 [12 February 1909]: 697. The difference between them is explained by the unreliability of both sets of statistics; in addition, the Ottoman figures did not include Jews of foreign nationality.

49. See Catherine Nicault-Lévigne, "Les juifs français et le sionisme de 1896 à 1920," *Yod* 3 (2) (1978): 30–41; Michel Abitbol, *Les deux terres promises: Les Juifs de France et le sionisme* (Paris: Olivier Orban, 1989), pp. 19–44.

50. Several files in the Alliance Archives testify to the extent of the conflict between the Alliance and the Zionists. See, for example, AAIU, Bulgaria I G 14,

M. Cohen, 8 August 1898; Central Committee of the Zionists of Bulgaria, 2 August 1903; AAIU, Bulgaria I G 7, G. Arié, 14 May 1911.

51. J. Bigart to H. Nahum, 26 November 1909, below.

52. *El Tiempo,* 23 August 1912; 11 September 1912; *Lloyd Ottoman,* 20 September 1912; *Ha-Herut,* 23 September 1912 (these periodicals reproduced extracts from that press and mention the steps taken by Nahum and some notables in government to bring these campaigns to an end).

53. Esther Benbassa, "Zionism and the Politics of Coalitions in the Ottoman Jewish Communities in the Early Twentieth Century," in Aron Rodrigue, ed., *Ottoman and Turkish Jewry Community and Leadership* (Bloomington: Indiana University Turkish Studies 12, 1992).

54. For the Alliance's refusal to make available to its sympathizers the necessary means to counterbalance Zionist propaganda, see AAIU, Turkey I G 1, J. Loria, 16 November 1910; AAIU, E. Nathan, 21 March 1911.

55. Gran Rabinato de Turkia, *Las eleksiones para el medjliss umumi* (Constantinople: El Korreo, 5671/1910), p. 4.

56. CZA, Z2/9, D. Wolffsohn to V. Jacobson, 20 June 1910; CZA, I. Auerbach to D. Wolffsohn, 25 June 1910; CZA, V. Jacobson to D. Wolffsohn, 23 June 1910.

57. It is even possible to speak of friendly relations, with the Ruppin couple, for example: CZA, A 107/84, Ms. Nahum to Ms. Ruppin, 13 December 1918.

58. See, among other works, Neville J. Mandel, "Ottoman Policy and Restrictions on Jewish Settlement in Palestine, 1881–1908, Part 1," *Middle Eastern Studies* 10 (3), (1974): 312–32; "Ottoman Practise as Regards Jewish Settlement in Palestine, 1881–1908," *Middle Eastern Studies* 11 (1), (January 1975): 33–46; and "Turks, Arabs, and Jewish Immigration into Palestine, 1882–1914," *St. Antony's Papers* 17 (1965): 77–108.

59. See the rather anecdotal book by Abraham Galanté, *Abdul Hamid II et le Sionisme* (Istanbul: Fratelli Haïm, 1933).

60. Neville J. Mandel, *The Arabs and Zionism Before World War I* (Berkeley: University of California Press, 1976), p. 225.

61. See *Ha-Olam,* 3 March 1909; *Ha-Zevi,* 15 Adar 1840 after the destruction of the Temple/8 March 1909.

62. *Hamevasser,* 29 Shevet 5670/8 February 1910; 20 Adar 5670/1 March 1910.

63. *Ha-Zevi,* 19 Heshvan 1841 after the destruction of the Temple/25 October 1909; *Ha-Or,* 11 Av 1842 after the destruction of the Temple/16 August 1910.

64. *Ha-Or,* 9 Sivan 1841 after the destruction of the Temple/16 June 1910.

65. *L'Aurore,* 27 December 1910; 17 January 1911.

66. *Jewish World,* 4 June 1909; *El Tiempo,* 7 September 1909; 9 September 1909.

67. CZA, Z3/45, V. Jacobson to R. Lichtheim, 16 January 1913.

68. CZA, Z3/66, H. Nahum to Victor Jacobson, 26 September 1913 (telegram).

69. H. Nahum to J. Bigart, 3 January 1910, below. For the booklet, see David Fresco, *Le Sionisme* (Istanbul: Imprimerie Fresco, 1909).

70. *El Tiempo,* 22 March 1911; *Univers Israélite* 30 (7 April 1911): 121–22.

71. CZA, Z3/66, H. Nahum to Jacobson, 12 February 1914.

72. During the First World War, the Ottoman Empire was on the side of the Central Powers.

73. Founded in 1914 by wealthy Jews of German origin to help war victims, it

later incorporated two other committees, hence the name. It is also known as the JDC, or the "Joint."

74. AAA, Turkey 195, K178268-178271, R. von Kühlmann to T. von Bethmann Hollweg, 15 February 1917.

75. CZA, Z3/66, extracts from a letter by Arthur Ruppin to the Central Zionist Office, 14 September 1917.

76. AAA, Turkey 195, K179259, J. Waldburg to Auswärtiges Amt, 27 July 1917; K179725-179726, H. Nahum to R. von Kühlmann, 29 October 1917; K179775-179782, R. von Kühlmann to H. Nahum, 13 November 1917 (draft).

77. CZA, Z3/66, J. Thon to O. Warburg, 1 June 1917.

78. AAA, Turkey 195, K178810, R. von Kühlmann to Auswärtiges Amt, 30 May 1917; *Univers Israélite* 40 (29 June 1917): 379.

79. *Journal d'Orient*, 25 March 1919; PRO, 371/3388/29730, memorandum on the attitude of enemy governments toward Zionism, received 16 February 1918.

80. Isaiah Friedman, *Germany, Turkey, and Zionism, 1897–1918* (Oxford: Clarendon Press, 1977), p. 354.

81. *El Tiempo*, 10 March 1919; *Ikdam*, 9 March 1919.

82. *El Tiempo*, 10 March 1919; H. Nahum to President of the Alliance, 27 April 1919, below.

83. For example, on his intervention in conjunction with Arthur Ruppin, see AAA, Turkey 195, K180486, J. H. Bernstorff to G. von Hartling, 28 May 1918.

84. AAIU, Turkey I G 1, A. Benveniste, 2 April 1919.

85. MAE, Levant, 1918–1929, subsection Turkey, vol. 112, H. Nahum to S. Pichon, 1919.

86. MAE, Levant, A. Defrance to S. Pichon, 31 July 1919.

87. Ibid.

88. PRO, 371/4168/145809, R. Webb to the Foreign Office, 17 October 1919.

89. CZA, Z4/1221 (I), I. Caleb to the Zionist Organization, 28 December 1919.

90. PRO, 371/4167/59630, A. Calthorpe to the Foreign Office, 15 April 1919.

91. CZA, Z4/888, M. Dizengoff to M. Ussischkine, T. Zlatopolski, I. A. Naiditch, 26 August 1919.

92. PRO, 371/4167/59630, Foreign Office to A. Calthorpe.

93. AAIU, Turkey, II C 8, A. Benveniste, 30 March 1920.

94. *La Nation,* 28 July 1920.

95. AAIU, Turkey II C 8, A. Benveniste, 2 April 1920; *Journal d'Orient,* 2 April 1920; MAE, Levant, 1918–1929, subsection Turkey, vol. 112, A. Defrance to E. A. Millerand, 7 April 1920.

96. MAE, Levant, 1918–1929, subsection Turkey, vol. 112, A. Defrance to S. Pichon, 31 July 1919.

97. AAIU, Turkey II C 8, A. Benveniste, 2 April 1920.

98. *Jewish Chronicle,* 23 July 1909.

99. AAIU, Turkey II C 8, H. Nahum, 14 November 1912.

100. MAE, Levant, 1918–1929, subsection Turkey, vol. 112, A. Defrance to S. Pichon, 31 July 1919.

101. MAE, Levant, 1918–1929, subsection Turkey, vol. 112, A. Defrance to E. A. Millerand, 7 April 1920.

102. MAE, Levant, 1918–1929, subsection Turkey, vol. 112, General Franchet d'Esperey to the Minister of Foreign Affairs, 5 August 1920.

103. The men in question were Oscar Straus (intermittently between 1889 and 1910), Henry Morgenthau (1913–1916), and Abraham Elkus (1916–1917).

104. For these visits, see the files devoted to them: AAIU, France XI 76; Zosa Szajkowski, "The Alliance Israélite Universelle in the United States, 1860–1949," *Publications of the American Jewish Historical Society* 29, pt. 4 (June 1950): 439–40.

105. AAIU, Turkey II C 8, H. Morgenthau to C. E. Hughes, 11 January 1922 (marked "confidential").

106. CZA, Z3/95, V. Jacobson to the EAC, 19 June 1918.

107. H. Nahum to President of the Alliance, 27 April 1919, below.

108. AAA, Turkey 195, K178268-178271, R. von Kühlmann to B. Hollweg, 15 February 1917.

109. H. Nahum to President of the Alliance, 27 April 1919.

110. *Ha-Or,* 8 Shevat 1842 after the destruction of the Temple/6 February 1917.

111. H. Nahum to J. Bigart, 30 January 1911, below.

112. *El Tiempo,* 20 March 1914; *Ha-Herut,* 6 April 1914.

113. PRO, 371/4141/47775, R. Webb to A. J. Balfour, 8 March 1919; *Ikdam,* 9 March 1919; *Le Moniteur Oriental,* 8 March 1919; *El Tiempo,* 13 February 1920.

114. MAE, Levant, 1918–1929, subsection Palestine/Zionism, vol. 10, Minister of the Republic of France in the Netherlands to the Minister of Foreign Affairs, 28 September 1918.

115. *Excelsior,* 24 July 1921.

116. *El Tiempo,* 14 August 1918.

117. MAE, Levant, 1918–1929, Ambassador of the French Republic in Berne to the Minister of Foreign Affairs, 28 August 1918.

118. MAE, Levant, 1918–1929, Minister of the French Republic in the Netherlands to the Minister of Foreign Affairs, 28 September 1918, enclosed with political dispatch no. 804.

119. William Yale, "Ambassador Henry Morgenthau's Special Mission of 1917," *World Politics* 1 (3), (1949): 308–20.

120. *Le Moniteur Oriental,* 8 March 1919; PRO, 371/4141/47775, R. Webb to A. J. Balfour, 8 March 1919.

121. MAE, Levant, 1918–1929, subsection Palestine/Zionism, vol. 10, S. Pichon to French Ambassador in London, 27 November 1918.

122. MAE, Levant, 1918–1929, subsection Palestine/Zionism, vol. 10, S. Pichon to French Ambassador in London, 27 November 1918.

123. PRO, 371/4141/6408, Lord Kilmarnock to the Foreign Office, 11 January 1919.

124. CZA, Z3/1489, notes on Haim Nahum's trip by R. Lichtheim, 3 November 1918.

125. PRO, 371/4168/82995, appendix 1, R. Webb to the Foreign Office, 20 May 1919.

126. *Archives de la Marine,* SS Ea 199, information sent from Geneva, 9 July 1917.

127. MAE, Levant, 1918–1929, subsection Turkey, vol. 112, A. Defrance to Paris, 23 September 1919.

128. These were the manifestos of Erzurum and Sivas in 1919.

129. 15 October 1919; 3 November 1919; 12 November 1919; 6 December 1919.

130. *Tasvir-i Efkâr,* 3 August 1922; *Tevhid-i Efkâr,* 3 August 1922.

131. 26 September 1922.

132. On his role, consult MAE, Levant, 1918–1929, subsection Turkey, vol. 283–318, passim.

133. Future prime minister (1923–1937), then president of the Turkish Republic (1938–1950).

134. Tenth-century Jewish doctor who took on important political and diplomatic responsibilities at the court of the Ommiad Caliph, Abd al-Rahman III.

135. Gabriel Valensi (1845–1915), general in the army of the bey of Tunis.

136. Kadir Misiroğlu, *Lausanne: Victory or Defeat?* (Istanbul: Sebil Yayinevi, 1965), pp. 111–14, passim (in Turkish).

137. *Tevhid-i Efkâr,* 23 July 1922.

138. On this campaign, see, for example, *Jewish Chronicle,* 22 December 1922.

139. For the Egyptian Jewish community under Haim Nahum's rabbinate, consult Gudrun Krämer, *The Jews in Modern Egypt, 1914–1952* (Seattle: University of Washington Press, 1989).

140. On the court Jew, see Selma Stern's classic book, *The Court Jew* (Philadelphia: Jewish Publication Society, 5710/1950); Jonathan I. Israel, *European Jewry in the Age of Mercantilism, 1550–1750,* 2d ed. (Oxford: Clarendon Press, 1989), pp. 123–44.

141. The age of the court Jews, properly speaking.

142. Later, the image of the court Jew became confused with that of the banker, who circulated in the higher circles of political power, advised the leaders, and became a symbol of economic success. See Pierre Birnbaum, *Anti-Semitism in France* (Oxford: Blackwell, 1992), pp. 29–33.

143. On the integration of the French Jews into the state and the state Jew, see Birnbaum, *Anti-Semitism in France,* pp. 17–32 and passim. I have adopted the term "state Jew" from this work.

144. Birnbaum, *Anti-Semitism in France,* pp. 15–17.

145. See Haim Nahum's statements in *Tevhid-i Efkâr,* 23 July 1922.

146. A descendant of the Sabbateans, Jews who followed the false messiah, Shabbatai Zvi, and converted to Islam in the seventeenth century.

147. *Encyclopaedia Judaica,* new English ed., vol. 14 (Jerusalem: Keter Publishing House, 1972), pp. 1462–63; Stern, *The Court Jew,* pp. 177–207.

148. Stern, *The Court Jew,* p. 181.

149. CZA, Z2/32, D. Wolffsohn to N. Leven, 21 February 1911; J. Bigart and N. Leven to D. Wolffsohn, 3 March 1911; D. Wolffsohn to N. Leven, 10 April 1911.

150. Chaim Weizmann, *The Letters and Papers,* vol. 9 (Jerusalem/New Brunswick, N.J.: Oxford University Press, Israel University Press, Rutgers University Press, 1968), Series A, Letters, January 1922–July 1923, C. Weizmann to I. Naiditch, 10 October 1922, pp. 184–85 (see also p. 184, n. 6).

151. Haim Nahum, "Jews," in Eliot Grinnell Mears, *Modern Turkey* (New York: Macmillan, 1924), p. 97.

152. G. Krämer, *The Jews in Modern Egypt,* p. 97.

The Correspondence

IN THE SERVICE OF A CAUSE:
THE ALLIANCE ISRAÉLITE UNIVERSELLE

As a young man, Haim Nahum applied to the Alliance Israélite Universelle for a grant so that he could continue his studies in Europe.

Constantinople, 4 January 1892

Honorable Monsieur Goldschmidt,
President of the Central Committee in Paris[1]

Monsieur le Président,

Having the good fortune to be able to rely on the philanthropy and generosity that are characteristic of you, I am taking the liberty of disclosing to your beneficent humanity the pitiful state of my terrible poverty, which I have been warding off for a long time.

My name is Haim Nahum, I was born in Magnesia, and I am eighteen years old.

From a very early age, people have noticed my rather unusual aptitude for study.

When Monsieur Vénéziani,[2] visited Magnesia ten years ago, he wanted to take me away and assume responsibility for my education, but my parents, who were comfortably off at the time, opposed my departure.

There is no educational institution in Magnesia, and as I passionately wanted to study, I went with my grandfather to Tiberias, where I learned Talmud and Arabic. The rabbis in that town gave me a certificate attesting to my knowledge in that area.

From Tiberias, I went back to my birthplace, Magnesia. The pasha of that town sent me to Smyrna at his expense to complete my studies in the Turkish language and French at an Ottoman high school.

I left with my baccalauréat in arts and science. Today, I am here in the capital in the greatest poverty. I came to study law and diplomacy and I do not have the means to do so (it is a day school).

I am taking the liberty of writing to you because I am certain that I will receive a favorable reply and I will be indebted to you for my material and moral life.

---

[1]Salomon H. Goldschmidt, philanthropist and president of the Alliance central committee from 1881 to 1898.

[2]Emmanuel Félix Vénéziani (1825–1889), director of the Camondo Bank in Istanbul, where he was a member of the Alliance regional committee and closely connected with the philanthropic activities of Baron Maurice de Hirsch.

In addition to the grant that the chief rabbi has given me, I still need a monthly subsidy of at least 40.80 francs.

Your good deeds are by now beyond measure.

In the hope of a favorable answer from you.

I have the honor to be, with the greatest respect,

Your very humble and very obedient servant.

P.S. I have the baccalauréat and the certificate with me. Otherwise, I would like to go to Paris to study law and diplomacy there and then finish my theological studies.

(AAIU, Turkey, XXX E)

Haim Nahum returned to the Ottoman capital after four years in Paris. He took up his post at the rabbinic seminary, which had just been transferred from Adrianople to the Hasköy district of Istanbul, on the Golden Horn. The relocation heralded a new stage in the westernization of Judaism in Constantinople, but the venture did not yield the anticipated results, and the seminary's position was jeopardized in the course of time.

19 January 1898

Monsieur le Président

As soon as I received your letter, I set off for the capital to take up the position you entrusted to me. After calling on the chief rabbi and the president of the regional committee, we busied ourselves with Monsieur A. Danon setting up the seminary, and we have drawn up its program.

. . . except for the classes in *Aggadah*,[3] *Yerushalmi*,[4] and homiletics, which necessarily have to be given in Spanish,[5] I propose to teach history and literature in French and science in Turkish.

For what there is of the latter, as there is only one hour a week, I think that the first year should be used to teach natural history, the second, physics and chemistry, and the third, arithmetic and geometry.

We start our lessons next Monday, the first of the month of Shevat.[6] The Jewish population in general is very enthusiastic about the work we have undertaken.

Since my arrival, I have been lodging with Monsieur Nabon,[7] who has really put himself out for me. While waiting, as my financial situation does

---

[3]Hebrew term designating the traditional homiletic literature, generally used to distinguish it from *halakha*, which designates legal literature.

[4]This is the *Targum Yerushalmi*, an Aramaic paraphrase of the Bible.

[5]In fact in Judeo-Spanish, the vernacular of the Jews in the Empire, who came originally from Spain.

[6]Shevat, the month in the Hebrew calendar corresponding to January/February.

[7]David Nabon (1859–1924), headmaster of the Alliance boys' school in Hasköy.

not permit me to rent a room and furnish it, I will be forced to stay at the school, despite the dampness that prevails.

(. . .)

(AAIU, Turkey, XXX E)

Haim Nahum was not content merely to teach. He was formulating a detailed strategy to advance his career.

Hasköy, 17 March 1898

Dear Monsieur Bigart,[8]

First of all, please forgive me for not writing since I arrived in Constantinople. I could have sent you only one letter and that a formal one. Now I am taking advantage of a rare free moment and hastening to fulfill my obligation and write to you personally.

Well, dear Monsieur Bigart, here I am embarked on working life and I am proud of it, because it is the work I wanted. At present I am tasting the pleasure of the bustle of activity, which adds to the happiness of life. For me, the pleasure is the teaching, which is taking up all my thoughts and all my energy at the moment.

. . . as far as my own position is concerned, I am very well thought of by the chief rabbi, who invites me to his home from time to time, by his son-in-law (leader of the entourage), and above all by the notables and by well-placed people who have asked me to give a lecture after the festival of Passover.

I am thinking of renting a furnished room with a good Israelite family in Galata,[9] where the cost of living is much higher but where communications are better than in Hasköy. Here I am losing a lot of time and I cannot work. It is constant coming and going. My ten hours of teaching at the seminary and seven hours at other schools already take up time; and in the evenings I also want to do a few hours of my own work. Here I am not able to do so, while in Galata, where I will be able to have a room of my own, I will be able to devote myself to work.

This week they wanted to appoint me honorary secretary of a welfare society in Hasköy; but I had to refuse because of my many commitments. Really I am comfortable; I am earning my living and I send the small savings I make over the month to my family. That is why I ask you to think of me, as you have ever done, any time you have the chance to cast an eye to my future.

(. . .)

(AAIU, Turkey, XXX E)

---

[8]Jacques Bigart (1855–1934), secretary-general of the Alliance from 1892 until his death.
[9]District of Istanbul with a large concentration of Jews.

The Alliance's work of training and education made headway among the lower orders. Nahum, who had faith in both its ideology and its work, embarked also on activity aimed at the Jewish bourgeoisie, whose support seemed to him crucial if the Alliance were to survive.

Hasköy, 3 May 1898

Dear Monsieur Leven,[10]

I want to talk to you about a matter that I think does not lack interest: this is the evening class, organized a few months ago at the Alliance school at Hasköy.

Two or three days before the Passover holiday, Monsieur Nabon, head of the aforesaid school, invited me to attend one of these evening classes. I went along. There were then twenty pupils, most of them twenty-five years old. They included two married men, aged forty. The lesson began at seven. It was a moving scene.

These unfortunate people (almost all of them are bootblacks, porters, ragpickers who barely earn their daily bread) looked very attentively at the board, on which the teacher was writing the letters of the Judeo-Spanish alphabet[11] and kept very still, like children brought up in a home.

They were utterly amazed the moment they began to decipher a word, in the process becoming aware of the importance of education.

When the lesson was over, I asked the teacher to give out to these pupils the little books written in Judeo-Spanish at the time of the twenty-fifth anniversary of the Alliance.

Then I gave a short talk to encourage them and make them understand the need for education. As a result of this little speech, pupils arrived in the hundreds on the day after Passover; this time their ages ranged from fifteen to forty-five. They were shouting at the school door: "We want to learn to read and write."

This party of pupils also comprised fishmongers, vegetable merchants, masons, road sweepers, etc. . . . Unfortunately, the room in which these lessons take place cannot hold a very large number of pupils, and what is more, several teachers are required. So far, Monsieur Nabon has been able to accept about 160 pupils.

Requests are now coming in daily, but they have to be refused. I go there from time to time to talk to them a bit about Jewish history.

The same thing is happening in almost every suburb of the capital. The class being instructed has also felt the need to be informed on Jewish ques-

[10]This is Narcisse Leven (1833–1915), president of the Alliance central committee since 1898.

[11]Sephardi Hebrew alphabet. *Rashi* for printed letters, *solitreo* for cursive, in which Judeo-Spanish was traditionally transliterated, before the belated adoption of the Latin alphabet.

tions. With this end in view, welfare societies have organized lectures in the synagogues on Saturdays.

Monsieur Danon and I speak about Judaism in general, and the headmasters of the Alliance schools talk about manual labor, arts and crafts, etc. . . . These lectures are given to large audiences. Last Saturday I spoke at Kuzguncuk;[12] next Saturday at Piripaşa;[13] and the following Saturday at Hasköy. During Pentecost, I am going to give a sermon in French at the Italian temple[14] in Galata.

In a word, the population that had completely lost hope for the future of Judaism is beginning to hold its head up high. For example, I take the liberty of translating for you the conclusions of an article covering three large columns that appeared in a Judeo-Spanish paper in Smyrna and was copied by papers in the provinces and in the capital. This article is the report of the lecture I gave at Smyrna during the festival of Passover, at the invitation of the committee of former pupils, an association of which you are president.

These are the conclusions:

> The people, like a child, need a good education. The preacher is for the people what the teacher is to the child. In the same way that the teacher can guide the child on the paths of good or evil, the preacher guides the people as he wishes. Everything depends on the way in which the audience is addressed. How many useful institutions owe their existence to the words of eloquent preachers!
>
> If the preacher counsels his audience to love God, to love his neighbor, to respect and practice truth, to love work, and if he also preaches by example, his sermons certainly strengthen unity, bring together those who are far apart; then enemies become friends, and the moral values of the people are improved.
>
> Convinced of all this, our mother, the holy Alliance, yes, the holy Alliance, has just founded a seminary conducted by the scholarly Monsieur Abraham Danon and our eloquent lecturer Rabbi Nahum. Thanks to the benevolence of this blessed mother, we will see the realization of the idea we cherish, which we were already thinking was utopian. We will have the good fortune to have good preachers who will be able to rekindle our religious feelings, for so long extinguished.

The lecture and the article have had some effect. We have just read in a Smyrna paper that the committee of the association of former pupils of Alliance schools at Smyrna has voted the seminary a small annual grant. Let us hope that other societies will want to imitate the Smyrna one.

---

[12]Kuzguncuk, the district of Istanbul, situated on the Asiatic coast.
[13]Piripaşa, the district of Istanbul (Hasköy).
[14]The synagogue of Jews of Italian nationality, the Francos.

The Jewish history lessons I give the first classes at Hasköy and Galata are being followed studiously. Twice a month I give them short lectures on Jewish ethics.

. . . the population continues to be very sympathetic. Several notables have put their names down to send the seminary a small annual subscription, and the society called "Dorshei Leshon Ever"[15] has promised to donate its little Hebrew library to us.

In a word, with practice, we hope to succeed in achieving something.

(. . .)

(AAIU, Turkey, XXX E)

The synagogue: a strategic zone.

Hasköy, 9 June 1898

Dear Monsieur Bigart.

This week the series of Saturday lectures concluded. Since the festival of Passover until after Pentecost, there has not been a Saturday without a sermon or lecture. We are pleased to see this passionate desire on the part of all our coreligionists to hear the ethical truth. They are not satisfied with an hour's discourse, they want one to speak to them for an hour and a half and longer if possible. We are also happy to see everyone hurrying to send in their subscriptions to the seminary. Propaganda committees have been formed in some suburbs of the capital. These committees are composed of very educated and respected people who work for this cause with love.

. . . this enthusiasm is spreading not only to our coreligionists in the capital but even to those who live overseas.

(. . .)

(AAIU, Turkey, XXX E)

Nahum was also well informed. His knowledge of Turkish gave him access to the local press and enabled him to follow Ottoman policy concerning both the Jews and the Alliance directly, without relying on interpreters, at a time when most Alliance teachers working in the Empire did not speak that language even though a fair number of them were natives of the country.

Constantinople, 26 July 1898

Dear Monsieur Bigart,

Today, the paper *Tercüman-i-Hakikat*[16] contains a very long article, filling four large columns, entitled "The Israelites and the Turkish Language." I do

---

[15]*Dorshei Leshon Ever,* in Hebrew: "The friends of the Hebrew language," a Haskala-type Istanbul association.

[16]Turkish nationalist paper (1877–1922).

not need to tell you that it is excessively flattering. It begins by paying homage to H.I.M. the sultan, from the day of whose accession relations between his different subjects became increasingly fraternal. Language is proof of this fraternity. The Israelites have felt the need to familiarize themselves with the Turkish language, which they have introduced into all their schools, and have thus become true Ottomans. "All Ottomans have an imperative duty to appreciate this devotion and this loyalty on the part of the Jews. What an honor for the whole Turkish nation to have in its midst a people as old as the world, a serious people who have been able to cross time and space amid countless sufferings and diverse vicissitudes! How many good and useful consequences are there for us in our relationships with the Israelites!"

The *Şule-i-maarif* school,[17] founded a few years ago, is, so the article claims, a striking example of the Israelites' goodwill. This love of the Turkish language spreading among the youth can easily be seen in all the Israelite schools in the Empire. It is thanks to the Alliance Israélite that our cocitizens are succeeding in raising their ethical level. This forms the second part of the article.

> The Alliance Israélite, whose head office is in Paris, has understood the moral and material situation of the Israelites in our country. It has seen that the Israelites have lived in security under the efficient protection of the Empire for long years, and it has always appreciated this imperial kindness and justice; it has not failed to demonstrate its feelings of appreciation and gratitude at every opportunity. It can be stated without fear of contradiction because it is the undiluted truth that the Alliance's works for the improvement of the intellectual and moral state of the Israelites are works resulting from very praiseworthy efforts that make for the glory, the pride, and the ornament of the annals of the Jews. Whenever Ottoman Jewry has turned to it to ask for help, the Alliance has not failed to give it very graciously.

Then it talks about the continual attacks of which the Alliance is the object and goes on to speak about the establishment of the seminary in very flattering terms, in relation to both the institution itself and its staff.

The author ends the second part of his article as follows: "We congratulate all our Israelite cocitizens on their efforts; and thank them once again for their love of our homeland, our government, and our language. We wish them every sort of success. To all Ottomans I give the good news that, God willing, we will in the very near future see a really useful people, devoted to the country, and raised and nurtured on a purely Ottoman education."

The author adds a long postscript to this article in which he censures and attacks anti-Semites.

---

[17]"Gathering for education" (in Turkish), a Jewish school founded in 1887, where teaching took place in Turkish.

This is the first time that I have seen an article so warmly favorable to the Israelites. I have tried to give you a brief summary. I am, if you wish, prepared to translate the whole article from beginning to end for you.

(. . .)

(AAIU, Turkey, XXX E)

It did not take Nahum long to inform himself on what was happening in the community. The Alliance took a close interest: far from the center, it depended on this information so that it could adjust its local policy to the situation.

Hasköy, 30 November 1898

Dear Monsieur Bigart,

It really is a long time since I had the honor of writing to you. I know that I was much at fault. But since the holidays there has been nothing new to report.

During the holiday month, I have been busy with a small piece I am preparing on the history of the Jews of Babylon, according to the Talmud. But unfortunately I do not have sufficiently serious sources to refer to. To be precise, I have only a Talmud at my disposal.

Classes opened immediately after the festivals, during which I gave no fewer than five sermons in different suburbs of the capital. Our style of preaching is most enjoyed in Galata, in particular, an aristocratic suburb. Yielding to the wish that the public has frequently expressed, I have contracted to write a sermon on the sabbatical sidra[18] every week for the paper *El Tiempo*,[19] under the title "The Religious and Moral Week." All this takes up a lot of my time.

Our seminary progresses daily. We note a great appetite for all religious knowledge among our pupils and above all devotion to their work. These good qualities make my task easier, because it is very hard to give a serious lesson to pupils whose knowledge varies. Today, thank God, the class is fairly homogeneous. I am continuing my series of lessons from last year.

. . . as to what is happening outside the seminary, I will add a word about the Constantinople community.

The Jewish population of the capital has already been showing signs of dissatisfaction for a long time, and this is gradually spreading to all the Israelites and has taken root in every heart. Not long ago a petition against the chief rabbi was presented at the palace, signed by several Israelites. This petition naturally came to nothing. In the eyes of the population, the chief

[18]Passage from the Pentateuch read at the Saturday morning service.
[19]*El Tiempo* (1872–1930), an Istanbul periodical that represented the sector of the capital's Jewry that was progressive and receptive to Western ideas.

rabbi's house has become a house of intrigues. His grandson, who receives 30 Ltq[20] a month by imperial *irade*[21] is accused of being a spy.

A campaign against the communal administration is now beginning. Several articles against this anarchy have been published in the Judeo-Spanish paper *El Tiempo*. Last week the chief rabbi appealed to some of our most highly placed coreligionists, asking them to form a council that could reorganize the community and promising them that their nomination would be officially recognized by the government.

As this promise has not been implemented so far, the members have begun by sending in their resignations. This is the state of affairs at present.

We still have a very good relationship with the chief rabbi, who is always prepared to help us. He it was who summoned me to his house during the holidays to tell me that it was time I set up my own home and finished with life in lodgings. It was he too who encouraged us to become engaged.

In fact, for the Orient, it was a major change just to see an unmarried rabbi mount the pulpit on the day of Kippur[22] and preach in public. But in any case, one must bow to all demands, so as not to arouse the comments of the rabbinic corps, which is steeped in the most absolute fanaticism. By acting in this way we have been able to win the respect and confidence of all the rabbis.

On the subject of setting up house, I have been thinking for some time of turning to you for advice. It is true that up till now I have lodged with a family and had my meals and my washing done there. But since then I have rented a small house so that I could start moving in gradually. Once the rent is paid, I will have just enough to pay a cook and be able to live. There are no restaurants in Hasköy. So I am not able to arrange for a little get-together. It is the custom here to visit the speaker after hearing a sermon: it is a sign of respect. I assure you that I feel very embarrassed. My position in no way resembles that of your teachers: the title of rabbi completely alters the situation.

I would be eternally grateful if you would be willing to act on my behalf with the central committee in order to improve my position so that I can set up house as modestly as possible.

Not long ago I heard that the chief rabbi of France intended to put my name forward as rabbi of the Sofia community. At present the aforesaid community has lost both a chief rabbi and a locum tenens, who has just handed in his resignation. I do not know if it would be a good idea to test the ground. I await your instructions on this.

(. . .)

(AAIU, Turkey, XXX E)

---

[20]Abbreviation of Turkish pounds.
[21]Imperial order (in Turkish).
[22]Fast of the Day of Atonement.

Nahum returned to Istanbul, and a year passed. He rapidly infiltrated the communal administration, an indispensable step toward eventually achieving the supreme office he coveted. It was also very much in the Alliance's interest that he be active inside the institutions in order to consolidate its work—all the more so as the rabbinate's position vis-à-vis the Alliance remained, if not hostile, at least ambiguous.

Hasköy, 18 January 1899

Dear Monsieur Bigart,

I am writing to give you some news that will surprise you but, I am sure, will please you. I have been appointed secretary-general of the higher administrative council (Israelite consistory)[23] and head of the chief rabbi's chancellery. I have only accepted this post provisionally while waiting for authorization from the central committee.

The last time I wrote to you, I spoke of the dissatisfaction with the chief rabbi and his administration that the public was evincing. In response to this movement, the chief rabbi is requesting the Porte's permission to form a council. The imperial irade promulgated on this subject entrusts the administration of the community to a higher council *(meclis-i cismanî),* composed of nine members. . . .

The council met for the first time last Sunday and gave the presidency to Béhor effendi[24] (the only able man among them all). No sooner was he appointed than he insisted that I be entrusted with the secretary-generalship and charge of the offices.

I have been promised five hundred piastres a month, but it is not the pay that tempts me, because not only is it minimal but its future is also uncertain, as I will explain in my next letter. I think it will not displease you if I plunge into communal affairs.

On Monday, the president showed me around and explained the type of work that I will have to do. I will have to supervise financial affairs with the president's help; see that the work of the employees is done according to the rules; take note of complaints made by the public and the decisions of the council, etc.

I have two to three hours of work every day apart from my work at the seminary and the other schools.

(. . .)

(AAIU, Turkey, XXX E)

---

[23]The reference is to the Jewish executive composed of nine lay members. The term is borrowed from the organization of the French Jewish community.

[24]Béhor effendi Eskénazi, former prefect of the capital and at the time when this letter was written a member of the Council of State (information supplied by Nahum).

Nahum's goal was still to obtain a position as chief rabbi, and he investigated various possibilities.

Constantinople, 2 February 1899

Dear Monsieur Bigart,

I have received your letter of January 27 in which you state your satisfaction with my entry into communal administration.

In one of my recent letters, I mentioned the vacant position in Sofia and asked you if it was a good idea to try and obtain this post. The time for the election of the chief rabbi has come. I have received the circular from the Bulgarian central consistory, on the one hand, and, on the other, a personal letter asking me to let my name go forward. It seems that I satisfy all the necessary conditions except that of age, which will not be too much of an issue.

I am writing to ask for your permission. I think that if I succeed in obtaining this position, it will be easy for me to obtain the one at Constantinople later. Because I will lose my status as a rabbi in the eyes of my people if I carry on with the administrative career.

But after having been rabbi in a place like Sofia, I will easily be able to obtain the position in Constantinople.

I would be grateful if you would be kind enough to give me your answer on this matter.

(. . .)

(AAIU, Turkey, XXX E)

At the same time that he was making these approaches, Nahum was also dealing with the current business of the Alliance at the local level.

Constantinople, 8 June 1899

Dear Monsieur Bigart,

In one of my recent letters, I promised to bring you up to date regarding the reforms that the Israelite consistory is proposing to make. The first question occupying the council is the communal budget.

. . . now I will mention a new question of particular interest to the Alliance because the Alliance itself is involved.

You know that we have not yet obtained official permission for the seminary.

Last year, the chief rabbi sent a request to the minister of public education to ask for authorization. This request has perhaps gone the rounds of all the ministries of Constantinople. Here in Turkey business always goes round in a vicious circle. But despite the approval of the competent ministers, in the last resort, the minister of public education (I was going to say of public ignorance, because the present minister is ignorance personified, ignorance mixed with blind fanaticism) turned to the grand vizier. . . .

. . . the grand vizier actually passed the question on to the Council of State. This latter, after having examined the chief rabbi's request and the note from the minister of education, asked the following questions (I am not trying to tell you that these questions were raised by an Israelite who occupies a seat on the Council of State; no, I would prefer to be wrong. It is simply a rumor that has been prevalent and that I am imparting to you as discreetly as possible):

1. What is the function of the Alliance?
2. Is it recognized by the state?
3. To what extent does it take part in running the schools?
4. What is the curriculum of the seminary?
5. What is its building plan?

The minister of public education informed the chief rabbi of these questions, and he in his turn informed the Council. This latter hastened to instruct one of its members, Lieutenant-Colonel Moïse bey del Médigo, Turkish language teacher at the school in Galata, to go and see Monsieur Fernandez[25] and draft the answers that should be given, in agreement with him. I do not know the result yet, but I can tell you that the response will be along these lines:

1. The function of the Alliance is to spread education among the Israelites.
2. The Alliance is recognized by the state; because some of its schools have been opened by imperial irade, and all without exception are recognized by the minister of public education, to whom they are subject as far as books and other things are concerned.
3. It takes part in school administration to support those schools that are all for the most part attended by very poor pupils.
4. The curriculum of the seminary had already been sent to the minister when it opened.
5. Does not apply for the simple reason that there is no new building.

This answer, which is still being written this morning, must be signed by the chief rabbi and presented, I believe by myself, to the minister of public education, in the names of the chief rabbi and Monsieur Fernandez.

---

[25]Isaac Fernandez, president of the Alliance regional committee in Istanbul.

I will not fail to keep you informed of all that goes on, down to the most minute details.

(. . .)
(AAIU, Turkey, XXX E)

Constantinople, 29 June 1899

Dear Monsieur Bigart,

Last week I was instructed by the chief rabbi to go to the minister of public education to answer orally the questions the Council of State sent to him.

. . . next Monday, I will go to the Council of State to find out what action will be taken on the chief rabbi's request. But I think the affair will drag on still longer because here in Turkey they have not the slightest idea of what duty is.

All the ministers are half asleep. They have to be prodded to move things along and get an answer.

The Council of State (the Senate), which according to the rules must meet four times a week, only meets once and then to skim over questions without ever making a definite decision.

Look at our so-called consistory. Soon it will be three weeks since it had a session. All the members are beginning to slack off, and communal affairs are suffering considerably.

There are hardly more than one or two members who are aware of their function, but the goodwill of two or three is not enough. The cooperation of the rest of the members is necessary, and these only attend the Council when there is a question to discuss concerning the chief rabbi, either to oppose it or to tell him everything that is going on—in a word, almost everyone is a spy.

We even give our lessons at the seminary with considerable tact and caution because it seems that we have spy pupils who are in frequent touch with the rabbinic body, the bitter enemy of our cause.

(. . .)
(AAIU, Turkey, XXX E)

The Alliance's blessings were required even in private life.

Hasköy, 20 July 1899

Monsieur le Président,

I have the honor to inform you that I am thinking of marrying Mademoiselle Sultana Danon in the course of next month.

This is a very good and happy occasion for me to express to you my deep gratitude and my eternal appreciation and at the same time to thank the central committee for the generous and benevolent help it so kindly gave me throughout my studies in Paris, help that it has not yet ceased to extend.

(. . .)

(AAIU, Turkey, XXX E)

Nahum's young wife also worked for the Alliance.

Hasköy, 3 September 1899

Monsieur,

I beg you not to attribute my absence from school in the five-day interval between the festivals of Rosh Hashana[26] and Sukkot[27] [*sic*] to laxity. A mild indisposition obliged me to go and take some baths at Bursa[28] after my wedding. I returned home yesterday, and classes start on Thursday. I need a few days to settle into my small household: my class will certainly not suffer thereby, because not only are the first days after the return taken up with registering the pupils, distributing books and materials, etc., but the children themselves return and resume their work seriously only after the festivals. I am nevertheless annoyed that I had to take this short leave because I deliberately arranged to get married during the holidays so that the school would not suffer from my absence. I had not reckoned on this bit of fatigue, which did not give me time to ask your permission for the short respite.

(. . .)

S[ultana] Nahum

(AAIU, Turkey, XXX E)

Constantinople, 17 October 1899

Dear Monsieur Bigart,

You are probably already suspicious of the excuses that I am going to make for the lateness of my letters. I would have found the time were it not for the activities that followed very closely on my marriage and setting up house.

I was recalled to Constantinople, which I had left for a few days, to give a sermon in French on the occasion of the inauguration of a temple at Haydarpaşa;[29] this was followed by another on Rosh Hashana, then at a distribution of clothing to poor children at the Tseror ha-hayim[30] Society, of which I am

---

[26]Jewish New Year.

[27]Festival of Tabernacles, commemorating the wanderings of the Hebrews in the desert, beginning five days after the fast of Yom Kippur (the Day of Atonement).

[28]Bursa, a town in northwestern Turkey, also famous for its thermal springs.

[29]Haydarpaşa, the district of Istanbul located on the Asiatic coast of the Bosphorus.

[30]*Tseror ha-hayim*, in Hebrew: "the gathering of the living" (cf. 1 Samuel 15:29).

president; then another on Kippur at the temple in Haydarpaşa, where Baron Edmond de Rothschild[31] and his family, Monsieur Straus (United States ambassador) and his family, etc. were to have been present.

Nor would my work have prevented me writing to you had I not wanted to wait until I had a definitive answer on the question of the seminary to communicate to you.

After having replied to the questions that the Council of State put to us, the inspector general of public education asked me for a list of all the Alliance schools in the Ottoman Empire, the dates when they were established, and the dates when they were recognized by the government.

I have been to see Monsieur Fernandez, who, like me, found the request slightly embarrassing in view of the fact that certain schools, the one in Tripoli, for example, do not yet have permission to operate. I have therefore asked the inspector to be content with the information that I could provide on the schools in Constantinople, on the pretext that it would be difficult for me to have data on all the schools. I presented him with the list of our schools in Constantinople, with the dates of the permits, and on this basis he sent the Council of State a favorable report on our schools and on the seminary. I even went back to the Council of State yesterday, where I was told that it will be necessary to wait another fortnight.

The new school term has left us with much to do: it has been very difficult to work out the timetable because of the preparatory class and the newly admitted pupils.

. . . before I conclude, one entirely personal and entirely selfish demand. May I ask you to approach the central committee for the loan of a sum of five hundred francs to be repaid in small quarterly installments. I do not need to tell you in what circumstances I have incurred expenses that have again left me with debts: you know that a wedding involves expenses and that it would have been impossible to do it more simply and more economically than I did.

(. . .)

(AAIU, Turkey, XXX E)

The rabbinate was suffering from chronic long-standing disorganization.

Hasköy, 21 December 1899

Dear Monsieur Bigart,

. . . but between ourselves, we know what happens inside the community. It is ever the same. One member, and unfortunately the most impartial, handed in his resignation yesterday. He could not stand for all the

---

[31]E. de Rothschild (1854–1934), a philanthropist, encouraged and financed colonization in Palestine.

irregularities. On the one hand, as an economy measure, certain small sub-sidies intended for widows, for the Talmud Torah,[32] for the food scheme in our schools for example[33] are being abolished, and, on the other, the chief rabbi is granted a bonus of 100 Ltq., on the occasion of the marriage of one of his granddaughters.

Just imagine, not all salaries are paid regularly because of lack of money. But what can you do, the chief rabbi always has the majority, because two-thirds of the members are doing nothing but working for him. These gentlemen are never present at the sessions: only when the issue concerns the chief rabbi are they there to vote. For my part, I have the task of introducing certain procedural reforms to stop the abuses; but by doing so I incur the jealousy of all these schemers.

I gave a sermon in Turkish last Tuesday on the occasion of the sultan's birthday, in addition I wrote one in Spanish that was read by the chief rabbi. You can see how little dignity these people have.

(. . .)

(AAIU, Turkey, XXX E)

Haim Nahum did not give up hope of becoming chief rabbi of Bulgaria.

Constantinople, 11 January 1900

Dear Monsieur Bigart,

A year ago at about this time, I sent you a letter in which I asked for permission to offer myself as a candidate for the chief rabbinate of Bulgaria, and you replied that "the central committee would wholeheartedly approve my appointment." The Bulgarian Israelites have had other things to do throughout the year than concern themselves with elections, but they did not want to begin another year without placing a spiritual leader at the head of their communities.

By a ministerial order, a general Congress, composed of delegates sent by all the Jewish communities, has been instructed to elect a chief rabbi.

We are sixteen candidates. The election will turn on one of three candi-dates who will be chosen from the sixteen. I have all these details from the president of the Philippopoli consistory, who came a month ago to ask for my decision unofficially and told me that general opinion is almost entirely in my favor, and that he had no doubt that I would be one of these three candidates. I did not show a great deal of enthusiasm: I will tell you why later on.

Again, the day before yesterday, Constantinople notables received letters

---

[32]Elementary religious school (here the author uses a singular for a plural).
[33]It dispensed free meals to poor children.

from a very influential member of the Congress asking for information about me: the reports sent were favorable.

. . . first, let me explain the reasons why I would be enchanted with my appointment and the reasons why I am not really enthusiastic about the position I would be offered.

The only advantage I envisage from accepting this position, a very important advantage, is that the time spent occupying it could serve as a transitional period so that I could acquire the actual status of a chief rabbi in office. Then, when the post of the chief rabbinate of Turkey stands vacant at some time or other, I will be able to offer myself as a candidate and to succeed on the basis of a well-established past record.

On the other hand, I think it my duty to explain the arguments that seem to me to outweigh this advantage and which can, I think, be usefully divided into two categories: (1) community disadvantages; (2) external disadvantages. As far as internal disadvantages are concerned, one should examine the character of the Sofia community itself, which has often shown itself unfavorable to the four rabbis who have occupied the rabbinic seat of Bulgaria.

. . . seeking the main causes, there is, first, a lack of awareness among the notables, a spirit of intrigue among the populace, and above all the existence of a disruptive party, the Zionists.

You must have realized the influence of this party from the trouble they caused Monsieur Danon, despite all his services on behalf of our coreligionists in Bulgaria, and from the emptiness of the communal coffers where salaries are concerned. All the more reason when it will be a question of being paid from local funds, as is the case with the chief rabbi.

All in all, the communities of Bulgaria cannot yet have shuffled off their oriental character, the ill effects of which we see in several communities in Turkey.

As far as the external difficulties are concerned, I have to mention the recrudescence of the anti–Semitic party, whose intentions are made manifest in the Sobranie.[34] As I would often have to sit in this chamber and continuously swallow the outbursts of this Judeo-phobe party, which is becoming increasingly powerful, I think I would cut a sorry figure, tranquilly witnessing the explosion of their lampoons without being able to say one word in reply because of my ignorance of the Bulgarian language. Likewise in official circles. It would be some consolation if I had some knowledge of the German language, which could serve in place of Bulgarian in certain circumstances.

I am not painting a gloomy picture of my future position in Sofia because I want to consider the matter from a pessimistic point of view.

[34]Bulgarian parliament.

It is a question of envisaging the consequences of accepting this post. In fact, as long as I do not venture into the unknown, I preserve my reputation intact and I may also perhaps be making progress in the esteem of the Ottoman populations, through my unceasing services and my knowledge of the languages of the country (Arabic, Turkish, Persian). It would not be the same if I experienced the slightest failure in my venture in Bulgaria; it would then become harder to return to Turkey, because my lack of success could provide a justified pretext for latent jealousies and ill will. Into the bargain, I lose my position at the seminary, and I am not certain of being able to find another position later on that would be equivalent from the moral and material point of view. If, despite these disadvantages, you think that the position should be accepted and that the consequences of this acceptance are nothing to worry about, I await your instructions as soon as possible, by return of post, so that I can give an affirmative or negative reply to the proposals of the Congress (in case I should be asked for documents and a photograph).

. . . P.S. If your response is in the affirmative, please send me my diploma from the seminary immediately.

(AAIU, Turkey, XXX E)

Despite all the precautions that Nahum took, he was not able to stay completely outside the divisions in the community. The factions took up their positions. In Jewish society there were individuals and groups desirous of change. Nahum was of them and recruited his allies from among them.

Constantinople, 27 February 1900

Dear Monsieur Bigart,

Before I wrote to you, I wanted to wait for the end of an affair that has taken place in our community and, if not important, is at least quite interesting. Here, briefly, is what it is about, but it may still be rather long.

An Israelite butcher in the capital has a shop at Balat[35] and wants to open another at Ortaköy.[36] He asks for authorization from the chief rabbi, who sends the question to the *bet din.*[37] The latter forbids it. Thereupon the butcher goes along and demands an explanation from the chief rabbi and ends up by insulting him. The chief rabbi has him arrested and consigned to the cells, and the bet din, for its part, excommunicates him. This excommunication arouses the indignation of the population, and particularly of

---

[35]Balata, a suburb of Istanbul, located on the Golden Horn.

[36]Ortaköy, a suburb of Istanbul on the European shore of the Bosphorus.

[37]Rabbinical court (in Hebrew). The slaughter as well as the sale of kosher meat (conforming to certain ritual commandments) was subject to rabbinic control.

Monsieur D. Fresco, who publishes a thundering article in his paper *El Tiempo* condemning, not only this unfair herem,[38] but the herem in general as being contrary to the spirit of the day and the Mosaic spirit.

You would think that the rabbis' infallibility had been questioned. How dare a simple newspaper editor condemn one of their judgments in public? They also took appropriate revenge: the day after the article appeared, the paper *El Tiempo* was suspended and remained so for a month as a result of measures taken by the chief rabbi. It would still be suspended if the party that formed around Monsieur Fresco had not begun to protest. It was then decided to hold a session of the communal council that the chief rabbi and the whole rabbinic body would attend. Monsieur Fresco had to appear before this high court to apologize and ask for pardon. He did in fact go; but they blanched when they saw his proud stance.

I did not intend to offend you, he told the members of the bet din; if you considered yourselves offended, it is because you did not really understand my article; I infinitely regret it. As for the herem itself, by virtue of what law might you be able to prevent me from expressing an opinion? Were not the rabbis themselves allowed to discuss the judgments emanating from the Sanhedrin?[39] Judaism does not acknowledge infallibility. . . . There is no way I could convey to you the comedy of our rabbis' replies. As secretary, I was present as a neutral and drew up my report. I can promise you that there was some amusing material in it. With all this, Monsieur Fresco still did not ask pardon: he bowed and took his leave.

Discussions took place among the members of the council, because the chief rabbi had just declared that he would do his best to suspend *El Tiempo* for good and prevent Monsieur Fresco from being editor of any other paper.

Fortunately some good soul went off to look for Monsieur Fresco, who came back just the same, still vehemently debating. There was an attempt to calm things down, and the chief rabbi turned to Monsieur Fresco and said: in other countries there are anti-Semites, here it is even more deplorable because the anti-Semites are in our own nation, they are those civilized young people who encourage you in your defiance; they are schemers. I beg your pardon, Eminence, answered Monsieur Fresco, there are no schemers among the Jews; what is sad is that our spiritual leader himself should go and denounce his flock as schemers. I know this happened once, and I deplore it. . . . This has weighed on my mind for too long, and I am glad that circumstances have allowed me to say it to you.

Obviously things were taking far too serious a tone; Monsieur Fresco was

---

[38]Excommunication (in Hebrew).
[39]High court of justice for the whole of ancient Palestine.

pushed toward the chief rabbi to kiss his hand. And that is how the reconciliation was effected.

So that the incident be closed, it had been decided that the council would make no official communication to the press on what had just occurred; but since affairs of personal and petty interest are always mixed in with general matters, the president wanted to send an article to the paper *El Telegrafo* by himself and on his own initiative.[40] This report said that Monsieur Fresco had apologized to the whole rabbinic corps and begged pardon. I was asked to sign this article. I opposed it because it was contrary to the report that I had drawn up at the time. They insisted, I was overpowered, and I signed after having toned down the article slightly. The next day I went back to the president. I told him that I had consulted the report again, that I was absolutely opposed to the impression given by the article with my signature. Thereupon the president told me that I had been wrong not to write in the report that Monsieur Fresco begged pardon and apologized, because a report must always be made in the council's favor.

Despite the countermand that the censor had given it, the paper *El Telegrafo* printed the article under my signature, and Monsieur Fresco was prevented from refuting it. I sent in my resignation the next day, though I took the precaution of going to the chief rabbi beforehand to explain my position and tell him that, as a rabbi, I was not allowed to play a part in affairs where there was, if not intrigue, at least disloyalty.

From the large number of letters of sympathy and congratulations that I received after my resignation I understood or rather was reassured, because I had suspected it, that my reputation would have been jeopardized. I am glad that I made this material sacrifice to my moral position, particularly as at the moment I need all of what I will modestly call my good name in Turkey for my candidature to succeed in Bulgaria. The Congress, which had been postponed indefinitely, will meet (according to the paper *La Verdad*,[41] which arrived from Sofia today) in a fortnight or three weeks. Dr. [Shimeon] Dankowitz (ex–chief rabbi of Bulgaria) is again a candidate. There are two others who are recommended by Güdemann[42] and Gaster,[43] respectively. Should I not also be recommended by Monsieur Zadoc Kahn? In that case, I should be very much obliged if you would ask him so that no time is lost.

You must have received the letter in which I thanked you on behalf of the

---

[40]Appearing in Istanbul (1886–1925), in Judeo-Spanish. At the time this letter was written, this paper was regarded as close to the chief rabbinate.

[41]Sofia (1898–?), a paper in Judeo-Spanish.

[42]Moritz Güdemann (1835–1918), chief rabbi of Vienna.

[43]Moses Gaster (1856–1939), a scholar, Zionist leader, and haham (chief rabbi) of the Sephardi community in London.

chief rabbi both for the paper and for the *Kehilat Shalom*.[44] Between ourselves, the paper itself informed the government that *Ha-Magid*,[45] as well as
the papers *Ha-Zefira*,[46] *El Progresso*[47] (from Vienna), and *El Dia*[48] (from
Philippopoli), were Zionist. We ourselves are obliged to have *Ha-Magid* sent
to us post restante.

. . . P.S. The chief rabbi has just appointed a high commission charged
with studying the means necessary to spread the Turkish language among
Ottoman Israelites. Although I do not agree with this, because I do not see
its usefulness for the future of our coreligionists, I have been obliged to
consent to form part of this commission so as not to displease the chief
rabbi. We have already held one session. For the moment nothing of importance and there never will be.

(. . .)

(AAIU, Turkey, XXX E)

*The defeat did not undermine his determination. He observed the society in
which he moved in order to adapt his behavior to it. A modernization movement was taking shape, at the instigation of an élite open to the West. As for
the chief rabbinate, it championed integration into Turkish society, which was
not as yet really part of the plans of the classes in process of westernization.
Later, Nahum, in his turn, would favor a similar option, but the circumstances
then would be more propitious. Even though its achievement was delayed,
integration was on the agenda for Jewish leaders at the end of the nineteenth
century. Was this a necessity dictated by the political facts of the day?*

Hasköy, 30 May 1900

Dear Monsieur Bigart,

You have probably been informed about the elections at Sofia. I should
have been the first to tell you, but I took the liberty of postponing my letter
because the result only reached me when my workload was at its heaviest, I
mean the time of our weekly lectures.

In particular, I waited for a few days before writing to you in order to
receive all the information and so know the indications that emerged from
this election.

[44]"Community of Peace" (in Hebrew).

[45]Lyck/Berlin/Cracow (1856–1903), the first modern paper in the Hebrew language intended
for the Russian Jewish public. It contributed to spreading the ideas of the Haskalah in the
Jewish world.

[46]A paper in Hebrew that appeared intermittently in Warsaw between 1862 and 1931. After
1876, the Zionist leader Nahum Sokolow took an important part in its publication. His name
became identified with this paper, which enjoyed a wide circulation in the Jewish communities.

[47](1895–?), a paper in Judeo-Spanish.

[48](1897–1914), a Zionist paper in Judeo-Spanish.

The appointment of Dr. Ehrenpreiss,[49] rabbi of Djakovav,[50] as chief rabbi of Bulgaria is no defeat for me. He was preferred for a variety of reasons. First and foremost, I must tell you that at the last moment I did not appear on the list of candidates: the commission charged with investigating the eighteen applicants rejected fourteen of them, including me.

Age was a great obstacle to my success. Although I am twenty-eight years old, my birth certificate only puts me at twenty-four. What is more the communal statutes require an age of thirty as a sine qua non. That being the case, my candidature naturally did not receive the approval of the Congress and the government.

As for Monsieur Ehrenpreiss, he owes his victory to some warm recommendations, his knowledge of two Slav languages (Polish and Croat), his title of doctor, and above all his Zionist sympathies.

Dr. Gaster's recommendation had considerable influence on the opinions of the electors and notably of the members of the commission. . . . Nevertheless I have had a chance to find out my deficiency and to think for a moment about how to remedy it in the future. I am hardly devoid of hope: I am following closely the activities inside our communities and waiting for the day when another post will fall vacant, such as Alexandria or Cairo, because I am better equipped for a Muslim country than for any other.

In any case the need for a religious leader who is literate, educated, and honest is beginning to be felt in the East, as the seminary's work increases and makes an impression on the public.

. . . because it is a well-known fact that here, more than anywhere else, the religious leader has to be shrewd and very capable. Few unexpected opportunities have presented themselves or will present themselves that can be used advantageously to raise the material and moral condition of Ottoman Jewry! But what can you expect? Our spiritual leader thinks of no one but himself and his family. Questions that do not affect him closely barely interest him. The basis of all his measures and all his actions is always the same: to please the Palace[51] (not the Porte).[52] I have already mentioned the commission that the chief rabbi appointed, charged with studying means of spreading the Turkish language among the Ottoman Israelites. This serious, lofty question always occupied the minds of his entourage. Hardly was the commission formed, when the chief rabbi sent a note to the minister of religions, a note that was read to the Council of Ministers and in which he informed the government that before long the Spanish language

---

[49]Marcus Ehrenpreiss (1869–1951), one of the pioneers of modern Hebrew literature, connected with the Zionists.

[50]Town in Croatia.

[51]The Sultan and his court.

[52]The Sublime Porte, the government.

would disappear and be replaced by Turkish. The commission has already held a few sessions. It has reached many conclusions: reorganization of the *Sule-i-maarif,* reorganization of Turkish in the Talmud Torah and in our schools, the introduction into girls' schools of one or two hours of Turkish a week, the establishment of a Jewish Turkish language paper.

The main question now is to find the necessary resources to meet all these needs and cover the costs. Several plans have piled up in the commission's office, plans that it is hard to implement. While waiting, all these fine plans will sleep peacefully in their boxes.

I would like to give you more details about the debates of this commission, of which I unfortunately form part (I wrote you in my last letter that I was forced to agree so as not to displease the chief rabbi), but I do not think that there is any point in talking about it to you at any greater length.

What is embarrassing about all these matters is that one cannot say everything one thinks. The present regime is becoming intolerable.

. . . you can therefore see that our task is of the most delicate; we have to be very circumspect. Perhaps the receipt of permission for the seminary will enable us to work more actively and more freely. At this precise moment it is the minister of police who is studying the matter. Once authorization is obtained, our aim will be to show the public and particularly the rabbinic body that future rabbis will be versed both in religious learning, such as Talmud and casuistry (indispensable subjects for the East), and in secular knowledge.

(. . .)

(AAIU, Turkey, XXX E)

Nahum was above all else a fieldworker, and he wanted to put down roots in the district where his clientèle lived, so that he could gain their attachment through a sustained effort.

Büyükdere,[53] 3 August 1900

Dear Monsieur Bigart,

(. . .)

I have never told you about the secluded life to which the interests of the seminary and my own interests have condemned us. My wife has only one day off a week, Saturday. She is obliged to spend it at home, with the result that months on end can pass, particularly in winter, when she can breathe no other air than that of the school and the house. This alone would be enough

[53]Büyükdere, the district of Istanbul on the European bank of the Bosphorus, a holiday resort.

to weaken a stronger nature than hers and you have had occasion to see that she does not err on the side of excessive good health.

I confess that we are not too keen on this change, which would occasion us increased expense, in view of the high price of apartments. At Hasköy we have a house for 500F; in the town our rent would rise to 800 to 900F.

I have been meaning to speak to you about this matter for a long time for my own needs and in the interests of the seminary. My father-in-law and I are in the same district and working on the same population. Our influence over the population of Galata is remote and consequently weak. Would it not be better to separate us? My father-in-law would continue his lectures at Hasköy, and I would work among the very apathetic Galata population, organizing a series of historical and literary lectures. And then, Galata is the center; and for my own future it is necessary for me to be right in the middle of it, that I study it from close up, if I am to understand it myself so that I in my turn can make myself understood.

I am very cross that I have left it so late to mention a subject about which I should have spoken to you at somewhat greater length. . . .

While waiting, I hope that you will not be annoyed if my wife does not resume her duties until after the festivals: the course of treatment she is following needs at least two months to yield effective results.

(. . .)

Hotel Büyükdere, Büyükdere,
Constantinople.
(AAIU, Turkey, XXX E)

Even though Nahum was the Alliance's man on the spot, it did not readily agree to his requests. An increase in salary, his wife's transfer, and his change of domicile demanded long negotiations and great perseverance. Still he spared no effort to settle the problems preoccupying the Alliance.

Büyükdere, 20 August 1900

Dear Monsieur Bigart,

(. . .)

You ask me if there is no way of living in Galata without it being necessary for Madame Nahum to work in the same district.

How would you suggest reconciling the two? Work at Hasköy would mean my wife's going out in winter in the rain, snow, wind, in the mud, in the drafts created by the boats from the Golden Horn arriving every half hour from Hasköy. Do you think she could stand such trials?

. . . to make her live in Hasköy again would endanger her health; the rest she is enjoying at present is, as you foresaw, leading to an improvement in her weak state of health.

. . . I can just see what would happen at the end of two months: fresh attack of anemia, fresh treatment, fresh need for rest, and so on; you can well understand that such shocks should not be repeated too often in her · state of health.

What I find surprising is your reason for refusing her the post that she is requesting: allow me to tell you that this criticism of her regular attendance, in however friendly a way you make it, is not entirely deserved. Would you have been able to say the same thing to her last year or even up to April this year? Why has her attendance been less regular in the more recent period? because she was ill. Why was she ill? because she was at Hasköy, because, apart from the fatigue of the school, she was deprived of fresh air and exercise. If you remove the causes, you remove the effects.

. . . by leaving Madame Nahum at Hasköy, you seem to be resigning yourself to the fact that she will do her job only intermittently, and that, I assure you, is impossible for her.

. . . after all the reasons I have just given for the need for my wife to live in Galata, I have scruples about speaking about my need to be in the town. I have left this subject to the end for fear of seeming to be using one cause to promote another. Setting aside this fear, I must tell you that my future is delayed, if not actually jeopardized, by seclusion in Hasköy.

As I have already told you, my presence in that district is absolutely useless. My father-in-law on his own can fulfill the task you entrusted us with, particularly as our young seminarians have already begun to preach.

. . . now look at the absolute necessity for my transfer to Galata.

The well-off class, which is influential in the progress of events within our community, if progress there will be, and there must be, is flocking to Galata. This section of the population knows me, from having seen me often and heard me sometimes; it is sympathetic toward me, and this is becoming more apparent every day (I notice it particularly when I target their purses for some welfare project or other: no one has the courage to refuse me, and this is no small sacrifice of my dignity), probably because I maintain a certain reserve. I think three years is enough to attract attention. It is now a question of turning this sympathetic attitude to advantage, and this is the way.

As well as a large number of rabbis and temples, the archisynagogues, every suburb of Constantinople—Hasköy, Balata, Kuzguncuk, Ortaköy— has its own spiritual leader, a member of the rabbinical court. He is there as the chief rabbi's representative. Only Galata does not have one, because it never wanted to have a rabbi of the old school. What is more, it possesses two large temples, including one placed under the protectorate of the Italian embassy, where the worshipers, mostly foreign subjects, belong to the most select class in the capital. The governing body of this Italian temple (I forgot to tell you that this latter voted the seminary an annual sum of 5 Ltq. =

115F), as well as the governing body of the Spanish temple in Galata, would have invited me to give sermons several times, but I have frequently been obliged to refuse because it means leaving on Friday and not returning until Sunday morning. It would be a favorable opportunity for me to be at Galata because, with the help of Monsieur Fernandez and the chief rabbi, I will succeed in being appointed rabbi-preacher of the temple, where sermons and lectures will be given more frequently and more freely. This would be a way of making myself officially acknowledged as a rabbi.

There is another major consideration. One of the reasons (perhaps the only reason) why the chief rabbi holds his head up so high, so well, so firmly, is because he has the support of the Palace. It would be no bad thing if, in view of a still remote future, I were to make myself known to a few influential personages. What I am thinking of at the moment is a post in the sultan's private library, a library full of valuable books and manuscripts. The letter I have written to H.M. asking for this favor is at present in the hands of the second chamberlain. Present events do not allow the chamberlains so much as to approach the sultan.

I hope that this letter will be handed to him after the celebrations of his twenty-fifth anniversary.[54] It is more than likely that the answer will be in the negative, but that will not discourage me, provided, that is, that I am at the center, in Galata, where all the foreign schools, the literary societies, the large Muslim libraries are situated. How do you expect me to take advantage of them, consigned as I am to Hasköy: I cannot study, it is too far away. I have recently obtained free entry to the museum, complete freedom to copy the inscriptions, etc. Can you believe that I have not once been able to use this right? And this is very harmful to me.

For all these reasons and many more, which are too minor to be worth mentioning, but are no less important for all that, it is absolutely indispensable that I be in Galata, and for this, it is necessary that my wife also has a post in that suburb.

(. . .)
(AAIU, Turkey, XXX E)

Hasköy, 30 October 1900

Dear Monsieur Bigart,

I have just received your letter of the twenty-fourth instant, in which you tell me of your satisfaction at the official authorization by the minister of public education. I no longer remember in what terms I reported this matter to you; perhaps I expressed myself badly. What it actually is, is not autho-

---

[54]Anniversary of his accession to the throne.

rization but a letter of appreciation in which the minister officially recognizes all our schools in the capital and appreciates their value.

Now I am busy with the girls' school at Tiberias. The letter I handed to the minister in Monsieur Fernandez's name, has been referred to the inspector general in order to proceed with the necessary formalities.

The permit for the seminary has still not been obtained. The blame must largely be attributed to the chief rabbi. About four months ago, the minister of religions asked us, through the medium of the chief rabbi, for certain information on the seminary.

We replied the same day. Now I have just learned that the minister is still waiting for an answer: the chief rabbi, or rather his grandson, his private secretary for Turkish, has lost this letter. We will write a second answer. In addition he is not proving energetic enough. Of all the ministers, the minister of public education is perhaps the only one to be a blind fanatic, anti-non-Muslim and, above all, anti-Jew. Consequently, we should be very satisfied whenever we obtain anything from that minister.

(. . .)

(AAIU, Turkey, XXX E)

Hasköy, 5 December 1900

Monsieur le Président,

In reply to the letter that I had the honor of sending you on 30 November 1898, in which I asked you to be so kind as to raise my salary, you were kind enough to give me hope of a decision in favor of my request when you wrote me on 23 December 1898, "Your salary could be increased later, it certainly will be."

I would have left the execution of the formal promise made to me to your discretion, if circumstances did not oblige me to repeat my request, the motives for which have become even more serious, particularly since my marriage. The many demands of domestic life (upkeep, rent, servants) on the one hand, the inevitable demands of my position as a rabbi, that is to say a public figure, on the other, necessitate expenses that my current salary, including Madame Nahum's, can never cover.

Last year, it is true, I did not consider it opportune to remind you: I was then holding the position of secretary-general of the consistory, a post that brought in 1,500F a year and that I had to give up following circumstances that are known to you. As for the justification of the case, I think it would be superfluous to bring up either the services that I endeavor to render to the work in general or the enthusiasm I bring to the conscientious accomplishment of my task, which is not all that easy.

I hope that the central committee will be kind enough to examine closely my position and the demands it makes, particularly in a large town like

Constantinople, and so give a favorable answer to the request that I have the honor of sending to you.

(. . .)

(AAIU, Turkey, XXX E)

Constantinople, 14 March 1901

Dear Monsieur Bigart,

Although vexed and discouraged by the refusal with which you replied to a request for a loan that I regretfully had to send you a year and a half ago, present circumstances oblige me to revoke a resolution I made never to take such a step again. But it is not on my own behalf. One of my sisters, engaged for two years, is obliged to postpone her marriage indefinitely for want of a thousand francs she promised to give her fiancé in cash.[55] As you know, I am my family's sole support and consequently the only person who could come to her aid in such circumstances.

But setting up house and Madame Nahum's successive indispositions, on the one hand, and my small resources, on the other, have not yet enabled me to save this sum, however minimal it may be.

I would be very obliged and very grateful to you if you would be so kind as to make me an advance of at least five hundred francs, which I pledge myself to repay by small quarterly deductions.

(. . .)

(AAIU, Turkey, XXX E)

Nahum's rise displeased the headmasters of the schools he taught at outside of the seminary; it offended them. The closed world of the Alliance staff locally also had its rules, which the future chief rabbi did not always respect.

Constantinople, 15 August 1901

Monsieur le Président,

It is very distressing for me to receive criticism from you when I am conscious of doing my duty even beyond the bounds you assigned me. You seem to believe the inaccurate reports that it pleases my amiable colleague to give of me.

I am very grieved, Monsieur le Président, to be misunderstood in this way, and I wonder anxiously what would have happened to my reputation had not Monsieur Bénédict[56] providentially arrived, with a reserved nature like mine in the face of headmasters, whose one aim is to put themselves forward, walk over anyone they find in their way, because they find them an obstacle in their morbid imagination.

---

[55] Young girls paid a dowry.
[56] Sylvain Bénédict, Alliance inspector.

. . . I am not up to sustaining petty and sterile conflicts, it is a waste of time, and I do not have too much of it.

(. . .)

(AAIU, Turkey, XXX E)

Constantinople, 18 October 1901

Monsieur le Président,

I am submitting to you straight away the proposal made to me by the Haydarpaşa community. They are asking me to take up the headmastership of the school in that suburb, temporarily, that is to say, until such time, probably soon, as a permanent headmaster will be engaged.

The situation is so urgent that my answer is required within four or five days. As teaching at the seminary leaves me two or three hours' leisure, I ask you, Monsieur le Président, to be so kind as to inform me of your affirmative or negative decision by telegram.

(. . .)

(AAIU, Turkey, XXX E)

Haim Nahum sought to gain a foothold at various strategic points. The suburb in question housed a comfortably off Jewish population that might be useful to him at the right time. Nahum was also desperately looking for new sources of income.

Constantinople, 1 November 1901

Monsieur le Président,

Whatever the reasons that led the central committee to reject the proposals made to me by the Haydarpaşa community, I have bowed to their decision and refused the post of temporary headmaster (November and December) that had been so urgently offered me.

In any case, the post scarcely attracted me; it would even have been too great a sacrifice for me to accept it. I know the suburb and its inhabitants and am perfectly well aware that it is never free from party struggles, and that is precisely the reason why the administrative committee considered my presence necessary, indispensable. But my position as a public figure prevented me from refusing it on my own initiative, at the risk of being accused in advance of indifference to communal matters.

I now come to the most important point in your letter, which touches me to the quick.

On the basis of the possibility that I could have put two hours a day at the disposal of Haydarpaşa, as I previously did at the rabbinic chancellery, with your authorization and for the same reasons that determined me to ask you for authorization to accept or not the post of headmaster, you ask me for a further hour of work a day, considering "that all my time belongs to you." I do not dispute the legitimacy of your principle and agree that a moral contract between the Alliance and myself joins us, without the need to discuss it or formulate its clauses.

However, there are times when its implementation requires some clarification. Deeply conscious of my duty and convinced of the inestimable results that our work could yield for the revival of the Israelite East, I am already devoting days and nights to my teaching. . . .

Disregarding the lessons you instructed me to give at Hasköy and Galata, my ten hours at the seminary require four times that amount of time to prepare.

. . . at what cost of effort, of fatigue, was I going to sacrifice two hours to the headmastership of the school? What I was going to give them was a large portion of my rest, my sleep, and above all of my personal work. Because, let me remind you, the career I intend to take up also requires more arduous study than the teaching profession, which is taking up all my time at present. I have on my desk the material that I collected with so much effort at the time of my stay in Paris to turn into a thesis for the École Pratique des Hautes Études, which stays there, dormant for want of time and intellectual tranquillity.

Yet I was still going to forgo one or two hours' sleep, simply to be able to live less wretchedly, because I am not going to manage to make ends meet on 2,400F (1,000F of which go for rent and 400 for insurance). I have my dignity and I hold a certain position that I must protect both in the interest of the Alliance and in the interests of the work and, if you like, for my personal future. I was still going to accept this post until December, confident that after four years of work, the Alliance would at last wish to improve my situation.

Monsieur le Président, it is with a heart filled with regret that I have to tell you that the proposal you have made me is materially impossible: I am too overburdened, and my teaching prevents me even from getting on with my personal work.

. . . P.S. I was born in Magnesia in 1873, but my birth certificate is dated 1878.

(AAIU, Turkey, XXX E)

The seminary was favored as a means of bringing about a deep-seated change in traditional society.

Constantinople, 30 April 1902

Dear Monsieur Bigart,

I have pleasure in informing you that I have just obtained the license for the seminary on very favorable terms that ensure the moral and material future of our work.

. . . I am very pleased that our efforts have not been in vain and that my activities have been crowned with success. This is a great triumph for us, particularly as the present regime is refusing to give a non-Muslim community a license for a primary school. The Armenian patriarch has worked for some years to found a large seminary, and the government is turning a deaf ear. In our case, no one has helped me in this matter; the chief rabbi has not so much as budged from his sofa; his has rather been a passive role.

What can you expect? He lacks spirit, energy, and often even goodwill.

. . . it is up to him to bring to their senses all those rogues of rabbis who are the shame of oriental Jewry. All they busy themselves with are intrigues, pettiness, pronouncing curses on people who are reported to buy *matza*[57] from the German community[58] or to drink milk at a *goy's*[59] celebration, etc. . . . And what an encouragement that is for our pupils and for anyone who wants to take an interest in our work!

Now the chief rabbi could place an official tax on the synagogues, the communities, to make an annual grant to the seminary. Neither the rabbis nor their supporters (however few they be) will be able to open their mouths again: *Dina de-malkhuta dina.*[60]

(. . .)

(AAIU, Turkey, XXX E)

Integration into surrounding society, another facet of westernization, also took place through knowledge of the Turkish language. There was no lack of resistance from one side or another.

Constantinople, 1 July 1902

Monsieur le Président,

In my last letter I promised to send you regulations for the seminary that would have been the beginning of the reorganization of the oriental rabbinate. But the chief rabbi's weakness, the implacable hatred of the rabbinic body, the apathy of our administrators, and the spirit of obscurantism of the government have filled me with the conviction that all the conditions on which our regulations would be based would remain dead letters.

. . . to be honest, I do not see what advantage we might gain from the adoption of Turkish. The government would be the first to be worried by this innovation, which it would regard with suspicion. Did not the former minister of public education let slip the following words in the course of

---

[57]Unleavened bread, eaten during the festival of Passover (in Hebrew).

[58]Ashkenazi community.

[59]Non-Jew (in Hebrew).

[60]*Dina de-malkhuta dina* (Aramean): "The law of the land is the law" (Babylonian Talmud, Nedarim 28a).

conversation: "Are they asking us for authorization to teach in Turkish so that they can compete with our imams?"

And then, do you think we would be allowed to mount the pulpit and give a sermon in Turkish? First and foremost, who would be our audience?

We are a long way, a very long way from the time—which will never come—when our coreligionists will adopt Turkish as their mother tongue. Innumerable difficulties and drawbacks prevent implementation. And even if they understood Turkish, we would not be allowed to preach. How would one talk about a dogma, a moral precept in general, or the Jewish religion in particular? Talking about the superiority of the Torah would imply the inferiority of the Koran or would rather contradict it. Praising Moses or his institutions, would be giving offense to Mohamed, "God's beloved." Explaining a passage from the Prophets concerning justice, righteousness, honesty, would be suggesting that we live at a time when these principles are misunderstood or abandoned. Believe me, Monsieur le Président, if the reading of the Bible or reciting of prayers are tolerated today, it is just because they are written in Hebrew. You may say that all this is temporary; I agree; but the race is too steeped in fanaticism to renounce its traditions. All legislation, administration, is based on religious foundations and their cement, as [Ernest] Renan nicely puts it, hardens as it ages; and the day when someone would take it upon himself to tamper with the religious soil, cultivate it or dig it up, on that day the whole edifice would collapse and be replaced by another construction. So, why waste our time teaching the language when we are not going to get any benefit from it?

(. . .)

(AAIU, Turkey, XXX E)

Haim Nahum persisted. This time his target was the chief rabbinate of Rome.

Constantinople, 29 July 1902

Dear Monsieur Bigart,

(. . .)

My candidature in Rome—You know, dear Monsieur Bigart, that I will never be able to obtain the position I want and that you also want before I have held a rabbinate elsewhere.

That is why every time the opportunity occurs I work toward this end. Two years ago it was Sofia, today it is Rome, where the post is vacant and I have offered myself as a candidate. In reply, the president of the community, the *cavaliere* Angelo Sereni, has asked for my diploma from the chief rabbi or a copy of it, a document that was not given to me when I left.

I have just written to Chief Rabbi Zadoc Kahn asking him for a written statement certifying my status and at the same time for a warm reference.

Please, dear Monsieur Bigart, be good enough to have a word with the chief rabbi so that he sends the statement and the reference as soon as possible.

I would like to hope that the central committee will write to its friends in Rome in support of my candidature.

(. . .)

(AAIU, Turkey, XXX E)

Constantinople, 13 August 1902

Dear Monsieur Bigart,

I have the honor to acknowledge receipt of your letter in which you "wish me good luck for the position of chief rabbi of Rome."

If the central committee wants my candidature to succeed, I do not understand why it has not had the kindness to support it by a recommendation, which I asked it to send to its friends in Rome.

Does it think me unworthy? Yet Chief Rabbi Zadoc Kahn was kind enough to accompany the certificate that I had the honor of asking him for with a letter of recommendation. Or does it really think that Rome is not the place for me to begin my rabbinic career, and in that case, I would have expected to receive a paternal word of advice.

As I have often had occasion to tell you, if the central committee wants to see me at the head of Ottoman Jewry one day, the only means of getting there is to hold a rabbinic post elsewhere first. Because, in the Orient, it is impossible to move straight from the teaching profession to the chief rabbinate of Turkey. I applied for the position in Sofia three years ago for the same reason, and then the Alliance did me the honor of recommending me.

I would therefore be very obliged, dear Monsieur Bigart, if you could give me your opinion on the above before the end of the month, so that I would have time to withdraw my candidature if the central committee is not in favor of it.

(. . .)

(AAIU, Turkey, XXX E)

Haim Nahum had a sense of family. He made use of the Alliance, his guardian angel, to help his family.

Constantinople, 19 March 1903

Dear Monsieur Leven,

Encouraged by the sympathy you have always been kind enough to show me, I am taking the liberty of writing to ask you a favor. I have a brother at *Mikveh*[61] who in a few months time will finish his five-year training course,

---

[61]Agricultural school of Mikveh Yisrael, founded by the Alliance in 1870 in Palestine.

where he has distinguished himself by his work and conduct and has nearly always been top of his class.

I would like him to be admitted to the Agricultural Institute at the Montpellier or Grignon schools for one or two years. By so doing you would secure his future and you would make all my family very happy. As my ecclesiastical position obliged me to marry early, it has been, and still is, impossible for me to help my family materially because of the scant means at my disposal. Today, it is impatiently looking forward to the progress of my brother, who is, I assure you, worthy of all your benevolence. Monsieur Niégo[62] can tell you about my brother's merits better than I.

Please be so kind as to grant me the favor that I have the honor to ask of you.

(. . .)

(AAIU, Turkey, XXX E)

Constantinople, 19 October 1903

Monsieur le Président,

Hardly eight months have passed since the death of my poor sister at the age of twenty-six, when today, the first day of the return to school, I received a telegram from Monsieur Brasseur.[63]

The blow is too cruel, doubly cruel particularly when I think of the consequences. My poor father leaves a family of five with no means. I can hardly manage with thousands of difficulties to make the ends of my small household meet. Now this heavy burden throws me into deep alarm. I do not know if I can bear it.

As I am obliged to set off for Smyrna today, I have asked Monsieur Fernandez for permission to be absent for two or three days longer than the traditional seven days if necessary.[64]

(. . .)

(AAIU, Turkey, XXX E)

Haim Nahum was beginning to set himself up as a genuine intercessor. This type of activity led him to describe some of the administrative machinery of the Empire from the inside.

Magnesia, 22 October 1903

Monsieur le Président,

The sad circumstances in which I left Constantinople in haste to rejoin

[62]Joseph Niégo (1863–1950), director of Mikveh Yisrael from 1890 to 1903.
[63]Adolphe Brasseur, headmaster of the Alliance school at Magnesia.
[64]The seven days of mourning.

my cruelly stricken family prevented me sending you a communication concerning the Jews of Kishinev.[65]

I learned during the festival of Succoth that an informal approach had been made to Memduh pasha, minister of the interior, with a view to obtaining imperial permission for the settlement in Anatolia of a thousand Jewish families from Kishinev and that, on payment of a *baksheesh*,[66] the minister promised his assistance in implementing this plan. It was then decided to send a request to the grand vizier. . . . I myself was asked to write it from the copy provided by the minister's assistant.

(. . .)

(AAIU, Turkey, I G 1)

To establish his power further, he enlarged the range of his contacts.

Constantinople, 20 April 1904

Monsieur le Président,

Permit me to report to you a matter that occurred during the course of last week, a matter that has some importance but which has not for the moment reached the desired conclusion. It involved having myself directly appointed by the Sultan as *muavin* (assistant) to the chief rabbi of Turkey, and here are the circumstances.

On Sunday, 10 April, I received a note from Monsieur Fernandez asking me to go to the Pera-Palace,[67] where Monsieur François Deloncle, minister plenipotentiary and deputy for Cochin China, was waiting for me, . . . in order to discuss some linguistic and philological matters with me. I went there at the time indicated, we chatted about oriental archaeology, epigraphy, and philology, and we decided to collaborate in preparing a study of Judeo-Spanish.

On Tuesday the twelfth instant, we had a second conversation, much longer and more interesting than the first, in the presence of Monsieur Lucien Perquel, a stockbroker with the Paris Bourse, who was accompanying Monsieur Deloncle on his mission. This time, the conversation led us from the domain of philology to the history of the Jews and their intellectual, moral, and social position. He was very interested in the organization of our schools and turned out to be one of their admirers and champions. He several times showed his desire to see the Israelites and their communities embark on the path of progress that the Alliance had already mapped out for them. I then told him about the obstacles and difficulties we meet in

---

[65]The allusion is to the pogrom that took place in Kishinev (Bessarabia) on 6–7 April 1903.
[66]Gratuity.
[67]A famous Istanbul hotel.

achieving our idea: the reorganization of oriental Jewry. Monsieur Deloncle was well aware of them and made me write the following note on a sheet of paper, which he handed to the sultan during his second and last audience the following day: "Request to appoint as muavin (assistant) to the chief rabbi of Turkey, Monsieur H. Nahum, born in Turkey, loyal subject of H.I.M. the sultan, qualified chief rabbi of the Israelite Seminary of France and recognized as such by the general government on the *takrir*[68] of the chief rabbi of Turkey dated 19 May [1903], graduate of the School of Languages, etc."

The next day I received the following note from Monsieur Fernandez, which he had received from Monsieur Deloncle: "The sultan is in favor of the appointment of Monsieur Nahum as muavin. He desires that the community take it in hand directly. Would you be so good as to ask Monsieur Nahum to come and talk to me tomorrow, Friday, at ten o'clock in the morning?" In fact, according to Monsieur Deloncle and Munir pasha, who was present at the audience, the sultan would be very inclined to do it, but he did not want to take the initiative so as "not to offend the Israelite community whose feelings toward me He did not know."

By way of continuing his propaganda, on the day of his departure, Monsieur Deloncle introduced me to Monsieur Bapst, chargé d'affaires at the embassy, who like myself had gone to the station to see him off. I spoke with Monsieur Bapst for some twenty minutes, and he promised me his assistance any time I would have occasion to request it. Monsieur Deloncle, while asking me to keep him informed on everything that was being done, promised to go and talk at length with Chief Rabbi Zadoc Kahn and the president of the Alliance.

So the project is excellent but difficult to . . . implement. In an interview with Monsieur Fernandez, Mentèche pasha[69] and J. Ménaché[70] stated that they were prepared to sign the statement to be handed to the sultan, they and the enlightened members of the council. Now it is a question of knowing who will take it upon themselves to present it. . . . In any case, even if the affair comes to nothing for the moment, it has been put on the agenda. I will write next time about the present situation of the community, which is in a deplorable state following arbitrary and tyrannical machinations by the chief rabbi.

(. . .)

(AAIU, Turkey, XXX E)

Nahum began to have allies inside the communal authorities.

---

[68]Official note (in Turkish).
[69]Dr. General Mentèche pasha Galimidi, president of the Jewish lay council.
[70]Jacques effendi Ménaché, secretary of the Jewish lay council.

18 May 1904

Monsieur le Président,

Monsieur Fernandez has already informed you of my appointment to the post—specially created—of director of the chancellery of the chief rabbinate of Turkey. In fact, last Thursday, the twelfth instant, I received the following letter from H. E. Mentèche pasha Galimidi: "Dear Rabbi, at its session today the central consistory, in agreement with the chief rabbi, unanimously appointed you director of the consistorial chancellery. We request you to take up your new post immediately. As for your emoluments, they will be fixed at our next session. Yours, etc."

The following day an official communication to the same effect appeared in the Judeo-Spanish papers, a communication that will also appear in the Turkish and foreign papers of the capital.

My salary was fixed today, insignificant for the work that I shall be undertaking, but I am glad to accept my post, since it will give me the chance of rendering some service to the community. My task, I admit, will be very arduous. Anarchy is widespread in all the consistory offices, whose employees, men completely lacking in education and, what is more, conscience, commit countless abuses daily. Will I be allowed to put this camarilla in order? I know not. In any case, I will try to win the favor of our spiritual leader. I will do everything possible to spare his susceptibilities.

As for general service to the community, this week I decided on a plan of action for a detailed study of the present condition of the three major branches of a well-organized community, namely: worship, education, and welfare, so that I can best determine the manner and the extent of the reforms to be introduced.

High in the intentions of the members of the consistory is that I should accompany and represent the chief rabbi in certain circumstances or on a visit, in order to facilitate my admission to the great religious council, whose members are the only people eligible as candidates for the post of chief rabbi.

This week I have already taken all the registers locked up in the archives for thirty years in order to examine all the reports, decisions, and firmans.

At this morning's session, the consistory decided to have me sit in on deliberations, where I will have a consultative voice. My other functions will be decided this week, but from today the treasurer has been told to make no expenditure without my signature. What I have just taken up is therefore a very heavy burden.

The chief rabbi appears well content for the moment. I am also trying to be pleasant to him. I went personally and took him the 1,000F that the council was required to grant him—by way of bounty on the occasion of a granddaughter's forthcoming marriage.

I hope that in this way I will be able to win him over so that he does not create difficulties for me in carrying out my duties.

. . . P.S. I would be very grateful if you would be so good as to let me know Chief Rabbi Zadoc Kahn's impressions or comments on my report of 26 March concerning the subjects I have taught during the first term.

(. . .)

(AAIU, Turkey, XXX E)

At the École Supérieure de Génie et de l'Artillerie, where he gave French lessons, he forged contacts with the future leaders of Turkey.

25 May 1904

Monsieur le Président,

I have the honor to answer your letter of 18 May.

In fact four years ago I was commissioned by Marshal Zeki pasha, grand master of the artillery, to give a French class at the École Supérieure de Génie et de l'Artillerie situated in the Golden Horn, not far from the seminary, and it happened in the following circumstances.

When my wife retired from the service because of her health and without salary, I was in a very critical position: I could not provide for all the household's needs, let alone the expense occasioned by the anemia from which Madame Nahum suffers. At that time, and on many occasions, I appealed to the central committee to be so good as to improve my situation in proportion to my work. But despite all my pleas and all the small services I have rendered the Alliance beyond the call of duty, I have not had one single bonus, and the only rise given me in the whole seven years was no more than two hundred francs!

Yet my courses, which took up ten hours a week when I began, now take up twenty. It is natural that I cannot continue to lead the same life of poverty.

It was then that I turned to Monsieur Fernandez personally, asking him to take some small interest in me, and he promised that he would think seriously about it. In fact, some time afterward, instead of private lessons, he procured me this class at the École de Génie through the good offices of a friend of his, Monsieur Marchand, a close contact of the grand master of the artillery. Since I began teaching there, I have tried to banish the anti-Semitic spirit that prevails in the military corps of this high school, which contains no fewer than eighty military teachers. Now, as a result of this new position, I have been obliged to hand in my resignation, which has been regretfully accepted. It is not because the consistory is paying me more; it is the same amount of 110F per month, and what is more, it obliges me to move to the town where the cost of living, rents, are very high, so that I have lost by the change. But I wanted to take up the career and make myself of use to the community.

As to your implied criticism that I did not inform you of it, I do not think it is merited, particularly as it was procured for me by Monsieur Fernandez, a member of the central committee and president of the regional committee, and then it is almost a private lesson.

(AAIU, Turkey, XXX E)

At the same time Nahum was trying to stem the anarchy that prevailed in the communal authorities.

Constantinople, 30 June 1904

Monsieur le Président,

With a great deal of difficulty I have managed to bring a little order into the inner service of the consistory, whose employees have been accustomed from time immemorial to living in complete anarchy and committing countless abuses. Expenses were not accounted for, the treasurer did what he liked, he advanced money to some and let others suffer because of it, particularly teaching and welfare projects, with the result that the latter have still to receive their subsidies for the month of January. Present income cannot meet ordinary expenditure. Consequently, we have tried to make a few small economies by retiring three or four employees whose services, far from being of use to us are, on the contrary, prejudicial. The chief rabbi was against this.

Monsieur le Président, you can have no idea of the way he behaves. He promises everything when the session is in progress but the following day, when the consistory has made its decision, he goes back on his word.

. . . it is impossible to describe the mentality of this man, of this traitor, I will say. His only grievance against me is that I belong to the Alliance and therein lies all his mistrust.

(. . .)

(AAIU, Turkey, XXX E)

Constantinople, 17 July 1904

Monsieur le Président,

The intrigues of the chief rabbi and his acolytes to hamper the forward movement of the seminary and the efforts of those who work in it, are unending. Every day we have a bone to pick with him.

Last week, just when the formalities for the transfer[71] were about to

---

[71]The transfer in question is to the Asiatic bank of the Bosphorus.

begin, the chief rabbi suggested first requesting authorization for it from the minister of public education, on the pretext that the new site is adjacent to a forest belonging to an imperial princess.

Although authorization from the competent minister is compulsory for the transfer of schools, the statement of the aforesaid reason is entirely prejudicial because, as you well know, Monsieur le Président, in Turkey anything requested is prohibited.

In any case, the request was made according to the prescribed laws without introducing the pretext he put forward. But it was agreed that I should take the letter to the minister myself so that I could speak to him in person in order to accelerate the usual formalities. The day after this decision, came the counterorder from the chief rabbi, who sent word to his *kapu-kâhya*,[72] an octogenarian, rotten with alcohol and incapable of properly pronouncing two words in Spanish,[73] to take the request by himself. The members of the council are furious, but their impotence forces them to accept everything with resignation. The request has been handed in, but given the chief rabbi's views and intentions on this subject, we do not know whether he has not ordered his man to take a different message to the minister. In any case, at the president's request, I went to the ministry the next day together with Monsieur Danon, to appeal to some friends to facilitate the procedure, which I will not fail to report to you.

This incident was barely over when another one arose.

Last Friday, Monsieur Isaac Gabay, editor of the paper *El Telegrafo*, published a very long article under his own name against the consistory, which he accused of inactivity and apathy and, most of all, against the seminary. First of all, he began by criticizing the council's decisions and the irregularity of its sessions and the subsidies which it granted (the author of the articles was hinting at the subsidies granted recently to a few Talmud Torahs and schools, and formerly to the seminary) and ended by throwing discredit on the new site. Our Rochefort[74] expressed regret that Pasteur had not invented a serum against seminary fever!

Jealous at observing the support that the consistory was granting to the seminary and, as far as it was able, the Talmud Torahs, Monsieur Gabay ended his article by saying that the future council would be obliged to abolish a large part of these subsidies!

Do not you see this, Monsieur le Président, as directly inspired by the chief rabbi and his clique?

In any case at the moment the article is causing quite a stir.

. . . the name Gabay is well enough known to us through the many

---

[72]Chargé d'affaires to the chief rabbinate.
[73]Nahum probably meant to say "in Turkish."
[74]Henri Rochefort (1831–1913), French journalist, politician, and writer.

articles he has published against the schools of the Alliance, its teaching staff and even its senior personnel; he is an ignoble creature, backed by the chief rabbi.

The paper *El Tiempo* is being very cautious about replying, because it has already been put on the index of the censorship department for progressivist ideas. . . . An article describing the chief rabbi's arbitrary actions, which cannot but lower us in the eyes of other nations,[75] will be placed in a Turkish paper.

(. . .)

(AAIU, Turkey, XXX E)

A brief pause in the race for power.

Constantinople, 12 January 1905

Monsieur le Président,

I have the honor to inform you that yesterday, Wednesday, the eleventh instant, Madame Nahum gave birth to a boy. She suffered greatly and continues to suffer from the crisis she has just passed through, but we hope that any complications will be averted.

(. . .)

(AAIU, Turkey, XXX E)

The war between traditionalists and supporters of modernization was not restricted to the capital. But as this was the seat of the central authority of Ottoman Jewry, the conflict was particularly virulent there.

Constantinople, 8 June 1905

Monsieur le Président,

(. . .)

When I arrived at Smyrna to spend the festival of Passover with my mother, the notables of Karataş[76] asked me to give them one or two lectures and to step in to reconcile the parties, which had been at odds since Palatchi died.[77]

The sermon has been given, but the reconciliation was impossible. The enlightened party refused to hear a word about Chief Rabbi Bensignor.[78] I did not want to stay one or two days in case I was suspected of partiality or appearing to have an interest in the matter. This week I received a letter

---

[75]The other religious groups in the country.

[76]Karataş, a district in Smyrna.

[77]Abraham Palacci (1809–1899), chief rabbi of Smyrna from 1869 until his death.

[78]Joseph Bensignor (1837–1913), chief rabbi of Smyrna from 1900.

inviting me to go and give two or three lectures over Pentecost. I refused, not without regret, but promised to make a trip during the long vacation or the festivals of Tishri.[79] I am afraid on all these journeys of arousing the chief rabbi's jealousy, more especially as the rumor has been spread around here that proposals have been made to me to remain in Smyrna. Consequently, we must spare his feelings.

(. . .)

(AAIU, Turkey, XXX E)

Zadoc Kahn, chief rabbi of France and Nahum's model, died.

Constantinople, 12 December 1905

Monsieur le Président,

I am still staggering under the blow of the terrible news that was conveyed by all the telegraphic agencies yesterday morning.

In the face of the immense grief that afflicts his dear family as well as French Jewry, the Alliance, and world Jewry, I dare not speak of my individual grief.

I have lost in him a venerated teacher, a guide, a counselor, a protector.

I have been appointed by the chief rabbi to give the funeral oration for the renowned pastor.

(. . .)

(AAIU, Turkey, XXX E)

Constantinople, 26 December 1905

Monsieur le Président,

Constantinople certainly is the town for unpleasant surprises. The governing body of Galata, which had been able to make so much progress within a few months that it had become the model for all our communities, offering the finest hopes for the future of Israelite youth in that large suburb, has been dissolved from one day to the next as if by a wave of a magic wand.

In actuality this outcome was foreseen and inevitable, what is more, it should already have come to pass at the time when the future of the school-age children of Galata had been broadly outlined and even partly implemented. Only we thought that the struggle with the obscurantist party would have been possible for some time yet. Although repeated experience has shown us with certainty that nothing in the present regime is lasting.

(. . .)

(AAIU, Turkey, XXX E)

---

[79]Month of the Jewish calendar corresponding to September/October, during which three major festivals occur: the New Year (Rosh Hashana); the Day of Atonement (Yom Kippur); and the festival of Tabernacles (Sukkot).

After the pogroms of 1903, Russian Jewry suffered a fresh wave of pogroms in 1905. The Ottoman capital was a stopping point for a certain number of refugees.

Constantinople, 17 January 1906

Dear Monsieur Leven,

After the success we scored with the promulgation of the imperial irade officially authorizing the organization of a subscription on behalf of our coreligionists from Russia, a subscription in which the sultan will take part, we have been working to realize a dream that I have cherished for a long time: the settlement of Russian emigrants in Turkey with the same privileges that Muslim emigrants enjoy.

. . . only I think this irade is being kept secret, since it has not yet reached us; the first secretary, it is said, is demanding certain sums of money.

(. . .)

(AAIU, Turkey, II C 8)

The seminary was moved to the Asiatic coast. Haim Nahum now had to give lectures on both banks. Given the size of the town and the transportation difficulties, his working conditions necessarily deteriorated.

Constantinople, 22 February 1906

Monsieur le Président,

(. . .)

At Hasköy because of the difficulties of communication I was already finding it very tiring, giving all my lessons at the seminary as well as at the schools, for in stormy weather I was obliged to make the journey on foot, via the hill of Ok-Meydan,[80] across rocky paths. Today these difficulties have become insurmountable because of the great distance between the seminary and the other schools.

The seminary is at Kuzguncuk, situated at the top of the hill. Not only is the crossing long, but the number of boats making the direct journey from the bridge[81] to Kuzguncuk is very limited, so that it takes exactly six hours to give two hours of lessons at the seminary, in view of the fact that the first departure from the bridge is at 8:30 and sometimes 9:00 in the morning and that I do not get back to the bridge until 2:00 in the afternoon, very late in the day even to go to the chief rabbinate, which is in the center, in Galata.

In these circumstances, you will agree, Monsieur le Président, that it is a material impossibility for me to spend all my time in boats, going from the Bosphorus to the Golden Horn, making connections, and particularly be-

[80]It is situated in Hasköy.
[81]Landing stage for boats for the Asiatic bank.

cause the time of arrival of one boat never corresponds with the time the other departs.

I will endeavor to retain the school in Galata because it is situated next to the chief rabbinate.

I await your instructions.

(. . .)
(AAIU, Turkey, XXX E)

Constantinople, 2 March 1906

Monsieur le Président,

I just (Friday, 4:30 P.M.) received during a session of our governing body, your letter of 26 February, informing me that you cannot release me from the classes I am at present giving in the schools (Hasköy and Galata); and you suggest that I move house to overcome the difficulties arising from the seminary's transfer to Kuzguncuk.

This solution, however practical and easy it may seem to you, has only one fault or disadvantage: that of not being possible, not just because of the removal itself, for by dint of money, by dint of sacrifice, leases could be canceled, damages, forced expenses borne, etc., for the sake of the goal to be achieved. Whether I live in Kuzguncuk, Galata, Şişli,[82] Hasköy, or any other suburb of the town of seven hills, the difficulties will be the same. . . . Yes, if I devote every day of the week, from 7:00 in the morning till 5:00 in the evening, I will be able to fulfill the task that people wish to impose on me. Monsieur le Président is very well aware that I am no odd job man to endure this fatigue beyond my strength, nor yet an errand boy to run from boat to boat, when the boats are not regular and when their hours of arrival and departure never coincide.

I have hitherto spared neither my body nor my time; I have always shuttled between the seminary and these two schools, because all three were in the Golden Horn. Today, the situation has changed completely.

(. . .)
(AAIU, Turkey, XXX E)

The communal leadership, bastion of tradition.

Constantinople, 19 June 1906

Monsieur le Président,

(. . .)

The present consistory has the power to do whatever it thinks good, because it has the effective support of the chief rabbi, whose tool it is, unlike

[82]Şişli, a northern suburb of Istanbul.

his predecessor, to whom the chief rabbi was not favorably disposed because of his very progressivist tendencies.

. . . some of our administrators, far from harboring feelings of gratitude toward the Alliance, are always ready to criticize its work, deny its services. Why? There are numerous reasons. But one of the most important is the following: never having sat on the benches of one of your schools, they are immersed in Turkish bureaucracy and in the degrading society of insipid and groveling pashas, ignorant of, even despising, the life of modern Jewry.

. . . these are the people I am dealing with, and you will agree, Monsieur le Président, that the small inch of ground won from this administration is an immense success, in view of the obstacles and difficulties that I encounter.

The chief rabbi and his camarilla curse anyone who takes the liberty of going out with an umbrella on Saturday,[83] reject someone who dedicates himself to Judaism as an administrator because he is liberal and a friend of progress, and give the presidency of the consistory of Ottoman Jewry to a bigamist, an immoral man, who has sullied the name of the Jewish family and does not scruple, if he so wishes, for his own ends . . . to overthrow a governing body, cast a threatening calumny on someone who has refused to bend to his will. There you have the present president. With a few Turkish books, he has gained the adoration of the chief rabbi and his acolytes and persuaded the hypocrites and the paper of evil causes, *El Telegrafo,* to laud him to the skies. I will revert very shortly to the moral work of this council.

(. . .)

(AAIU, Turkey, XXX E)

The repercussions arising from the appointment of new chief rabbis in the provinces bore witness to the growing politicization of communal questions, all the more so as divergent social plans were at stake.

Constantinople, 9 August 1906

Monsieur le Président,

(. . .)

Chief Rabbi of Jerusalem: Two or three days after the death of Chief Rabbi Elyashar,[84] I received the following telegram from Monsieur Antébi:[85]

---

[83]The commandments connected with the observance of the Sabbath as a day of rest in particular forbid the transfer of any object from the private to the public domain and also forbid the opening of an umbrella.

[84]Jacob Saul Elyashar (1817–1906), Sephardi chief rabbi of Palestine.

[85]Abraham Albert Antébi (1869–1919), headmaster of the Alliance vocational school in Jerusalem and politician.

"Haham başi dead! Request effective support candidature Rabbi Jacob Meïr.[86] Population and colonies categorically reject candidature of Rabbi Elyashar, Jr.[87] Act quickly and advise." This telegram was confirmed by a long letter on the twenty-sixth of last month.

I immediately went to the chief rabbi, who then and there received a telegram from a Jerusalem rabbi. This telegram asked in the name of "all notables, both Sephardim[88] and Ashkenazim,[89] that Meïr's candidature be categorically dismissed and that Elyashar, Jr., be nominated locum tenens by vizierial irade." We already know the consequences of these temporary appointments—which always last until the death of the incumbent. I explained to the chief rabbi that the question of the temporary appointment should be postponed, and I succeeded. By waiting, we gain time. Monsieur Antébi for his part, has succeeded in thwarting the maneuvers of the Elyashar syndicate and has persuaded the government to nominate the chief rabbi of Hebron as locum tenens.

It remains to be seen what will be the result of the forthcoming election.

From what I could understand of the chief rabbi's attitude when I suggested Rabbi Meïr to him, it seems that our spiritual leader, influenced by his camarilla, will oppose this nomination, not only because Rabbi Meïr is relatively more learned and rather less ignorant than his Palestinian colleagues, but simply because he has heard that this rabbi "draws a subsidy from a Jewish society in Europe. . . ."[90]

. . . I already arranged for an article in favor of Rabbi Jacob Meïr to be published in the paper *El Tiempo* last Monday. I will wait for information from Monsieur Antébi and act accordingly.

(. . .)

(AAIU, Turkey, XXX E)

The war against the Alliance was a war against westernization, which represented a genuine ideological and economic threat to the rabbinic body. The latter was increasingly being supplanted in the educational field by secular teachers trained by the Alliance. With the creation of the seminary, there was a risk that it would also be replaced in the religious domain by young progressivist rabbis. The evolution of a society toward modernity, with all the changes that that involves, contained the capacity to disrupt the conservative strata of which the rabbis formed part.

---

[86](1856–1939), elected chief rabbi of Salonika in 1908 and of Palestine from 1921. At the time this letter was written, he had been a candidate for the chief rabbinate of Palestine.

[87]Haim M. Elyashar (1845–1924).

[88]Plural of Sephardi (Hebrew).

[89]Plural of Ashkenazi (Hebrew).

[90]The Alliance Israélite Universelle.

Constantinople, 19 September 1906

Monsieur le Président,

You must have heard via Monsieur Antébi of the success gained in the Jerusalem elections, a partial success, it is true, since the chief rabbi's approval is indispensable before the firman can be handed over to the newly elected candidate. Here the chief rabbi, as usual, is undecided, particularly as he claims that every day he receives protests against the "epicurean"[91] Jacob Meïr.

While we were trying to commit the chief rabbi to recognizing Rabbi Jacob Meïr, the minister of justice and religions sent the chief rabbi a letter in which he said that, according to the many rabbinic protests that had reached the ministry, not only were the elections illegal but Meïr himself ought not to figure among the candidates in view of his previous foreign nationality.

That is how things stand today. The chief rabbi, his pride and amour propre already wounded, has postponed his reply. The public and the newspapers here have already been won over in favor of Rabbi Meïr.

. . . what is regrettable is that the present consistory, as I have had the honor to mention to you on three occasions, is largely composed of people who are not kindly disposed to the Alliance's work. This council conceals everything: they have regarded me as suspect from the moment I belonged to the Alliance and cried out against injustices and the arbitrary actions committed by the rabbinate here and principally its monstrous judgment of 18 Av 5654,[92] which decreed that "according to our holy religion it is categorically forbidden to make communal funds available to the Alliance." On this subject, I will take the liberty of informing you that for some time I have been receiving anonymous letters and threats—I received a sixth inviting me to quit both the chief rabbinate and Turkey on pain of excommunication. I was granted a fortnight's grace.

(. . .)

(AAIU, Turkey, XXX E)

Constantinople, 22 November 1906

Monsieur le Président,

Allow me to give you, purely as a curiosity, the literal translation of the anonymous letter that I have just received. I have so far received several, but in the one today the "rabbis" have taken the liberty of talking about their sanguinary threats and of associating me with Monsieur Danon. I take no

---

[91]Here, as in Rabbinic terminology, the term "epicurean" *(epikoros)* denotes an unbeliever. The word does not, in Hebrew, mean "devoted to sensual pleasures," as it does in English.

[92]July–August 1894 in the Hebrew calendar.

notice; I know they are poltroons and cowards, but it is no less true that these blood threats make one think.

> Monsieur le Rabbin Chaim Nahum,
> (it is a sin that you bear that title)
> Wretched, shameless; in *La Vara*,[93] an unscrupulous rag, you had the courage to designate us by the titles you deserve. You have insulted the rabbis of Constantinople who are your teachers, and the teachers of your father-in-law Danon, the man who glories in his knowledge and prides himself on his secular science.[94] We are going to invite you to the bet din and show you how badly you have conducted yourself toward our rabbis of Constantinople. Perish the day that gave you birth.[95] Cursed be the day when you came to Constantinople! You have made our town impure,[96] you and your father-in-law, the man who wraps himself in a rabbinic cloak[97] and deep inside himself detests the Jewish religion. Rivers of blood will flow if you and your father-in-law try to rule over us. We are already ready to show up your conduct, whenever your protectors like to put you forward.
> Consequently, for the last time we tell you to withdraw from the chief rabbinate; otherwise we will make you quit by the force of the Law.
> Signed: the same rabbis.

There is no point in translating all the other letters I have received for you. They are equally stupid. That is why I am refraining from taking any action with the authorities.

(. . .)
(AAIU, Turkey, XXX E)

Constantinople, 17 December 1906

Monsieur le Président,

(. . .)

We know that with energy and perseverance we will succeed in dissipating the clouds that envelop our institution and in averting the storm that our enemies so much desire. Our constant concern is to strengthen the unsettled and unstable base on which the seminary is built; and to extend more force-

---

[93]"Paper published in Cairo to which several anonymous correspondents in the capital and the provinces sent articles against the chief rabbi and his camarilla. They wanted the articles to be attributed to us in order to be able to attack us" (note by Nahum). This paper had been founded by an Istanbul intellectual, Abraham Galanté, a champion of the Alliance and of westernization. It appeared from 1905 to 1908.

[94]Abraham Danon was a *maskil* (member of the Jewish Enlightenment movement), a distinguished orientalist whose scientific approach to the traditional heritage was not to the liking of orthodox Jews.

[95]Verse from Job (note by Nahum). See Job 3:3.

[96]Verse from Leviticus (note by Nahum). This verse does not appear in this form in Leviticus.

[97]Talmudic expression (note by Nahum).

fully our reforming activities outside, around and within the circle of which our institution is the center. In these difficult times, our task is therefore arduous and hard.

. . . what method should we use to succeed in introducing a new re-generating current into our teaching, particularly into the study of religious subjects, in making our seminarians true and worthy *"tsurva merabanan"*?[98] More than anything else, this means succeeding in giving our pupils a new mental discipline, an upright conscience, and an honest heart, then directing their minds toward rationalism and, as far as possible, nurturing them on a useful and varied knowledge of modern Judaism. These are the methods by which we will succeed in changing in them the extreme mobility of opin-ion, so common among rabbis in the Orient, in moving them away from the subtle, servile, and shabby discussions of routine and obscurantist rab-binism and in making them take a broad view of the depth, the interest, and the different aspects of the mission they are assuming. This is the target we all aim for and thanks to which we succeed in establishing homogeneity and unity in education and teaching, in theory and practice.

(. . .)

(AAIU, Turkey, XXX E)

Constantinople, 1 August 1907

Dear Monsieur Bigart,

The chief rabbi has just received a letter from the minister of religions in which the latter informs him of the grand vizier's decision based on a detailed report by Hilmi pasha, inspector general of the provinces of Macedonia, relating to the appointment of Rabbi Meïr to Salonika re-quested by the chief rabbinate. The Sublime Porte imposes its catagorical veto on this appointment, because this rabbi, the letter from the vizier says, "was affiliated with certain Jewish societies in Europe and principally with the Alliance and with its representative in Palestine and was consequently inclined to safeguard the interests of foreign Jews! . . ."

This is where the chief rabbi's accursed regime, the spying and the denun-ciations of his camarilla, have brought us. I cannot describe to you all the infernal intrigues and maneuvers that have been carried on behind the cur-tain. I cannot go on. I am literally exhausted. I will give you all the details when I arrive in Paris, where, with your permission, I am thinking of going for a short rest.

In the face of this monstrous calumny that makes the Alliance a suspect society, I am told that the chief rabbi will remain silent!

(. . .)

(AAIU, Turkey, XXX E)

---

[98] *Tsurva merabanan:* Aramaic expression designating someone who has been intellectually "fired," or "burned," by contact with the rabbis.

As early as 1862, the Alliance took an interest in the case of the Falashas, Ethiopian Jews, whose Jewishness was long subject to controversy. It sent the scholar Joseph Halévy[1] to visit them in 1867, but the war raging in the country prevented him from completing his investigations.[2] From January 1904 to August 1905, it was the turn of one of Halévy's students, Jacques Faitlovitch, to carry out a mission of this sort. On his return, he founded a "pro-Falasha" committee in Italy. The Alliance associated itself with this work but wanted the terrain to be explored anew by one of its own before embarking on the actions that Faitlovitch advocated. Faitlovitch claimed that the Falashas unquestionably adhered to Judaism. He therefore appealed to the Jews of Europe to save them from decadence and assimilation, to establish schools and to procure books for them. In 1907, the Alliance sent Haim Nahum to investigate the Jews of Ethiopia. It counted on removing him temporarily from the scene of communal conflicts that might harm his career in the long run.[3]

Nahum's mission arrived in Addis-Ababa on 16 February 1908. It turned toward the interior of the country only after it had been received by Menelik on 6 March. In fact, it only set out in April and was back in Paris in July 1908. Nahum did not know Amharic. The aim of the mission was the "relief" of the Falashas: however, Menelik's suspicions must not be aroused.

While Nahum was traveling north, Jacques Faitlovitch traveled south. They met in Addis-Shoa on 21 June 1908. A further source of conflict was added to the already considerable friction between the Alliance and the pro-Falasha committee: the conclusions of the two missions were radically opposed.

What were Nahum's conclusions, and how could they arouse the wrath of Jacques Faitlovitch at this juncture?

Constantinople, 23 October 1907

Monsieur le Président,

(. . .)

Mission to Abyssinia: As the "dry season," that is to say, the season propitious to journeys of exploration in Abyssinia, particularly the north-

---

[1]Joseph Halévy (1827–1917), an orientalist who made a career for himself in France, where he began to teach Amharic (Ethiopian) at the Ecole Pratique des Hautes Etudes in Paris in 1879.

[2]*BAIU,* 2d semester, 1867, pp. 17–19; *BAIU* 1st semester, 1868, pp. 67–70; *BAIU,* 2d semester, 1868, pp. 85–102; Joseph Halévy, *Excursion chez les Falachas en Abyssinie* (Paris: E. Martinet, 1869).

[3]Jacques Faitlovitch, *Gli Ebrei d'Abissinia (Falascia)* (Acqui: Tirelli, 1907), pp. 6–7; *BAIU* 30 (1905), pp. 96–104.

west region, has already begun, I am waiting for your instructions, as well as the necessary advance to make my preparations for the journey and set out for Florence. I would like to take advantage of my brief stay in that town or in Paris, if you think it necessary, to attend some courses in anthropometry and to arrange all the details of the organization of the mission with you. As for the art of photography, I intend to learn that in Egypt.

(. . .)

(AAIU, Turkey, XXX E)

On 28 November 1907 Haim Nahum embarked for Cairo, joined shortly afterward by Monsieur Eberline, house surgeon at Bicêtre. The Jewish press immediately seized on the story. The pro-Falasha committee in Florence accused the Alliance of trying to rob it of the fruits of all its efforts and activities. In self-defense, the Alliance invited the committee to participate in the scheme.

Cairo, 11 December 1907

Monsieur le Président,

When, on Thursday, 19 September, the day after Kippur, during the long conversation that I had the honor of holding with you about our work in the Orient, you suggested that I go to Abyssinia to make a detailed study of the Falashas' condition, I did not pause a second before joyfully accepting the immeasurably difficult but infinitely sacred mission offered me. Perhaps it was very presumptuous of me to rush straight into this exploration, which brought fame to Luzzato[4] and above all to our oriental scholar Halévy, to mention only our coreligionists. The spontaneous enthusiasm with which I lightheartedly accepted this mission did not arise from love of the unknown or curiosity or the urge to travel and see new countries and peoples. I had a much more definite, more specific purpose: the ardent desire to work for Jewry and to contribute, in however small a way, to the regeneration and rallying of its different groups.

It is incumbent on everyone . . . to contribute, according to the prompting of his heart, a small portion of his activity, his intelligence, his thought, his soul to this fine task that requires many workers, and no one . . . should shirk his duty. The mission that you have done the honor of entrusting to me, however arduous, however hard it may be, frightens me not at all. However many the difficulties, privations, sufferings of every type to which I may be exposed, nothing will stop me from pursuing the goal I have set myself.

[4]Philoxène Luzzato (1829–1854), Italian orientalist. On Luzzato and the Falashas, see Archives Israélites, 1851–1854.

It was in this frame of mind that I left Paris on 7 October to spend a few weeks at Constantinople with my family. On 28 November last, after a last farewell to my dearest loved ones, I embarked on board a khedival[5] boat for Egypt, where, as you know, I must organize my equipment.

When I arrived in Cairo I went straight to Monsieur de Valdrôme, chargé d'affaires at the French legation, armed with a recommendation from Monsieur de Nalèche, editor of the *Journal des Débats,* with whom I have long had good relations. Monsieur de Valdrôme gave me the warmest possible welcome and very kindly undertook to help me make our venture succeed.

. . . in addition Monsieur de Valdrôme promised me, with a willingness for which I am extremely grateful, to introduce me to the marquis Salvago Raggi, his former colleague in Cairo and at present governor-general of Eritrea, who is due to return from Rome in the next few days to go and rejoin his post. This recommendation was indispensable to me, particularly as the Italian ambassador to Constantinople apologized that purely administrative reasons prevented him from effecting it. Thus everything bodes well.

As for the program of my mission, I will try to outline the plan to you, if not completely at least as clearly as possible and ask you to be kind enough to study it carefully and correct its failings.

1. Are there Jews or Judaizers in Ethiopia?
2. Are they scattered here and there in the plains or in the mountains, and approximately how many of them are there?
3. What is their religious, intellectual, moral, economic, and social condition?
4. A few thoughts on the most immediate means to be employed to relieve their poverty to some small degree and to extricate them from the state of intellectual isolation in which they find themselves.

. . . you know from the telegram I sent this evening that I have first to go to Addis-Ababa via Djibouti. H.M. Menelik[6] desired this. As a result, I have to travel across the lands of the Gallas and the Somalis, the whole plateau of the Chercher, etc.

. . . if you telegraph me the funds I will be able to get my equipment ready in four days and leave as soon as the reply to this letter reaches me.

I think it would be very useful if the central committee wrote a brief memorandum or a flattering letter to Menelik "king of kings of Ethiopia." What should I take as gifts?

I will wait for your instructions and your assessment of the program that I have set myself.

[5]Belonging to the Khedive, a title borne by the Egyptian ruler.
[6]This was Menelik II, emperor of Ethiopia.

... N.B. I have not received Monsieur Mondon's textbook.[7]

(. . .)

(AAIU, France, XI A 80)

As the Alliance and the pro-Falasha committee did not succeed in reaching a compromise, negotiations were broken off. Nahum was still unaware of this at the beginning of January. The committee for its part sent Jacques Faitlovitch.

An additional source of conflict was added to the already numerous causes of friction between the Alliance and the pro-Falasha committee because the findings of the two missions were radically opposed. What is more, Faitlovitch's mission had been partly subsidized by a rival society to the Alliance: the Hilfsverein der Deutschen Juden.

Faitlovitch had brought two young Falashas back with him from his earlier mission (1904–1905) and placed them in the École Normale Israélite Orientale, subordinated to the Alliance. As he wanted to have control of their education, he withdrew them, against the wishes of the Alliance, which never forgave him.

This time, Faitlovitch set off with the intention of founding a school in Eritrea. It was obvious that, if his plan succeeded, the Alliance was unlikely to be the organization to assume responsibility for this establishment. The Alliance even feared that it would be run by the Hilfsverein.

aboard the *Enna,* Thursday,
9 January 1908

Monsieur le Président,

In accordance with the arranged program, we left Cairo on Saturday the 4th by the 11:00 A.M. train and arrived in Suez at 4:00 in the evening. (Allow me at this point, to open a bracket, Monsieur le Président, to explain our religious conduct.[8] Since one of our greatest casuists the Radbaz[9] regarded the Falashas as *Shevuim,* prisoners, captives,[10] it is our duty, according to our religious traditions, to transgress the Law if need be and even sell synagogues and Torah scrolls to obtain the necessary funds and go to their aid. Consequently there is nothing in our religious conduct that might offend the convictions or beliefs of a pious Israelite.)

---

[7]C. Mondon-Vidailhet, professor at the Ecole des Langues Orientales Vivantes and councillor of state of the empire of Ethiopia. The reference is to his book, *Manuel pratique de langue abyssine (amharique), à l'usage des explorateurs et des commerçants* (Paris: Rouam, 1891).

[8]Nahum had actually had no hesitation in setting out on his journey and taking a train on Saturday!

[9]The initials of R. David ben Salomon ibn Abi Zimra (1479–1573), talmudist, authority on halakha, and cabbalist.

[10]In Hebrew.

After we had taken a few minutes rest at Suez to shave and brush our clothes, which were literally covered in sand, I went to the customs, in the company of a Muslim notable from Suez . . . who was recommended to me, in order to be present when our parcels were examined; there are already fourteen of these at present, apart from your two cases, which I never let out of my sight. With one baksheesh, our luggage was given a certificate exempting it from inspection. We had it carefully placed in a large sailing barge that was to take us to the boat expected at dawn at 6:00 the next morning and then set off to look for a hotel, followed all the time by a Barbary who carried our two small cases containing the speech and the present. We did not even have much trouble finding a trustworthy hotel in this dump of Suez, which is the hideout of thieves and vagabonds. A room was prepared for us at the Hotel Victoria, kept by an Israelite from Russia.

During dinner, the boatman came along to warn us that we would need to show our passports to the police in the morning. This caused us the greatest perplexity. We each had our passport, but we no longer knew which case contained them. The thought of going there in the early morning, ripping open our bags, declaring our cases, and disarranging our belongings, was intolerable. After a few minutes' reflection, I recalled that I had on me, in my overnight bag, the letters of recommendation to the governor of Djibouti and Monsieur Brice, French minister at Addis-Ababa, that Monsieur de Valdrôme had given me; in these circumstances, these letters were real "credentials" for me.

It was already nearly nine in the evening. Without delay, I went straight to the French consul to explain my problems. With no hesitation and with very courteous willingness, Monsieur le Consul handed us a pass and escorted us as far as the port, wishing us bon voyage.

We went straight back to the hotel to rest. At five in the morning our boatman knocked on our door. Half-shaved, half-dressed, with a heavy overcoat over our shoulders, we went to board the boat, which was some hundred meters from the hotel. This was the second "exodus" and the start of our future peregrinations. There was absolutely no breeze, and our barge, which sailed very slowly, was propelled by two Arab oarsmen, who implored the help of Abu-Salama and Abu Al-Afiyya, the two saints of the Red Sea, by chanting the song of the indolent Arab sailor to a languid melody; and even so our barge hardly moved. At last, after sailing for an hour, we arrived on board the *Enna*.

My first concern once on the boat was to have all our luggage brought down to the hold and then to find a good cabin to make ourselves comfortable in: the crossing to Djibouti took eleven days instead of the five with the Messageries line.

All the first and second class passengers were Italian officials or officers who were going to Eritrea. (The marquis Salvago Raggi had boarded a different boat.) As a precaution and to be absolutely free, I had to pay a supplement[11] in order to have a cabin for just the two of us.

. . . the only thing that has begun to trouble us is the heat. We take a cold bath every morning and eat on the bridge at midday and in the evening: it is almost unbearable to stay in the cabins or the dining room. Fortunately we are beginning to approach Massawa, and the heat is already less tropical. We are told that Abyssinia has a very good climate; the only thing to guard against is the difference in temperature between day and night. I have taken every precaution on this score, particularly for Monsieur Eberline, who is of a delicate constitution and slightly rheumatic.

In any case, be reassured on this point; thanks to your paternal care, we are traveling in the best possible conditions, and everything is proceeding auspiciously, despite the announcement of the possible or probable arrival of Monsieur Faitlovitch.

His arrival, although not very pleasant, frightens me not at all. Here, face to face with immensity, and with the prospect before me of the goal I have set myself, the meanness and small-mindedness of a schemer will have no effect on me. Believe me, I will be able to remain entirely calm and serene and at the same time enforce respect for the superior authority to which I am responsible. I will begin by behaving toward him in a friendly fashion that I will change, depending on his conduct, to a conciliatory or defensive manner but never an offensive one. I do not want to change my disposition or damage my morale at any price, particularly at the moment when I need it most. Let Monsieur Faitlovitch come, at the time you have judged necessary, for reasons of a higher order; you can be sure he will be greeted like a good friend.

My program: I am very glad to hear that the views I set out in my study plan correspond to your own, and I thank you for your comment regarding anthropometric measurements. In fact, this was an omission, because the ethnographic question cannot be solved without help from anthropometry. This is how I envisage that part of my study.

I will exclude from our framework any examination of the two theories, the orthodox one, monogenism,[12] and the heterodox one, polygenism,[13] that aim to seek the origin and the relationship of the different peoples mentioned in Genesis (chaps. 9 or 14, I do not exactly recall).[14] Instead, I

[11]The journey, food for eleven days, including the supplement, will cost about 450F to 500F more than by the Messageries line (note by Nahum).

[12]Doctrine of the unity of the origin of man, whereby every human race derives from a common original type.

[13]This doctrine claims that the human species appeared at the same time in several points of the globe.

[14]It actually comes from chapter 10.

will make a particular effort to compare the two types, the Ethiopian and the Falasha, and the latter with the Jewish type.

. . . as for the anthropologists, they themselves do not agree on the place to be assigned to the Ethiopians on the scale of human species.

. . . if we go back to the source, I mean the explanation of the stock from which the different peoples (Shem, Ham, Japhet) are descended, there again, scholars, linguists and physiologists disagree.

. . . Weak laymen that we are, we cannot be exclusive; we have to draw on all the sources, weigh every consideration, and succeed by methodical analysis of the diverse material and information to determine the origin of the Falashas from the ethnographic point of view, without giving too much offense to the overgullible staff of the pro-Falashas[15] or the "Falashists."

Craniometry, to which we should have recourse in order to solve the problem, requires quite special training and mathematically precise processes. But both are lacking. I will therefore settle on the simplest method, the most practical that anthropologists advise in these circumstances: this is the study of the external structure of the body, which consists of examining the descriptive characteristics (skin color, type of hair, organs, senses, etc.) and anthropometric characteristics (methodical measurements of the bodily proportions). I think that this will be sufficient for us.

Conversation between Monsieur le Secrétaire and Monsieur Mondon: The advice of this professor, who has spent so much time at Menelik's court, is unquestionably of very great use to us, since he, more than anyone, because of his impartiality, his experience, and his deep knowledge of the men and things of Abyssinia, is in a position to warn us of the serious difficulties we could be exposed to. From now on, therefore, we are complying with his advice and are strictly following the instructions that you have added to it.

In all our conversations either with Menelik or with some court or provincial official, I will clearly and positively state that the sole purpose of our mission is to make a historical, archaeological, and ethnographic study in the country. In accordance with your warnings, I have destroyed all your letters and do not even keep a copy of those I sent you.

(. . .)

(AAIU, France, XI A 80)

Djibouti, 17 January 1908

Monsieur le Président,

We have been at Djibouti since yesterday morning after a twelve-day crossing. We suffered badly from the sea between Massawa and Aden and

---

[15]Nahum is referring to the committee founded by Jacques Faitlovitch.

particularly in the Bab-El-Mandeb straits. But even so, despite the storm, I took advantage of our four-hour stop in Aden to disembark and spend a short time in the town. In the company of Monsieur Messa, a notable of the town, I had time to glance at the old cemetery, which has no historical interest since the oldest epitaph only dates from 150 years ago. They tried to tell me that there was a very ancient one on the top of one of the surrounding mountains. I did not have much faith in it.

(. . .)

(AAIU, France, XI A 80)

Dire Dawa, 23 January 1908
Addis-Harar (on the map)

Monsieur le Président,

As I had the honor to write you in my letter dated the 17th instant, we left Djibouti on the eighteenth at six in the morning and arrived at Dire Dawa at six in the evening. Despite driving rain, which still continues, the governor of the town, Ato Negato, informed by telegraph by Ato Joseph of Djibouti, was at the station. He received us very courteously and ordered all our luggage and cases of food be allowed to enter without passing through customs.

We put up at the Hotel Emile, a French hotel next to the French consulate, which had been recommended to us at Djibouti.

On Monday, the twentieth instant, we went to call on the French consul, Monsieur Naggiar (probably a coreligionist).

. . . the whole countryside from Djibouti to El-Bab (an Abyssinian port, on the map), the penultimate station before Dire Dawa is mountainous; immense black rocks packed tightly together cover the entire region. Thus the heat in all these places is stifling. There is no vegetation or plantations. Now and again one sees trees completely bare of leaves, dry mimosa, chestnut husks, etc.

All the villages situated along the railway line and in the neighborhood are inhabited by Somalis and Issas, nomad tribes who profess a sort of Islamism mingled with pagan and fetishist rituals.

The resemblance between these regions and the groups who inhabit them is extremely striking.

All of them are reddish black, slim, graceful, with very wiry limbs and spiky hair. They look fierce. They walk about all along the line, large spears in their right hands, leather shields in their left, enormous knives in their belts, wearing no clothes bar a piece of material or oxhide to cover their sexual organs.

Although of a warlike, even bloodthirsty, nature, they are generally very cowardly; I have been assured that they never strike except from behind and regard assassination as the supreme act, highly esteemed by the women. Once they have achieved this goal, they proudly plant an ostrich feather in their hair: ready to marry! . . . But today wearing this feather is pure fantasy.

They all feed themselves on milk from their goats or camels (this milk is used by the tribes of the Danaki desert in particular); once every three or six months they go to the market in a large village to sell a few goats and in exchange buy *dura,* a type of Abyssinian corn, to make bread.

All these Somali tribes live in an independent fashion on territory belonging respectively to France, England (Somaliland), Abyssinia, and Italy (Benadir). But in religious matters they obey a chief, a judge called *ugas,* who normally lives at Warof, near Adda-Galla, in the province of Harar (Abyssinia).

This chief is elected in exactly the same way as our judges. When the chief dies or when he has been acknowledged to be remiss in the exercise of his duties, all the "elders" meet under a large sacred oak (the *elon* of the Bible), which is situated about thirty-five kilometers from Zeila (English territory). I am told that the governor of Zeila is present at this conclave. The man elected immediately receives a sword of honor, which is offered him by England, and then goes to Warof to be recognized by the Abyssinian government.

How interesting it would be to live among them, with them, for some time, to get to know their customs, beliefs, and rituals! Because those who live in regions in contact with Europeans, those on the French coast in particular are beginning to be tamed and are slowly discarding their traditions.

One evening we were walking in the Somali village, in Djibouti, when suddenly some twenty urchins of both sexes, aged between eight and ten, completely nude, came and surrounded us to ask for baksheesh. In gratitude for the four sous they received they formed a circle and sang to us . . . the Tonkinoise! and gave an imitation of a ballet.

Dire Dawa: At the penultimate station, El-Bab (the Abyssinian port), a radical change is apparent; vegetation shows signs of life, the temperature is cooler and there is running water everywhere; this is Dire Dawa or Addis-Harar (the new Harar).

Harar is the chief town of the province of the same name. According to Arab historians, it was founded at the beginning of the ninth century . . . and was an important center of Islamism. . . . In 1875, it was taken by Reuf pasha, sent by the khedive Ismail pasha,[16] and on 2 January 1887 it was conquered by Menelik, who put his nephew Makonen in charge of its administration. Today it contains 35,000 inhabitants.

[16]Khedive of Egypt, 1863–1879.

In view of the splendor and brilliance it already displayed at a very early period, Harar became the town serving at the link between Abyssinia (the Shoa and the Galla) and the coast and consequently the most important center for commerce.

But when the railway came into operation, Addis-Harar was created at the end of the line. Six years ago, it was nothing but a simple village composed of some twenty huts; today, according to the governor, it has 15,000 inhabitants, including 180 to 200 Europeans (French, English, Swiss, Indians, and Greeks).

Here at Dire Dawa, there is a French consulate, an English consulate, a Greek consulate, a French postal service, an English postal service, a branch of the Bank of Abyssinia, and five hotels, including three French ones.

The majority of merchants in Dire Dawa are Indians who transport all sorts of import and export goods via . . . Aden. The imports include everything from cotton goods from Manchester, silks from Bombay, and German hardware to conserves from Amieux brothers. But everything is horribly expensive; first because of the distance, then because of the high cost of rail transport and the petty annoyances of the Abyssinian customs.

Exports primarily consist of ivory, skins, and civet bought by representatives of Belgian and Swiss firms. But the largest lots are always bought by the Messas from Aden, who are said here to be worth some forty millions! From time to time a few Yemenite Israelites, who have settled in Aden, come and buy ostrich feathers: that is their specialty!

Vegetables and fruit grow in abundance, particularly pineapples, bananas, and lemons. There is no question that since time immemorial Abyssinia, and especially this province of Harar, has always produced large quantities of lemons and even exported them to Syria, since the Talmud forbids their use during the festival of Sukkot.[17]

Industry: for the moment there is none. . . . Once the railway has been built up to Addis-Ababa, every branch of human activity will undoubtedly be greatly increased. The Abyssinians will gradually begin to imitate the life of the people around them; they will have stone houses built and adopt European dress.

There already is an invasion of Greeks who are scattered all over the place, from Egypt and the Red Sea ports (Suez, Port-Sudan, Massawa, Aden, Djibouti) to Abyssinia. Almost all the hotels, restaurants, cafes, bakeries, and groceries are run by Greeks.

Why the expected trade expansion has not yet occurred is first and foremost the matter of the railways and then the Abyssinian law, which forbids the sale of property to a foreigner. Moreover, the inalienability of land is

[17]See *Mishna Suka* III, 6, *Babylonian Talmud, Suka* 36a, and *Jerusalem Talmud, Suka* III, 6.

adhered to in Abyssinia. The Emperor has the "high ground"; he gives it away but never sells it. The first Europeans who settled here, at Dire Dawa, have obtained certain concessions over the years that they are authorized to sell, but they find no buyers. At this time when they are setting about forming a ministry in Addis-Ababa, it is said that the property law will be completely changed.

I did not want to do any research on the existence of a few Falashas in Dire Dawa or on certain things concerning them before I had set foot in the Abyssinian capital.

(. . .)
(AAIU, France, XI A 80)

Addis-Ababa, 28 February 1908

Monsieur le Président,

In accordance with my letter from Dire Dawa, we left that town on Monday, 27 January, at 3:30 in the afternoon and arrived at Addis-Ababa on Sunday, the sixteenth instant at 6:30 in the afternoon, after twenty-one days of peregrinations across the mountains and plateaux of the Chercher.

. . . the peace of mind, safety, and well-being that we have enjoyed were first and foremost due to the homogeneity, devotion, and loyalty of the men whom the governor of Dire Dawa gave us, and then to the precautions that we took to procure ourselves appropriate comfort.

. . . the success of a venture or a mission in Abyssinia largely depends on the choice of men.

As all our men were Abyssinians, there was no occasion to fear a disagreement among them, a frequent occurrence when they belong to different religions or races: Somalis, Dankalis, Abyssinians, and Gallas. In that case, it is common to see conflicts break out for childish reasons between bearers and servants, which sometimes end in a real battle and leave the traveler where he is, in the backwoods, with the animals and the burdens.

As for our small degree of comfort, it was organized methodically and very practically. We cannot claim to have had perfection . . . , but thanks to your gifts, we were able to procure the essentials, I will even say, the necessities: a model medicine chest, comfortable equipment, a complete canteen, and an excellent cook. Thus we can confirm that we have enjoyed all the comfort that is as welcome in the backwoods as in the town.

. . . when the *nagadi*[18] inspected our luggage on the eve of our departure, he reckoned on eight mules to carry our 560 kilos. When the caravan was setting off, this number proved insufficient, and another one had to be hired immediately and an additional third soldier engaged before we began our

[18]Merchant.

journey to the capital across "African Switzerland." The countryside is in fact very picturesque and very fertile, so much so that it can yield two harvests a year regularly. However, the Gallas prefer to leave their land fallow rather than allow it to be devastated by their conquerors, the Abyssinians. But barely 150 of the 580 or 600 kilometers that we traversed from start to finish were over flat ground. The rest were beds of dried-up mountain streams, bounded by immense boulders, ravines, steep mountains, slippery ascents, and sharp descents that gave us vertigo and the sensation of falling down a deep precipice at every turn. As for the paths, they were so narrow and twisting that our men often needed to unsheathe their long curved sabers to cut the branches of the prickly mimosa to let our mules get through, and even so we always kept our heads down. We frequently preferred to walk on foot across the enormous rocks, amid the crevices cut by watercourses, rather than be balanced between life and death on muleback. But our beasts of burden, our poor animals, how often did they lose their loads and end up injured. When we got to the camp, there were enormous wounds on their backs which our nagadis, empirical veterinary surgeons, thought they could tend . . . by passing a red-hot iron over them. You can imagine the sound of the plaintive cries and the suffocating odors that rose up from hairy hide and bleeding flesh being grilled!

. . . after crossing the river Awaçh, you enter the burning desert of the Karayus, about fifty kilometers. The nagadis are normally accustomed to make this journey by night, first because the heat there is murderous and there is a complete absence of water, also because the Karayus, nomads and plunderers par excellence, almost always attack small caravans. . . .

But at our "Council of State" held near Awaçh, we decided to take to the road at five in the evening in order to arrive at Tadisha-Malka after a nine-hour forced march.

We divided our servants into an advance guard and a rear guard and proceeded very peaceably in this formation, helped by very beautiful moonlight. At about eleven in the evening, after traveling for six hours (not to mention the four hours in the morning), stop! Our overtired mules would not, could not, carry on, and we decided to camp in the heart of the desert. The ground was stony, and it was impossible to drive in our tent pegs. We simply put our beds up under the stars. Unfortunately, we did not even have a drop of water to make a cup of tea. Cheer up! We stretched out on our beds, still with our clothes and shoes on, revolvers at the ready within reach. In any case we were thinking not of sleep but of watching. But we were overcome by weariness and our whole camp fell into a deep sleep.

At about four in the morning, a warning shout rang through the camp and all our men jumped up: seven mules were missing! Cries of distress and tears from the nagadi. In fact, our anxiety was all too sharp. If the Karayus had laid hands, or wild animals' teeth, on our mules it would be impossible for us to continue the journey for twelve or eighteen hours, and how could we camp amid these inhospitable neighbors, withstand the heat and thirst? Without losing a minute, our men set off in different directions, and Monsieur Eberline and I remained with two soldiers. Six in the morning, eight o'clock, ten o'clock, nothing; our men did not reappear. At around eleven o'clock a long . . . call was heard: our mules had been found behind a nearby mountain. They were quickly and successfully cornered, saddled, and loaded with the luggage and we left at midday en route for Tadisha-Malka.

We journeyed for four hours in the desert without a drop of water. Progress became increasingly perilous; we feared a bad attack of sunstroke. At last we arrived at Tadisha-Malka, where a very pleasant surprise was waiting to make us forget "the Karayu crossing." The *shum* (tax collector and village chief) came out to meet us and took us to his home, a round earth hut with a conical roof covered with thatch, which seemed like paradise to us at that moment. He sat us down on mats and served *tej* (hydromel). We no longer gave a thought to the millions of microbes those prehistoric black jars contained, or to the contagious diseases of the people who prepared and served us with this drink, or to the repugnant filthiness of the persons around us. We were consumed with thirst. Ah! Cunning old Mohamed was right when he promised his followers the future reward of "a clear, fresh drink, served by nymphs under trees giving eternal shade."[19]

When we were restored to ourselves, we thanked the shum and went off to rest in our tent. The shum's—slightly self-interested—kindness did not end there. He came to visit us in the evening and brought with him: one sheep, five kilos of butter, ten liters of milk, forty lemons, a chicken, eggs, honey, tej! The next morning, as we were leaving, we had, in accordance with tradition, to give him baksheesh.

Thank God, apart from these little adventures, which are not unusual in themselves, nothing else has happened; all the rest of the journey was pleasant and we arrived in the capital of the King of Kings of Ethiopia in perfect health and as dashingly as real horsemen (we had a ten-hour forced march on the last day).

. . . when the pursuit of animals does not break the monotony of these journeys in Africa, every day is the same.

Our first concern when we stopped was to select a camping site in order not to sleep in proximity to stagnant water on swampy plains. More often than not we preferred mountaintops, despite the altitude.

As soon as we arrived at our chosen camp, all our men, bearers, servants, and soldiers began to put up the tents and beds. Then one of the men set out

---

[19]Nahum is quoting from memory. Several verses in the Koran allude to it; see, for example, XXXVII, 45–49.

on water fatigue, another on wood fatigue, while the cook made a start on preparations for the evening meal. . . .

At about seven o'clock our table was well and plentifully served, thanks to our provisions and the abundance of poultry. As for the water, it was carefully prepared by Monsieur Eberline. . . . At nine we went to bed with three flannel jerseys . . . , three heavy blankets, and most often with over-coats and waterproofs on top of them. Despite all these precautions we shivered for the first half of the journey. Our servants, wrapped up in the blankets I bought them, mounted guard in succession and kept a small watchfire going to frighten off the animals, principally hyenas, who prowled around our camp.

In the mornings we had coffee at about six-thirty and at eight. After letting the sun warm our limbs and joints, sore from the daytime fatigue and numb from the intense nighttime cold, we ordered preparations for depar-ture to begin. We did not find it difficult to enforce our wishes. . . .

At midday a cold lunch under a tree, a half hour's rest, and on the road again. As for the servants, they procured their own food with the 0.50F I gave each of them every day.

The second day of our trip Monsieur Eberline and myself experienced the onset of dysentery. You can imagine how frightened we were by our early symptoms. . . . Fortunately it was rapidly averted; and for the remainder of our trip, only a few minor and passing attacks of fever for Monsieur Eberline. At the moment we are very well.

(. . .)

(AAIU, Turkey, XXX E)

Haim Nahum reached the Abyssinian capital on 16 February. He prepared for his introduction to the Menelik.

Addis-Ababa, 28 February 1908

Monsieur le Président,

Please be so good as to excuse me for the delay in writing to you. Ironically, the very day that I sent you a telegram informing you of our perfect health and our presentation to the emperor, I was the victim of an accident that might have had very serious consequences for me.

At about six-thirty that evening, we were returning from the home of Monsieur and Madame Katz in Fury (situated ten kilometers from Addis-Ababa), when a hundred meters from the river Akaki, which is surrounded and edged with rocks, the horse I was riding, young and still unused to long journeys, suddenly bolted at the sight of a caravan of camels. It bounded off so impetuously that I lost control. When the bit, bridle, and stirrups became inaccessible, I was in imminent danger of falling off. Thanks to the ten lessons in horsemanship I took in Cairo, instead of letting the horse throw me and hitting my head on the rocks, I was able to slide under the animal's stomach by a semicircular movement from right to left. As I fell, I was kicked right in the chest, which left me stunned for a few minutes. When I returned to my senses, I noticed that my right hand and the index finger of my left hand were injured, my morning coat and my trousers torn to shreds, my watch and my second pair of spare spectacles broken.

Leaning on Monsieur Eberline and an Abyssinian, I was able to walk quite a long way and reach the hotel, where my first concern was to make sure that I did not have a fracture. I was afraid not of the pain but of the three months' immobilization to which it would have condemned me. Fortunately, all I had were bad contusions in the two tibial regions. But all the same I have been obliged to stay in bed for ten days. Although my hand is still bandaged, I have been able to pick up a pen and write to you today.

(. . .)

(AAIU, France, XI A 80)

With the help of the French minister of Foreign Affairs, Nahum was received by the Menelik on 6 March 1908. The purpose of the mission was actually the "relief" of the Falashas, the thrust of the Alliance's ideology. To avoid arousing the Abyssinian leader's suspicions, it was described to him as a mission of a historical, archaeological, and ethnological nature. The Alliance made much in the press of Nahum's reception by the Menelik, which was accompanied by an investiture. Good relations with the rulers of countries with Jewish populations, in which the Alliance was taking an interest, formed part of its usual strategy.

Addis-Ababa, 12 March 1908

Monsieur le Président,

I have the honor of confirming my letter of the sixth instant, the day of our reception, in which I had the pleasure of informing you in haste of the warm welcome the mission sent by the Alliance received from H.M. Menelik. The next day, Saturday, the master of ceremonies and first court interpreter, Ato Haile Mariam, came to the hotel and said to us: "I am here officially on behalf of H.M. the empress to bring you the imperial greetings, to thank you for the beautiful gift you offered her and to congratulate you warmly on the speech you made. H.M. the empress would be very glad if you would be kind enough to send her a full copy of it. At the same time you are invited to come and partake of the imperial luncheon next Sunday"; I am reporting what he said word for word. On Monday the ninth instant, the same delegate came on their majesties' behalf to ask for news of us and I kept him for dinner. He repeated that H.M. talked of nothing else but my speech. To tell the truth, I do not know what was so extraordinary about it.

Speaking in front of an orthodox emperor, a fervent worshiper of the Bible, and the Psalms in particular, I began and concluded by expanding on the verse in Genesis: "And through you, all the nations of the earth will be blessed."[20] On the one hand, I showed the moral greatness of Israel's mission and, on the other, the lofty power of ancient Ethiopia, and how the first had been able to preserve its religious unity during the centuries of ignorance and persecution in the Middle Ages; and the second its independence and its integrity despite the various invasions. I then went on to speak of the renaissance of Israel and the blossoming of Ethiopia in modern times. The Israelites and Jewish knowledge continue their march toward progress, thanks to the living organism represented by the Alliance, which, in working toward this end, is also working for humanity in general. And Ethiopia is embarking on a new road toward civilization, thanks to the intelligence, tolerance, and goodness of their majesties, who seek to make justice, union, and peace prevail, in accord with the words of the psalmist.[21] This verse so pleased the emperor (probably because of the last word), that he immediately asked for the reference. Naturally, I adapted myself to my audience, employing figures of speech and poetic metaphors in the oriental manner, just what was required to appeal to the intelligence of primitive peoples.

Monsieur Brice who had been kept informed of the welcome given us, both by Monsieur Roux, French consul, who was present at the audience, and by the palace itself, made a point of congratulating us by word of mouth, particularly on the empress's marks of favor. The latter in fact keeps a harem, and when she goes out—which is rare—she is veiled. She almost never sees a stranger. This is very important for us, because the provinces we are going to visit are all situated in "her country" (the Shoa and the Amhara are the Aragon and the Castille of the Catholic kings) and are governed by her brother and her nephew.

Yesterday, the French legation asked the palace secretariat for the promised letter of protection; the answer it received was that H.M. first wished me to visit the ruins and inscriptions, which are situated three days away from the capital, as well as the ancient objects (with inscriptions) preserved in the treasury of the *guebi*.[22] I will go to the palace tomorrow to see these objects and to find out exactly where the ruins are. I will do everything possible to hasten my departure; but you certainly know the slow ways of the Abyssinians. At this very moment, there is a German mission here that has brought a quantity of presents with it, even an automobile and that has been waiting two months to be received by the emperor.

---

[20]Genesis 12:3. In Hebrew in the text.

[21]"Love and fidelity have come together; justice and peace join hand": Psalms 85:10. In Hebrew in the text.

[22]The royal palace.

My itinerary:

It is very unfortunate that A. d'Abbadie was not able to confirm, de visu, the presence of Falashas in the provinces that he mentions but did not visit. He himself states that he wrote down all this information "at the dictation of a priest from Kayla-Meda, near Gondar."[23] J. Halévy only visited the Wolqayt. . . . I would very much like to see the list he drew up of a hundred and sixty sites,[24] which should be in the Alliance archives.

As for Monsieur Faitlovitch, you know, Monsieur le Président, that all he does is repeat the names of the provinces Halévy mentions. Furthermore, he has copied the latter word for word in his conclusions. . . .

For my itinerary, I will take the data of d'Abbadie and Halévy as my base and will prepare to travel through all the provinces mentioned by the two scholars.

There is a revolt in the Gojam at present and also in the Tigre. I will make inquiries at the guebi tomorrow in order to arrange my final itinerary.

In any case I must engage a total of some fifteen men, whom I will arm with Gras rifles.

(. . .)

(AAIU, France, XI A 80)

Addis-Ababa, 20 March 1908

Monsieur le Président,

Last Sunday, the fifteenth instant, at the very gracious invitation we had received on His Majesty's behalf, we betook ourselves to the palace, where Ato Haile Mariam pasha (the Negus had given the latter permission to bear this title, bestowed on him by the sultan at the time of his mission to the Porte) received us with his customary kindness in the hall specially reserved for foreigners of note.

After a few minutes' rest, he took us into the *aderash* (the large throne room), which is used as a dining room for the ceremonies of the geber. Before telling you about the quite exceptional honors of which we were the object, permit me, Monsieur le Président, to give you a few details about the aderash and the geber.

The aderache is a vast hall, built ten or twelve years ago, which is 80m long, 50m wide, and 25m high. Despite the harmonious nature of its architecture, its general appearance has the look of an engine room (or rather a large block in Les Halles) because of the large number of girders running across the walls and the iron columns supporting its triangular roof.

The roof, covered on the outside with sheet metal, is very skillfully, I will

---

[23]*Revue de l'Orient* (1845), 222 (note by Nahum).
[24]*BAIU,* 2d semester, 1868, p. 98.

even say very artistically, decorated inside: the reeds of bamboo that form it are arranged symmetrically and joined by bands of yellow, green, and red fabric (the colors of the Ethiopian flag), which produces a charming effect.

The walls, like the façade, are painted with small blue and red flowers to imitate mosaic.

At the back of the hall, opposite the large portal, there is a dais (24m × 12m) about 0.7m high, with four steps. The throne, called the throne of David, is situated in the center of this dais, under a superb canopy surmounted by a crown and supported by four gilt columns. The dais and the room are covered with rich oriental carpets. It is in this room that the emperor gives his solemn audiences and the geber.

The geber is the meal, the luncheon that the emperor gives on Sundays and on great feast days, to all the high dignitaries, ministers, military leaders, and soldiers in the capital, to about 15,000 or 16,000 men. In normal times, some hundred oxen are slaughtered for this purpose, and it is then one of the most interesting sights there could be in Abyssinia. There are all these soldiers holding lumps of raw meat—still twitching, sprinkled with salt and pepper—in their hands, hungrily chewing it. This is the national dish par excellence: the *dergo*. We did not have the pleasure of being present at this savage scene: it is Lent at the moment.

From the hall, we were taken through a corridor leading to the dais itself. After we had washed our hands according to Abyssinian tradition, at a bowl that three soldiers of the guard offered us in front of the door, we greeted the emperor and took our places at the table that had been put up for us on his left.

Behind Menelik stood twenty military chiefs lined up in two rows, with shields, curved sabers, and rifles; opposite, the minister of war, saber poised; on his right, the *afa negus* (literally, the emperor's mouth, because all his orders are communicated through him); and on his left, the *nagadi-ras* (minister of trade and foreign affairs); they were all standing up. Below the dais, at ground level, all the high dignitaries, governors of provinces passing through Addis-Ababa, about a hundred all in all. On very low tables in front of them were their respective rations of *injera* (bread), sardines, and a salad of green pimentos: this is the menu of the emperor and all his subjects during a fast. We Israelites, delegates of the greatest Jewish institution of modern times, that is to say of world Jewry, we were seated on gilt chairs in front of a table and a menu royally served. Not the smallest detail of etiquette had been neglected: tablecloth and napkins embroidered with the imperial arms and silver vases furnished with blue, white, and red pinks!

Immense garnet red curtains, with long cords, cut the dais off from the rest of the room during the luncheon. The Abyssinians believe that it is during the performance of animal functions that the evil eye is to be feared. Thus the page boys, surrounding the emperor, cover him with their *sham-*

mas when he blows his nose, coughs, yawns, or sneezes! During the meal he was cut off only from the crowd, not from the court grandees.

A large seven-branched candelabra on gilt plinths lit the dais while the curtains were closed. When the imperial luncheon was finished, the curtains were drawn and the doors of the room opened. To the sound of long trumpet blasts, reminiscent of those of Jericho, the thousands of soldiers who were stationed in the courtyard were led in by their chiefs and took their respective places at ground level next to their tables, served by Shangallas slaves.[25] At dessert, the emperor asked, through Ato Haile Mariam, who remained standing between him and us, if I wished to propose a toast, which I accepted with alacrity. Champagne had been brought in, and as if by magic, all those 5,000 pairs of jaws came to a halt. I rose (Monsieur Eberline did likewise), glass in hand, and amid deep silence delivered a short speech in the name of my superiors, emphasizing their majesties' broad tolerance and love of progress. I mentioned the services France had rendered to civilization (as my speech at the official audience had been purely Israelite, this time I spoke mainly about the good services of France, in view of the semiofficial character our mission had assumed), and I concluded by wishing their majesties a prosperous reign and a prolongation of their days. When this short speech had been translated word for word by the first translator interpreter, Ato Haile Mariam, H.M. replied that he had been much moved by my words and thanked me warmly for them.

A few minutes later, a little man came onto the dais and took up a position opposite the emperor and us. He was plump and puffy, with fuzzy hair, a shirt down to his knees, tied at the waist with a green belt, and he had a small three-stringed instrument resting on his hips: he was one of the *azmaris (mezamerim),*[26] or troubadour poets. He had come along to improvise songs in honor of the "King of Kings of Ethiopia" and his guests, your servants. I much regretted that I was unable to grasp anything of that guttural rhapsody performed with the verve and liveliness of a positive crescendo because of the distance and particularly because of the hubbub of 5,000 soldiers devouring their injera. Before this first batch was finished (the whole army is fed in three batches), we took our leave of the emperor, who this time absolutely overwhelmed us with friendship.

He shook my hand for over three minutes, thanking me for my brief speech, with a more than usually gracious smile. He asked me (always through the medium of Ato Haile Mariam, whom we used as interpreter) if we could stay for a further three weeks so that we could be present at the great festival of the Ark of the Covenant. I replied that time was pressing

[25]Shangallas: region of Ethiopia.
[26]In Hebrew.

and we had to complete our mission before the rainy season. He asked me yet again to go to Soddo, three days away, south of the capital to visit the ruins in that region and to send him my report, and I consented with alacrity. The first interpreter conducted us to the door of the second chamber.

When we returned to the hotel I made it my duty to send a letter to Monsieur Brice, French minister, to thank him warmly for all he had done for us and particularly for the assiduity with which he had requested our audience on the second day of our arrival and arranged for the French consul to accompany us.

On Monday morning Ato Haile Mariam came to call on us. He informed us that H.M. was still very moved! by my speech and that he had told the empress to say prayers for my toast to be fulfilled.

This morning I received, via the legation, the letter from H.M. the emperor, accompanied by another letter from the French minister, asking me for acknowledgment of the receipt of the emperor's safe-conduct and at the same time thanking me for the letter I sent him. I do not want to miss today's post. I will write to you at length next Tuesday, the eve of our departure.

. . . P.S.: Now that the first part of my mission is completed, I am congratulating myself on having asked you in my first letter from Cairo for a speech that I could make to the emperor. It is true that I took great responsibility for the tact that had to be used toward the Negus of the Abyssinians, whose character is, as Monsieur Mondon said, all ups and downs. But I worked out a plan. Here I took advantage of the fifteen days I spent in bed and in the hotel lounge to study the mentality of some Abyssinian chiefs who came to see us. As a result of this small bit of research I succeeded in getting to know something of their weak point and in grasping the extent of their awareness of it, which helped me in my two speeches to use ideas capable of interesting the emperor and to gain his confidence and favor. Today it is he who says to me: "Go and visit all the Falashas and see that I am informed of their grievances." In my next letter I will give you a literal translation of the emperor's safe-conduct. I am very pleased with this result, but I will be infinitely more pleased if this result corresponds to the desiderata of the Alliance and gives it complete satisfaction.

(AAIU, France, XI A 80)

Addis-Ababa, 3 April 1908

Monsieur le Président,

I have the honor to confirm the telegram I sent this morning: leave-taking audience warm, leaving for Gojam.

Last Saturday at about four-thirty in the afternoon, just when we were getting ready to go out to make a few duty calls, Ato Haile Mariam, first interpreter to the palace, came in haste to tell us that the emperor granted us a leave-taking audience at five o'clock. We went straight to the guebi and at the agreed hour were taken in to H.M. This final welcome was exceptionally warm. First he informed me that he had just bestowed on me the title and insignias of knight (which he raised today to those of commander) of the order of the Seal of Solomon. I made a brief speech, thanking the emperor in the name of the Alliance for all the honors of which we were the object and offering him good wishes for a prosperous reign. Menelik replied in the following terms: "Give my imperial greetings to all the members of the Alliance Israélite, and tell them that I thank them for the prayers they have said for me; prayer in fact is the strength of kings. Go and visit the Falashas and the archaeological monuments, and make sure to send me long reports via the French minister. I wish you a good journey and ask that you send me a telegraph to let me know that you have reached home in good health."

. . . we have at last made up our caravan. We have eleven pack mules that will carry our equipment and provisions for three months, three soldiers, and four servants engaged at the same price as at Dire Dawa. In addition, six bearers to be paid for by the nagadi. I have armed my men with Gras rifles.

. . . I will first go south, to Soddo, to please the emperor and will continue along the road from Gojam to get to Agaumeder.

(. . .)

(AAIU, France, XI A 80)

Nahum's mission set out for the interior of the country in April 1908. When it returned to Paris in July of the same year, it provoked a controversy. The Alliance pressed Nahum to submit a detailed report in order to silence his critics. But no sooner had he returned from Abyssinia than Nahum was recalled to Istanbul by the Jewish progressives. The important duties that were given him at this point delayed the submission of the report.

What were Haim Nahum's conclusions, and how could they make Faitlovitch and his supporters so angry? Nahum, who thought that the Falashas were probably of Greek origin, dismissed the idea of creating educational schemes for them and underestimated their numbers. The opposing party was very far from sharing his views. On one hand, it estimated the number of Falashas at tens of thousands; on the other, Faitlovitch advocated the creation of local educational infrastructures. To this end, he produced a letter from the Falashas themselves asking their coreligionists to open schools for them and send them books.[27] Moreover, he brought Falashas back with him and settled

---

[27]Archives Israélites 22 (3 June 1909), pp. 171–72.

them as colonists in Palestine,[28] to the great satisfaction of the Zionists, who had already ranged themselves on his side against the Alliance.

Constantinople, 17 March 1909

Before you read this letter, please be so good as to forgive me for my delay in sending you a detailed report on the mission in Abyssinia, which you did me the honor of entrusting to me. But you know the important reasons that obliged me to postpone this task: they must be my excuse.

To tell the truth, the account that I am sending you today is less a systematic, methodical, skillfully arranged overall report than a draft, a tidied-up version of my travel notes, accompanied by an outline of the conclusions that I felt should be drawn from what I had seen and heard relating to the problem of the Falashas.

In addition, this problem can be viewed from several aspects. My first task was to determine as far as possible the number and geographical distribution of a population that has commanded the attention of explorers and scholars on various occasions without their ever succeeding in reaching complete agreement on these questions, for reasons that will emerge. My investigation was also concerned with the moral, religious, and economic condition of the Falashas. You will find the substance of the positive data on this subject that I gathered on my journey further on. This was the purely practical aspect of my mission, but it was only one of its aspects. Since the attention of the Israelite world has been called to these distant brethren, deprived of all contact with their coreligionists, and since praiseworthy efforts have been made to draw closer to them, the question has arisen as to the possible origin of the Falashas. Are they native Africans converted to the Jewish beliefs of their day by Jews or Judaizers who came to Abyssinia two or three centuries before Christianity? Conversely, do they form a population of Jewish ethnic origin that might have invaded Abyssinia at a still unknown period? I can only touch on this problem of origin here, reserving it for later treatment in a more documented study, which will emerge to some small extent from the framework I have outlined for this report.

Before introducing you to the Falashas, I think it a good idea to set them against their background, to show you the country they inhabit, to give you some information on the broad outlines of the general life of its inhabitants.

In the Capital

My earlier communications informed you of our arrival in Addis-Ababa and the welcome we received there. The leisure allowed by a forced stay for a few weeks in that town permitted me to study the life and customs of the

---

[28]Ibid. 19 (13 May 1909), 148.

Abyssinian capital. Let us stop for a few moments at this point before continuing our journey.

Menelik formerly lived in Entoto, but that town, situated on the mountain of the same name, is exposed to all the winds, and access by caravans is difficult. The empress Taitu persuaded her husband to transfer his capital to Addis-Ababa in 1886. The present capital has retained the appearance of a vast camp covered with some 12,000 huts, with here and there a few houses built in the European style.

Connected with Dire Dawa and Djibouti by a telegraph line and a telephone network that cross the Chercher, to Eritrea by another line that crosses the Tigre, Addis-Ababa already has a quite well organized weekly postal service with the eastern coast. Commercial transactions there are in the hands of a bank (the Bank of Abyssinia); there are two hotels, and a hospital is at present being built. Two major roads run through the town and lead to the guebi (imperial palace); a roadway suitable for vehicles, sixty-five meters long, leads from the guebi to Addis-Alem, the Abyssinian Versailles, to which the emperor travels by automobile. As the town is situated on a height, the European, or rather the white, usually travels by horse or on muleback. There is no regular police force to keep order in the town, and the native population is not allowed to move about after nine o'clock in the evening; only the European enjoys this privilege, but it is still necessary to carry a lantern. Despite persistent efforts by all the European merchants who have been settled in the capital for a number of years, trade has so far made no perceptible progress; the reason is primarily the enormous distance between the town and the coast and the few needs of the Abyssinian population. But the opening of the railroad from Addis-Ababa to Djibouti has reduced distances, and the Abyssinians, in contact with civilization, will probably gradually become accustomed to commercial transactions and familiar with European industrial products.

The transport of goods, such as it now is, either by mule through the Chercher or the Assabot, or by camel through the desert of the Denakil, constitutes a considerable expense that can be calculated at an average of sixty centimes per kilogram. Add to this the loss incurred through the frequent late arrival of caravans, deterioration, breakages, and sometimes total loss of merchandise through the death of a camel, and baksheesh that have to be given to the customs (not to mention the 10 percent of the ad valorem charge) in order to avoid any petty harassment, and you will have some idea of the enormous cost of these goods.

What also has to be taken into consideration is that only a limited number of goods, mainly food products, are suitable for export; in addition, life is extremely expensive for the European, and there is an extraordinary contrast between the living conditions of the foreigner and those of the native. The latter is content to make his home in a hut that he builds for himself out of branches of trees and straw, at no cost; he feeds on *berberi* (red pimento) and *injera* (a sort of bread); the European has greater food requirements. Also, he cannot put up with such a primitive dwelling.

The population of the capital is estimated at 50,000 to 60,000 inhabitants, including 12,000 to 15,000 *askari,* or soldiers; there are barely a thousand whites (Europeans, Armenians, Hindus); the remainder are a mixture of Abyssinians proper, Gallas, Shangallas, and Guragis.

En Route

Departure from Addis-Ababa; our itinerary: In the letter that I wrote you from Addis-Ababa on 12 March I told you how I had drawn up my itinerary on the basis of the data of d'Abbadie and M. Joseph Halévy. Gabrukantiba (a former Falasha and mayor of the Gondar; at present interpreter at the German legation and at the palace) was kind enough to give me even more precise information on the roads I had to travel, on the regions where I would find Falashas; I was thus able to fix the timetable for our small caravan's journey in advance, and on Sunday 26 April we left Addis-Ababa with a strength of fifteen men, three saddle mules, and twelve pack mules.

Earlier experiences had already taught us that one should never count on the Abyssinians. Their character is full of contradictions, oddities, duplicity. The Abyssinian spends the best part of his time in discussions, in harassment; for the most trivial reason, he is capable of abandoning in the middle of a desert the European who has engaged him. We took a roll call as we climbed into our saddles. One of our men was missing: he had slipped away, taking with him a rifle, a full ammunition pouch and eight thalers.[29] We were going to have our share of this sort of incident. The first day of our great journey began badly. Our caravan did not take the same path that we did, and when night fell, M. Eberline, the caravan chief, and I found ourselves in a vast plain. Torrential rain was falling, and we were without tent, without bed, without the slightest covering, without so much as a bit of biscuit to put in our mouths. Nonetheless we continued on our journey, bracing ourselves to fight weariness and the weather. At last we saw a few Gallas huts; this was our salvation; we ran toward them and asked for hospitality. We were offered a stable; we went inside with our mules. That was an unforgettable night. As drenched as human creatures can be, we stretched out, exhausted, tortured by hunger, in a corner beside our mules and the oxen of our amphitryon. Our host made us a fire with damp cow dung, which smoked without burning, and he grilled us some barley; we thus shared our animals' food; this was our whole meal.

The next morning, after walking for an hour, we met up with our caravan and set off toward the plains of Salale, renowned for their horses. After

[29]Local money.

having crossed the Mugher, where a violent cyclone caught us by surprise during our halt, we entered the Salale. There was no shortage of incidents on the journey. One morning we found a very dangerous snake under my bed, which our men killed. Another day we had a difference with Abyssinians who were pursuing us; one of them claimed that our caravan chief's mule was his property and demanded its return. We made the acquaintance of Abyssinian justice on that occasion, and we had to take the matter as far as the minister of foreign affairs and trade, supreme judge of disputes.

Before reaching the Blue Nile, we had to cross a very rough region. Instead of the humid plateaux of Salale, we were faced with steep mountains intersected by deep ravines. This was the most difficult, the most dangerous, route in all Abyssinia. To scale the precipitous slopes we literally had to turn ourselves into lizards. From the top of one of these mountains, one has a view of a vast chain stretching as far as the eye can see with formidable variations in height. Between two spurs, we found the Blue Nile. It was time. The reflection of the sun off the granite rocks had given me the first symptoms of sunstroke; we had no water. By a supreme effort of will, I reached the Abbai (the Blue Nile) and fainted. They carried me to the water's edge and plunged me fully clothed into the river several times. This bath and the knowledgeable and devoted efforts of M. Eberline restored me. A short rest, a siesta under a tree, set me on my feet again within a few hours and we resumed our journey.

It took us eight days to cross the region of the Gojam that is irrigated by the Blue Nile.

The Abbai, or Blue Nile, a torrent with its source in the mountains situated in the center of Gojam, travels northward, flows into Lake Tsana and reemerges in the east, borders the Gojam and the Damot, and flows into the White Nile near Khartoum. We were able to cross the river by the old bridge built by the Portuguese, and we turned our steps toward the Begemeder.

At the entrance to the Begemeder, the country of the Guxa ras, we were received with great kindness by the *dejaj* (governor) Makonen, who was kind enough to give us one of his men to accompany us to Debra-Tabor, the residence of the ras.

Debra-Tabor, at an altitude of 2,945m, has a population of 6,000 to 7,000 inhabitants; like all the other towns in the country, it consists of a large camp covered in huts. Ras Guxa is the empress's nephew and at the same time the emperor's son-in-law. About thirty-six years old, the ras is powerfully built, with regular features and very bright eyes. Like all the other ras, he leads a similar life to Menelik's; he has his guebi (palace), his aderache (reception room where he gives a banquet for his chiefs and soldiers on public holidays). The ras Guxa gave us an enthusiastic reception. He kept us in his capital for four days, and when we left, he had us escorted by an officer of his household, followed by two soldiers, made us a present of two superb mules, and gave us a letter for the *durgo*,[30] of which this is the translation:

> The *ras* to all the chiefs of his country:
>
> Messieurs H. Nahum and Eberline, who have been recommended to me, have come into my country to see the Falashas; I order you to be kind enough to receive them and to bring to their camp every day: 100 injeras (a sort of bread), 3 *gombos* (jars) of *talla* (Abyssinian beer), 3 saucepans of sauce, 1 sheep, 1 jar of honey, 1 jar of butter, milk, eggs, and poultry, according to their needs. Show them everything they want to see in my country and have them escorted to the next shum by the most practicable route.

From Debra-Tabor, we descended to Kurata (1,900m), to return along the east bank of Lake Tana, where, according to the information Gabrukantiba gave us in his itinerary, a few Falasha families were to be found. We then entered, via the plains of Fogera, the Dembea, and the Sekelt, provinces inhabited by Falashas.

We went along the whole eastern bank and encountered ten villages, one after another; it was only from the eighth village, the village of Atshera, that we began to meet Falashas.

In Falasha Country

Atshera belongs to Gabrukantiba, who, like the missionaries Aragawi and Stefanos, from Djenda, is of Falasha origin. Converted to Christianity in his youth by German missionaries, he was taken to Basle and then London to complete his studies. When he returned to Abyssinia, he was appointed mayor of the town of Gondar and held this office for fifteen years; he was then summoned to Addis-Ababa, where he became attaché at the German legation. It was he too who accompanied Professor Rosen, the diplomat's brother, on his journey to Gondar.

Gabrukantiba's daughter is settled on a property situated half an hour away from our camp and has three Falasha families in her employ, two of whom engage in agriculture. These were the first Falasha people we met. On the road from Shenker we had had occasion to see two huts in the plain inhabited by two Falasha widows who are engaged exclusively in weaving fabrics intended for the native clothing, called *chomas*.

It was in the villages of the provinces of Dembea and the Sekelt that we encountered settlements of Falashas at varying distances from one another. Let us cast a brief eye over them in the order in which we visited them.

The first we met was:

Shenker, two and a half hours to the north, that is to say about 10 km from Atshera. There is quite a large Abyssinian population there in com-

---

[30]Upkeep of the caravan at the state's expense (note by Nahum).

parison with that of other villages; but it only contains three Falasha families. The men are weavers; the women work in pottery production.

Three hours from there, we reached the Djenda valley. This is a large plain surrounded by hills, on which six small villages are established. This is where the missionaries Aragawi and Stefanos live, and also the mother of Taamrat, the young Falasha whom Monsieur Faitlovitch brought back to Europe and who is now studying at the rabbinic seminary in Florence. This woman, converted to Protestantism, performs duties similar to those of a deaconess. According to authentic information that we gathered locally, all the families in these villages are of Falasha origin and were converted to Christianity by Aragawi. The number of converted Falashas in this district was 200 to 300. Several probably perished at the time of the last invasion by the Dervishes. The natives themselves told us the sorry tale of these raids and showed us the ruins they had left. Today there is not a single Falasha in Djenda.

Fendja is situated three hours from Djenda. In the vicinity of the Abyssinian village there are two distinct clusters, one inhabited by Falashas (five families) and the other by converted Falashas (seven families). They are all weavers. They even own a small *tukul* (hut), which they use as a *mesgid* (temple), but have neither a *kahen* (priest) nor a *debtera* (teacher).

Guraba is four and a half hours away from Fendja. We set up our camp on a distant hill half an hour away from the Falasha district.

This village contains twelve Falasha families (two farmers, two carpenters, and eight weavers). It is famous for its Falasha priests. There are eleven of them, including eight priests and three subpriests. The high priest, an octogenarian called Abba-Teyyim, asked us for news of M. Halévy, whom he had seen at Vohni, in the vicinity of Wolqayt, in 1868.

Gana-Yohanis, about three and a half hours from Guraba, is inhabited by five Falasha families (two blacksmiths and three weavers).

Amba-Walid, four hours from Gana-Yohanis: This village is the birthplace of Guetie, the second Falasha brought back by M. Faitlovitch and who, like Taamrat, was taken in by the Alliance. In the absence of his father, summoned to Addis-Ababa for a lawsuit brought against him by Guetie's father-in-law, his mother, accompanied by her other sons, came to our camp to bring us injera, talla, eggs, and live poultry and to ask us for news of her son; she entrusted us with a letter for the young man, which we were able to give him when we met him with M. Faitlovitch at Addis-Shoa.

Abba-Finhas, the village debtera, told us that a few days before our arrival a fire had destroyed five huts and the mesguid with the few manuscripts that it contained. Amba-Walid has fifteen Falasha families; the heads of families are divided among the professions as follows: three blacksmiths, two masons, and ten weavers. Although it was Friday, a holiday for the Falashas, a blacksmith specially lit his forge to show us how he worked iron.

Sekelt: This village, which has the same name as the district, is two hours away from the previous one. The ten Falasha families who inhabit it are all engaged in weaving.

Dirmama (Ezezo), an hour from Sekelt, has only one Falasha family.

Gudi-Gudi, on the road leading to Gondar, contains two Falasha black-smiths.

Amba-Atshera, two hours from Sekelt, is inhabited by ten Falasha families, five weavers, and five blacksmiths.

Tadda, an hour south of Gondar, possesses fourteen Falasha families; two heads of families are masons and two blacksmiths; the rest are weavers.

Kaddus-Yohanis, half an hour from the town of Gondar: This is a new village built by Falashas who came from Simen at the empress's orders to repair the churches of the town. All of them are masons. The *kantiba* [governor] of Gondar had them brought to us; they gave us information on their life and that of their coreligionists in Simen.

After Aksum, Gondar is historically the most important town in Abyssinia. We camped there in the vicinity of the palace called Atie-Fassil, built by the Portuguese in the fifteenth century. It is a castle flanked by a massive, high, square tower and other, round turrets. Facing this castle and at some distance from it, several other small crenellated buildings, used as churches or seminaries, can be seen. This town contains the largest number of Abyssinian Muslims. They inhabit a separate district and have as their leader a certain sheikh-Said. All the Abyssinian Muslims are nagadis, or merchants. They carry on trade between Gondar and Metemma (on the Sudanese frontier). There is not a single Falasha in the town itself.

After resting for three days, we left Gondar by the road from Wagara in order to enter the Simen and cross the river Takazze before 30 June; after that date it overflows and becomes impassable, and we would have had to stay on this side of the river until the end of October.

On this road we encountered:

Walaka, five leagues northeast of Gondar; eleven families of Falashas live there and engage in farming or weaving.

After four days of uninterrupted travel, we arrived at Dobarik (the entrance to the Simen), where the dejaj was then staying; he is the empress's nephew and governor of the Simen and the Wolqayt; he arranged for three chiefs to escort us for a few days.

From Dobarik we set off for Shevada (Simen). We camped at Barna at an altitude of 4,200m. The night there was terrible: penetrating cold prevented us from sleeping, and the violence of the wind condemned us to immobility. Faced with the impossibility of continuing our journey, as much because of the cold as because of the difficulty of climbing these high mountains, we turned back and retraced our steps toward the Takazze via Woldebba. According to the information given us by the Kinyazmatch Ilma, a native of Simen, which corroborated what we had gathered at Gondar, Simenite

Falashas are employed in building work undertaken by the empress. The villages of the Simen inhabited by Falashas are as follows:

(1) Malata, fifteen families; (2) Bashgue, three families; (3) Mount-Shanegzi, four families; (4) Dibil, three families; (5) Shevada, eight families; all the heads of these families are blacksmiths; (6) Aiva, six families; (7) Tiena, five families; the heads of these eleven families are masons.

After six stops, we crossed the Takazze and went straight on toward Adenkato, which we thought was populated with a considerable number of Falashas.

Adenkato is the name of a district that, like other Abyssinian districts, is made up of several small villages, or rather several small clusters of huts, the largest of which bears its name. The day after we arrived, guided by an askar of the dejaj, Gabro Sallassi, chief of the whole country up to Eritrea, we went to visit the place inhabited by Falashas. We were absolutely taken aback to see that "this great Falasha community owning a synagogue"[31] was no more than an ordinary small piece of land like the rest, with a total area of 100 square meters, containing precisely ten huts; the "synagogue" was no more than a small round tukul with a diameter of about 4m. The ten or twelve Falasha families who inhabit these thatches earn their living as blacksmiths or farmers. At the time of our visit they were plunged in despair: cattle plague, which was raging throughout the countryside at that time, had robbed them of the few animals they owned. From there we went to Addis-Shoa, where we found Monsieur Faitlovitch.

Addis-Shoa, two and a half hours from Adenkato, is the largest Falasha village we encountered in the whole of Abyssinia. It contains *thirty-two* families and possesses a larger mesguid than the other villages. Almost all the men are blacksmiths; very few of them are engaged in farming. The insides of their dwellings denote relatively comfortable circumstances, something which we had not met among their coreligionists in the Amhara. Their moral level is also higher; we were struck by the dignity of their characters; they say that they are proud never to have known conversions.

After leaving Addis-Shoa, we struck camp at Dembagina. Two Falasha families inhabit this village, where they work as blacksmiths.

From there, we continued our route toward Aksum, crossing the plain watered by the river Selakleka, where there are some ten families of Falasha blacksmiths and farmers. After a forced march of four days via the road from Belis, we came to Aksum, the most famous town in Ethiopia.

Today Aksum contains 4,000 to 5,000 inhabitants, including 800 priests, who are the real lords of the town. It was here that the Aksumite kingdom

---

[31]J. Faitlovitch, *Notes d'un voyage chez les Falachas* (Paris: E. Leroux, 1905), p. 14 (note by Nahum).

was founded in 290 before the Christian era. . . . The Abyssinians exagge-
rate the antiquity of their religious town and date its founding back to
Abraham. The obelisks we saw testify to the ancient splendor of this "refuge
town,"[32] which today is entirely under the dominion of the priests, whose
leader, called *nebrid*, is regarded as the guardian of the Tables of the Law. The
"Great Church" is situated at Aksum; from the architectural point of view it
is different from the other churches in Abyssinia. Its restoration was entrusted to Italians from Eritrea; they also built a palace designed to be used
as a residence for Menelik during possible visits to the town. On our arrival
at Aksum, we camped at the approaches to this palace, and the agent for
these buildings was kind enough to invite us to his home and to offer us
hospitality in one of the five bedrooms in this palace. This was the first time
for two and a half months that we found shelter under a real roof.

The next day the headman of the town came to see us, and we had a long
conversation about the Falashas with him; he told us that the latter, numbering some fifteen families, inhabited a small district in the south of the town,
they are all honest workers; as everywhere else, they work as blacksmiths,
but during the rainy season they leave Aksum and settle in the Shire, at
Akabrat, where the village chief rents them land that they cultivate.

The Return

After two days of rest, we left for Aduwa, where we were very kindly
received by the dejaj Gabro Selassi, chief of the Tigre. He speaks and writes
Italian very fluently and has an appreciation of European civilization.
Thanks to Monsieur Stefanin, head of the Italian telegraphic bureau, we had
no need to pitch our tents; we lodged in a tukul of the resident, to whom we
had been recommended by the Italian minister at Addis-Ababa.

From Aduwa, we set off for the Mareb, a river that separates Abyssinia
and Eritrea and is known for its unhealthful water. We crossed it after
stopping twice and entered Gundet (the first station in the Italian colony).
Here we were the guests of the frontier guards, who invited us to spend the
night with them in an attractive building situated on a knoll overlooking
all the plain watered by the Mareb. It was a real treat for us to sleep in a
comfortable room at last.

From Gundet, we went to Adi-Ugri, our last stop on muleback. There
again we received the warmest welcome from the Italian authorities. Two
rooms were prepared for us, and we were offered luncheon on the "Square."
The royal commissioner, Monsieur de Rossi, told us about a few Falasha

---

[32]Murderers and deserters from the army who, during the war, took refuge in the sacred
enclosure of the town containing the great church saved their lives; this is almost like the
"refuge towns" mentioned in the Pentateuch (note by Nahum).

families, natives of the Wolqayt, who had settled in the colony at Mai-Tukul, and gave us a copy of the report he had sent to the governor-general of Eritrea, the marquis Salvago Raggi, on the information these Falashas had supplied on the Wolqayt.

The following morning, we got into the carriage that we had ordered by telegraph and, after a journey of five hours, arrived at Asmara.

Asmara is a very pleasant small town; it has hotels, cafes, small boulevards, clubs, a theater, and schools, one of which is run by Swedish missionaries. The Jewish colony there consists of some fifteen families, including two who are natives of Constantinople, five from Smyrna, and the rest from Aden. The first engage in wholesale and retail import trade, and the remainder are gold- and silversmiths and watchmakers.

The day after our arrival we called on the governor-general, the marquis Salvago Raggi, to whom I was recommended by Monsieur de Valdrôme. He gave us the warmest reception. I have already had occasion to inform you of the conversation we had with him. He stated very clearly that he could not conceive of the usefulness of creating a school for the Falashas at Asmara, as Monsieur Faitlovitch had planned. He did not really see, he told us, where and how pupils would be recruited; and even assuming that these pupils were found, they would become déclassés, because once they left the school they would want to be employed in the governorate; in that case, they would be regarded as complete natives and never as Europeans. In addition, the foundation of a school of this type would be badly received by the natives and would only arouse hatred of the Falashas. As for the creation of an agricultural colony at Asmara, the governor thought it would be impossible to do for the simple reason that the government has no land. All the colony land is private property that could only be bought at very high prices. However, according to the marquis Salvago Raggi, Falashas might set up as craftsmen or farmers in various places in the colony but as individuals and not as groups.

———

After having leafed through my travel notes with you, mentioned a few of the minor incidents on our voyage of discovery, listed the places we visited, and taken a census of the Falashas in all the places that we encountered on our route, it remains for me to offer you an overall view of the moral and material life of the Falashas, based on both our personal assessment and on information we were in a position to gather at first hand from a large number of them.

Regions inhabited by the Falashas: It follows from the preceding discussion that the Falashas are clearly confined to a limited number of regions. They appear to have deliberately chosen those that offer fewest geographical and climatic disadvantages.

Abyssinia has two major seasons: the dry season, which begins in November and ends in June, and the rainy season, which begins in June and ends in October; during this latter period, called *tekemt* in Abyssinian, active life is necessarily interrupted; rivers overflow; roads become impassable as a result of continuous torrential rain, often accompanied by cyclones, etc.

Abyssinia is divided by altitude into three zones: the tropical zone, 200–1,200m; the middle, 1,200 to 2,500; the upper, 2,500–4,300. The Falashas mainly inhabit the middle zone, with a tiny number in the upper zone. The Chercher, the Galla lands, the Shoa, the Gojam, the Begemeder, and the Tigre proper contain no Falashas. They are settled to the east and north of Lake Tana, in the Dembea, the Sekelt, the area around the Gondar, the Wagara, the Simen, the Shire, districts that we visited. We have been told that there are still some of them in a few villages in the Lasta, and a few scattered families west of Lake Tana (Tagossa, Atshefar); the Kauara, which formerly contained a few Falasha villages, is completely abandoned today because of the malaria that rages in this region (Gabrukantiba's evidence). As for the large province of Wolqayt, which was thought to be still populated by a very large number of Falashas, not a single family can be found there today.

According to Bigirudi-Mebratu-Wold-Aianasghi, native of Sherkos Mai Lomomo (Wolqayt): "At Tukul, we are five Falashas: myself, one Lilai Ouald Salamon, and the brothers, Merra, Taccaligne, and Meheret, sons of Abraham. I left my native land twelve years ago; I spent four years in the Addiabo, working iron, and for eight years I have been at Tukul with the Balambaras. My four coreligionists settled in Tukul five years before me. They are natives of Addi-Remez (Wolqayt). When I left my homeland twelve years ago, the whole of Wolqayt barely numbered twenty Falasha families."

The external appearance of the Falashas: We did not have the opportunity to take measurements to establish the exact anthropological nature of the Falashas. Like all Abyssinians, they are of average build, slender, dry, and wiry and have relatively long hands and feet; the color of their skin varies according to altitude. They are paler at higher levels, darker in the plains. Like the Abyssinians, they also have woolly hair. Because of interbreeding, it is difficult to establish an absolute Falasha type.

Religious Life and Practice

The Bible: The Falashas' holy book par excellence is the Bible. Their priests in their ascetic life continuously meditate on it; they teach the children its lofty ethics. The Falashas do not know Hebrew; depending on region, their everyday language is Amarina or the Tigrina language. The latter is a derivative of Guez. The Bible is written in Guez, and as the Falashas no longer understand this language, the priests translate it into the local idiom for the children.

The Bible is written on thick sheets of parchment divided into two columns. The copies the kahen uses in the mesguid are different from those in use by laymen in that they have several annotations in the margin in the form of *massora,*[33] which serve as commentary on certain difficult words. The Pentateuch is generally in one volume, the Psalms in another; the Prophets and the Hagiographa are combined with a few apocryphal books, particularly the one by Ben-Sira.

The kahen has the greatest veneration for the book of Enoch. On the first page of this book, which we found with the kahen of Guraba, we saw pictures of Moses and Aaron on the same page in the dress of Byzantine priests, colored red and blue, Moses holding the traditional rod in his hand and Aaron the censer.

The Ethiopian translation of this Bible must have been made from the Greek text, like the one used by the Abyssinian church; I need no further proof of this than the names of the various books, the order in which they are placed, the transcription of certain Hebrew proper nouns. The Falashas call the Bible *Werit.* This is the word *berit* ("alliance" or "testament," the term used by St. Paul in the Epistle to the Hebrews[34] and in his Second Epistle to the Corinthians).[35]

The books of the Falasha Bible are the canonicals, plus those called apocryphal, which are found only in Greek versions. They are placed in the same order as the Septuagint version. The books of the Bible that the kahen of Guraba showed us were arranged in the following order: Job, Kings,[36] Judges, Proverbs, Isaiah, Jeremiah, Ezekiel, Daniel, Hosea, Jonah, Haggai, Joel, Nehemiah, Habakkuk, Zephaniah, Zechariah, Micah, Ezra, Ben-Sira. The transcription of proper nouns is also Greek: Finhas for Pinhas, Isaias, Irmias, Anvakum (Habakkuk), etc.

Religious books: We have seen few books in the possession of Falashas, other than "the Saturday Commandments," which M. Halévy has already made public, a summary of biblical regulations on the laws of purity, some treatises containing legends of the lives of Abraham (Galla Abraham), Isaac, and Jacob, and prayer books.

All these books are very carefully preserved by the kahen (priests) in the mesguid.

Priests: The kahen wears the same costume as the layman, that is to say, shorts and a shirt down to the knees, covered by a white robe, choma, edged with red. But while laymen are always bareheaded, the priests wear white cylindrical headdresses wider at the top than at the base.

---

[33]Critical note made in the margin of the biblical text by the Massorites (in Hebrew).

[34]VIII, 18 (note by Nahum). It actually appears in VIII, 13.

[35]III, 14 (note by Nahum).

[36]These are four books, two of which correspond to the books of Samuel (note by Nahum).

They lead an ascetic life, never marrying. Meals, prepared by one of their number, are eaten communally, and they live in a community in small huts built around the mesguid and separated from the rest of the dwellings by a wooden fence about 70 cm high. What primarily struck us about the priests of Guraba was their completely black complexion and their virtually Sudanese type. They are all beardless. The Abyssinians assured us that all the kahen are eunuchs and that fathers who consecrate their children to priestly office have them operated on at an early age.

D'Abbadie[37] reports that, according to information given him by a priest, the kahen eat certain roots that destroy their virility. This is the only explanation for their ability to maintain celibacy in such a hot country. They have a horror of women; they would not taste a dish prepared by one, and they make their ablutions whenever they are handed an object by a female hand. We did not see the kahen of Abba-Yared (Simen), but we were told that they have even more austere customs: they make their ablutions every time they touch a married Falasha man. Apart from their religious duties, the priests write amulets, practice a little thaumaturgy, like the Essenes of old, and sometimes spend their leisure working a small piece of land to provide for their needs. But their real life is spent in the mesgid.

The temple: The mesgid, like the other dwellings, is a round hut, 4m in diameter; the walls are sometimes made of wooden posts, the gaps between filled with earth, sometimes of stones placed on top of each other; the roof is conical in shape and covered with thatch. At the back of the mesgid, facing the door, is a small table on which the holy books are placed and which is separated from the rest of the hut by a curtain. Near the mesgid is the altar; this is a simple pile of rough stones round a center cavity into which the animals to be sacrificed are placed.

Prayers: The kahen prays seven times a day:[38] (1) at dawn; (2) before midday; (3) at midday; (4) in the afternoon; (5) at sunset; (6) before midnight; (7) at cockcrow. Laymen only pray twice: morning and evening. Furthermore, their prayers consist only of these simple words: "We bow down before our God, the holy God, creator of all creatures, blessed be He."

Saturday prayers are longer. They start reciting them on Friday evening and continue throughout the day on Saturday. The worshipers chant these prayers in chorus; they start with the words: *Yetebarak Egziabiher emlak Israel.* Praise of God plays a very large part in them: they are made up of verses mainly taken from the Psalms and in that respect are reminiscent of the thanksgivings of the Karaites and Muslims; they contain other passages demonstrating their love for Jerusalem and their hope for its future restora-

---

[37] *Revue de l'Orient* (1845), 225 (note by Nahum).

[38] The Abyssinian priests also recite seven paternosters every morning, and they do this in accordance with the verse "Seven times a day I praise thee": Psalms 99:164 (note by Nahum).

tion. It is worth noting that the Abyssinians too have not ceased to extol the holy city.[39] All these prayers must certainly have undergone several transformations, hence the variations in the texts.

In accordance with the Abyssinians' tradition, the Falashas turn toward the northeast (the site of Jerusalem) to pray; they pray bareheaded.

Festivals and fasts: The Sabbath is strictly observed. The majority of Abyssinians also abstain from working on Saturday, for which they have a genuine respect. The Falashas also abstain from work on Fridays, the eve of the Sabbath. In the afternoon, they carefully wash their bodies and put on clean clothes. Like the Karaites,[40] who take the biblical precepts literally, they stay in the dark on Friday evenings and only leave their dwellings on Saturday to go to the mesgid, where they remain in prayer the whole day. The kahen gives a talk in Guez on certain biblical passages and, like the *metargemim* in olden times,[41] he translates them into Amarina, the common language, adding a few homiletic commentaries taken from the traditional teachings.

Apart from the Sabbath, the Falashas observe the five biblical festivals, namely:

a. Fassika (Passover): seven days when they eat *kitta,* which is very simply prepared. This is the bread (unleavened) that all the nagadis (merchants) generally make themselves when they are on a journey and when they cannot find anywhere to buy injera.

b. Mairer (Pentecost): one day.

c. Tazcar (corresponding to Rosh Hashana): one day, in memory of Abraham.

d. Asterio, or Segdet (Kippur): According to Falasha tradition, it was during this memorable day that God appeared to Jacob.

e. Babe Mazelet (Sukkot): This festival lasts seven days, but they know nothing about the *sukka.*

In addition, they have semifestivals based on their traditions or on the apocryphal books, for example one celebrated in the month of Tahsas (De-

[39]The Guxa ras told us in the course of conversation: "I await with the greatest impatience the completion of the railroad between Addis-Ababa and Dire Dawa so that I can go to Jerusalem, holy city of our ancestors" (note by Nahum).

[40]The literal observance of the commandments concerning the Sabbath and their total ignorance of the oral law convinced our former casuists that the Falashas were Karaites . . . (note by Nahum).

[41]Translators (in Hebrew).

cember) called *zeberabu senbet*. The historical festivals of Chanukah[42] and Purim[43] are unknown to them.

On the other hand they observe the fast of Amatsu (17 Av) very strictly, in memory of the destruction of Jerusalem and the Temple by Nebuchadnezzar.[44] They are also accustomed to fast on 9 and 12 Tammuz.[45]

Religious practices: The Falashas observe the most important of the religious commandments that are peculiar to the descendants of Abraham, namely circumcision. The Abyssinians also practice it. *Periya*[46] is not practiced.

Circumcision takes place on the eighth day after the birth of the child; as with the Karaites, it cannot be performed on the Sabbath. The Falashas do not have special *mohelim*.[47] Anyone can carry out circumcision; generally, the father circumcises his child. The instrument used is a small knife with a crescent-shaped blade. Daughters are also circumcised but, according to Abyssinian custom, only at the end of the second week; this operation is carried out by women. First-born males are offered to the kahen, who dedicates them to priestly duties, likewise, first-born animals are offered to the priests at the age of one.

The Falashas are totally ignorant of the other external practices of Judaism, such as *tefillin*,[48] *tsitsit*,[49] *tallit*,[50] and *mezuzah*.[51] However, some Falashas wear a sort of white cord round their necks with several amulets that they buy indiscriminately from Falasha priests or Amharas, in the same way that Abyssinian Christians have a *mateb* (blue cord) round their necks holding a cross, a ring, and several amulets, and Abyssinian Muslims hold a rosary.

Religious hygiene: The biblical commandment that the Falashas observe most strictly is the one concerning the purity of women. The woman who is *nidda*[52] remains in complete isolation for seven days. Every Falasha village has a small room separate from the rest of the dwellings for this purpose. Here nidda women are shut up for the whole of this time; they use special

---

[42]Festival of lights commemorating the victory of the Maccabees (2 B.C.).

[43]Festival of Esther, who saved the Jews of Persia from the extermination decreed by Haman, King Ahasuerus's minister.

[44]It is undoubtedly through a mistake that they fast on 17 Av instead of the seventh (2 Kings 25:8) (note by Nahum).

[45]Jeremiah, 52:6–11 (note by Nahum).

[46]Rending (in Hebrew).

[47]Circumcisors (in Hebrew).

[48]Phylacteries (in Hebrew).

[49]Ritual fringes worn on the corners of a garment (in Hebrew).

[50]Prayer shawl (in Hebrew).

[51]Parchment fixed to the lintel of the doorpost (in Hebrew).

[52]In a state of sexual impurity (in Hebrew).

utensils to cook with. On the eighth day, they have to wash their clothes and bathe in the river.

Women in childbirth who have given birth to a boy observe forty days of isolation in this thatch, eighty days for a girl.[53] At the end of this period, a goat is offered as a sacrifice to God. One priest drains the blood, while another recites the customary prayers. Falashas from the Chenker told us that in olden times a small red cow was offered as a sacrifice and the ashes were thrown into *purifying* water.

Death: The Falashas have quite specific death rituals. Like the Abyssinians, they shave their heads as a sign of mourning and professional mourners come at fixed times for eight days to chant elegies in chorus. Here again what distinguishes them from their cocitizens of the Christian faith is sacrifices. After death, four people come into the thatch, wash the body of the deceased, dress it in a new shroud, and carry it to the cemetery, which is situated in the vicinity of the village. The grave is dug to a depth of about one and a half meters. The close relatives observe seven days of mourning, then they carry out fresh ablutions and offer a sacrifice.

Food laws: The Falashas observe a sort of *shehita,*[54] but they are completely ignorant of *bedika.*[55] Providing he is married and monogamous, anyone can carry out the duties of the slaughterer. The knife used is pointed and has two cutting edges. One curious thing: the Falashas know the tradition whereby shehita must be carried out in *halala* and *haavaa* (backward and forward movement). The slaughterer first makes the usual blessing: *Yetebarak Egziabiher, emlak Israel,* then he slits the animal's throat and covers its blood with a small quantity of earth. The Falashas abstain, as do all Abyssinians, from eating pork and game.[56] They are ignorant of the prohibition on cooking and eating dairy products with meat. Before eating, they perform ablutions, as do all Abyssinians; they recite a prayer before the meal[57] and another before leaving the table.[58] In the absence of water, they, like the Israelites and Muslims, take a handful of earth, which they rub between their hands.

Moral and Economic Condition

Intellectual and moral life: The Abyssinians regard the Falashas as educated men. Perhaps this reputation was justified in former times; it has no

---

[53]Leviticus, 12:2, 3, 5 (note by Nahum).

[54]Ritual slaughter (in Hebrew).

[55]Examination of the organs of the slaughtered animal.

[56]The Abyssinians are allowed to eat the slaughtered animal on condition that its throat has been cut according to their ritual immediately before death (note by Nahum).

[57]Blessed be the Eternal, the God of Israel (note by Nahum).

[58]Eternal God of heaven and earth, blessed be Thy name for ever (note by Nahum).

foundation today. What probably earned them this prestige, was, on the one hand, the knowledge they had, first, of the Guez language, the language of the Holy Books and prayers, and second, of the Scriptures, with which they seem to have been very familiar; on the other hand, the fact that they were frequently blacksmiths,[59] which the Abyssinians regard as an élite occupation. But today, only the priests can claim the title of "sage," because they alone know Ge'ez and Amarina writing. In Amhara the kahen speak to each other in the Agau language, particularly when they are in the presence of Abyssinians, and although they know Ge'ez, they translate the sacred texts and give instruction to the children in Amarina.

The Falashas have a good knowledge of biblical history, particularly up to the time of Kings, but are totally ignorant of later periods and do not seem to have really authentic traditions based on their own history.

The family: The Falashas, on the Abyssinian model, marry very young; parents arrange matches and engage their children to be married before they are nubile. Monogamy is scrupulously observed; anyone transgressing this law would be excluded from the community. Concubinage is almost unknown. Because of their customary chastity and their attachment to the ideal of family, the venereal diseases that cause such ravages among the Abyssinians are very rare among the Falashas. Falasha women are fairly infertile. What are the causes of this stagnating birthrate? A lengthy scientific study would be needed to elucidate this difficult problem and above all quite a long stay among these populations.

Religious marriage does not exist; the marriage is concluded solely in the presence of witnesses. The two partners combine their respective property, which consists of goats, oxen, etc. This joint possession is dissolved by divorce or by the death of one of the partners. Separation or divorce is pronounced by the *dania*.[60] Justice is generally administered by the village *shum* (tax collector), assisted by two individuals. When a woman is found guilty of adultery, and cases of this sort are very rare among the Falashas, the guilty party is punished by beating before the divorce is pronounced. Then her property is shared out: one-half of it falls to the husband, the other to the dania. If there are children, the eldest son is entrusted to the woman, the eldest daughter to the husband; the rest are equally divided.

On her husband's death, the inheritance falls to the wife; if the children are minors, she has ownership of the property, must raise the children, and must take the responsibility of arranging marriages for them; only then is she permitted to remarry. If the children are adult and married, the mother has to live with them; if she should wish to remarry, she loses all rights to

---

[59]In Abyssinian, *tabib,* which means "wise" (note by Nahum).
[60]Judge.

her husband's estate. The property of someone who dies without an heir falls to the district chief.

Litigation: Apart from the religious traditions that distinguish the Falashas from the Abyssinians, nothing differentiates them from their cocitizens of the Christian religion, with whom they live in perfect harmony. If there is a dispute between them, they take their case before Abyssinian magistrates. If they are not satisfied with the judgment given, they appeal to the shum, the dejaj, or the ras or even lodge an appeal with the *afa-negus* in Addis-Ababa to be decided according to the *feta negest,* or imperial code.

Abyssinians in general, the Falashas included, have great fluency of speech; consequently they think of themselves as very eloquent; everyone pleads his own suit personally before the dania. In large villages, this latter administers justice at the foot of a tree, generally on a riverbank; all Abyssinians have to be familiar with legal functions because they can be called at a moment's notice to pronounce on some case or other. We have often been present at these curious hearings. The two litigants stand facing each other in front of the dania; both spring into action, gesticulate, stamp their feet, lie down, stand up, throw their cloaks off their shoulders; after hearing them, the dania gives his judgment in accordance with tradition. Violence and assault and battery are punished by a fine of one thaler; an unprovoked attack on one person by two or three others earns a punishment of seven thalers for the principal aggressor. In the course of our journey, we witnessed this sort of sentence pronounced by the chief of our caravan on one of our servants. In former times, the Falashas themselves settled disputes between one another, but today they readily abide by the justice of the Abyssinian danias.

Economic situation: The economic situation of the Falashas is relatively good, particularly compared with that of the Abyssinians among whom they live. Truth to tell, they are ignorant of trade, properly speaking, practiced by the nagadis and consisting of the transport of local products to commercial centers such as Aduwa, Asmara in the north, Addis-Ababa, Harar, and Dire Dawa in the south. From time immemorial they have pursued manual trades, particularly those of the weaver, potter, blacksmith, carpenter, and mason. Some of them, but a limited number, engage in agriculture.

The women work like the men: they sometimes help their husbands in their trades, sometimes they have their own professions, but this does not cause them to neglect their domestic occupations. At Shenker, for example, the husbands weave the chomas while the women work in the potteries; as for the children, they go off to the meadows and guard the few goats, mules, and other animals that constitute the family's patrimony.

The weavers: Next to the thatch he lives in, the Falasha weaver builds a very small hut. Inside this hut he digs a sort of pit about a meter deep in which he installs his loom. He drives it by foot. The cloth he produces is used to make chomas, shorts, and shirts. He takes three days to weave a piece 3m long by 90cm wide, which he sells for three thalers (7.50F).

The nagadis import cotton from Metemma (Sudan-Abyssinian frontier, six days away from the districts inhabited by the Falashas). The raw material needed to weave one item costs the Falashas one thaler (2.50F). Their profit is therefore two thalers, or 1.65F, a day.

The Falasha weavers do not go to the markets in the large towns to sell their cloth; the merchants come and collect it from them.

The blacksmiths: The Falasha blacksmith's equipment is of the most primitive. He works outdoors in the vicinity of his hut. Using bellows composed of two water skins, strengthened with iron, he heats up the items to be worked over a wood fire; he then hammers them on a very odd type of stone anvil. We saw them at work in Amba-Walid. They manufacture in the main spears, plowshares, knives. The Abyssinians bring them the iron to be worked and deal with them on a contract basis. They earn an average of 1.25F to 1.50F a day.

Other trades: Most of the masons and carpenters are employed in building churches or aderaches; we are sorry that we were not able to see them at work. But according to information we collected, their daily wage varies between 1.25F and 1.50F. The demands of their trade put them in frequent contact with Christian Abyssinians. Consequently they are in much greater danger than their coreligionists of breaking the religious laws. Thus it is that Falasha masons and carpenters, engaged to work with their ras or the dejaj, often convert.

Other trades, like pottery and basket making, are more specially the preserve of Falasha women; they do this with great taste, and their work is much appreciated for its delicate execution.

As I have already said, agriculture is not widespread among Falashas. Moreover they no longer own land and are employed as workers or farmers by Abyssinian cultivators.

As I will show below, the daily upkeep of a family composed of father, mother, and three children costs barely thirty-five to forty centimes; as a result the economic condition of the Falashas is relatively good: in several villages we saw Falasha families owning slaves, who are to be bought at an average price of 150 thalers (375F) per head; this is relative wealth in a country where money is scarce. Moreover, the total absence of beggars proves better than any argument the satisfactory state of their economic condition.

Habitat: Every village consists of a few groups of dwellings or huts. The Falashas form one of these groups, which have between five and thirty families, each of which owns one or sometimes two huts, often situated near a small stream or a simple ditch fed by rainwater. From the standpoint of building, the Abyssinians have scarcely progressed for centuries. The ruins we saw bore witness to the fact that the huts in olden times were made of stones and clay. The walls are almost never more than one and a half meters high and one always has to bend down to get inside a hut. There are no windows in these huts. As a result of the rudimentary nature of these dwellings, combined with the insignificant cost of building them, the Abyssinians are not particularly attached to them and leave their place of residence quite easily. It is therefore not uncommon to see whole groups abandon their homes to settle in other regions, either after an epidemic or following a fire or because of unhealthful conditions. In these huts they live, eat, and sleep. The furnishings are absolutely basic: a bed *(angareb),* sometimes made of clay, sometimes of straps mounted on four pieces of wood; small stools, a few skin rugs, one or two saucepans, jugs, a few wicker baskets, glasses *(berlie)* for drinking tej, etc. There is a small cavity in the center of the hut in which a wood fire for cooking, heating, and lighting burns constantly. There is no outlet for the smoke from this hearth, so it accumulates in the hut and produces the eye diseases that are very common among the Falashas, as among Abyssinians in general. Outside the huts, there is a hollowed-out bole of a tree and two large stones that are used as millstones. Here the women crush the grain from *taj, dura, dagussa,* etc. (types of corn), to prepare kitta or injera.

Food: Kittas are absolutely identical with the *uggot matsot*[61] mentioned in the Bible. The *taf* (corn) is crushed, then mixed with water until it forms a sort of paste. It is then poured onto an iron disk placed on a wood fire. It is smoothed out by hand, turned over, and the kitta is made. Cooking a kitta takes about two or three minutes. It tastes excellent when it is fresh; we ate it on our travels when our supply of biscuits was exhausted.

Injera is fermented kitta and in fact always has a sourish taste.

The dishes the Falashas serve are *shiro,* or stew, on the exceptional days when they eat meat, and *wog,* a sort of thick sauce, on other days. Shiro is a dish made of meat cooked in butter with a sauce made of flour. Like all Abyssinians, the Falashas first arrange several kittas or injeras at the bottom of a very closely woven wickerwork basket; then they pour in the shiro.

As for wog, this is a sauce made from *shimbera* (pea) flour, oil or butter, and *berberi* (powdered red pimentos). The Falashas soak their kitta in this sauce, and this is their only food on ordinary days; they eat two meals daily, one in the morning and the other in the evening.

Their drinks are *birz,* tej, talla, and occasionally *boza.* Birz is quite simply honey mixed with water; it is a very pleasant and above all very refreshing drink. Tej is fermented birz, in the proportion of one liter of honey to five

[61]Unleavened bread (Exodus 12:39), in Hebrew.

liters of water. The mixture is placed in gombos, or immense earthenware vases. After adding a few bits of leaves from a bush called guecho, the vases are hermetically closed and exposed to the sun for three days. The lemon-colored drink is pleasant but exceptionally overstimulating because of the relatively large quantity of alcohol that accumulates during fermentation. It is in greater demand than talla, particularly when it is carefully prepared. Talla is less alcoholic and yet less pleasant; it is prepared with fermented crusts of dura bread. It does not have an appetizing look because no attempt is made to strain it. Boza is a sort of beer and is in more general use than the other drinks. It is brewed with grilled barley; consequently it always retains a burned taste. These drinks are consumed in large quantities at any hour of the day.

Among the Falashas, as among the Abyssinians, the women attend to the housework, which does not prevent them from helping their husbands with their occupations.

Their diet (the Falashas do not eat *brondo,* raw meat), their sobriety, their habit of chastity, their monogamy, and particularly the hygienic measures they impose on themselves make the Falashas a healthy, robust group, exempt from many of the diseases that ravage the Abyssinians.

Conclusion

Though brief, the sketch that I have just drawn you will enable you to understand the findings of our journey to the Falashas. Later I hope to be able to devote a detailed study to the problem of the origin of the Falashas, their history, and in a general way to everything related to the ethnography of the peoples among whom they live. For the time being, let the broad outlines of the conclusions that I have drawn from my investigation be enough.

The Falashas must have been converted to Mosaism by a group of Judaizers who came from Egypt in about the second or third century before the Christian era, probably at the time when Ptolemy Euergetes[62] founded the Aksumite kingdom. Like all Greek expeditions, the immigrants, would have followed the course of the river Atbara (the Greeks' Astaboras) and settled west of the Takazze. They would not have crossed the river because, with a few exceptions, the great majority of Falashas are at present settled on this side of the Takazze, that is to say, in the west of Abyssinia. This is perhaps the reason why the Falashas of this district, and those of Atshefar in particular, are called Kailas.[63]

At first this group of immigrants would have formed an ethnic and not a

---

[62]Ptolemy III Euergetes (246–221 B.C.).

[63]A word that, in the dialect of the province of Qwara, means "do not cross" (note by Nahum).

religious group, since the Falashas today still call those of their members who embrace Christianity by the name "Amhara" and almost never call them "Christian."

What confirms the hypothesis of the Greek origin of the Falashas is the order in which their biblical books are arranged, the system of transliteration they have adopted for proper nouns, the adoption of the apocryphal books, the ascetic life and austere customs of their priests, etc. Moreover, according to information provided by d'Abbadie, Falashas who claimed to be scholars had, in former times, to know how to read prayers written in Greek.

This small group of immigrants who settled in Ethiopia would have found natives already well prepared to accept Mosaic principles; circumcision in particular had been practiced by the Ethiopians from a very remote period and was their distinctive sign, a sign that they did not abandon despite the introduction of Christianity (fourth century). The group would have grown and given birth to warlike tribes who would have established an independent principality in the Simen. For several centuries there were continual battles between innumerable and powerful enemies, and this bellicose life must have intensified their religious faith, which withstood every assault. But with time, particularly after the many wars between Muslims and Christians in the sixteenth century, persecutions, forced conversions, and epidemics, the Falasha population has much diminished, and today there are barely more than 6,000 to 7,000 souls.

They can be divided into four geographic groups: those in the neighborhood of Lake Tana, those in Lasta, those in the Simen, and those in Shire (on the other side of the Takazze). These four groups are separated by distances of four, five, or six days at a rate of five hours' travel a day, or an average of twenty to twenty-two kilometers. These clusters or villages are far from densely populated; they are scattered over groups of five, ten, or fifteen families. The most populous village, and it is the only one of its type, is Addis-Shoa (Shire), which numbers thirty families.

It seems to me that the most effective means of saving the remnants of this population, whose past, little known though it is, cannot fail to excite our interest and arouse our admiration, is by the gradual creation of two emigration movements for them: one northward, I mean toward the Italian colony of Eritrea for those from Shire; the other southward to Addis-Ababa, the capital of Ethiopia, for those from Amhara proper. In these large agricultural, industrial, and commercial centers, living in the midst of European populations, they would be safer, would practice their religion freely, and would succeed in improving their material and economic condition.

Not for one moment should there be any idea of creating any educational project whatsoever in Abyssinia or even in Eritrea. The fact that the Falashas are very widely dispersed would make it impossible for a foundation of this sort to succeed. Even assuming that this plan could be realized, it would never yield appreciable results in practice. At the most, what would be created would be a class of déclassé individuals.

Let us not deceive ourselves with dangerous illusions: we are dealing with a people whose intellectual capacity is generally undeveloped, and whose social and economic conditions we cannot change too suddenly without danger to the people. One cannot and must not seek to improve them except in the direction of their natural tendencies and their centuries-old past. To act in any other way would be to risk upsetting the mental balance of the Falasha race: and the result would be infinitely regrettable.

Attempts of a different nature, and of more immediate practical application, might perhaps be tried.

The distance that separates the Falasha districts from Eritrea is not very great. Depending on locality, it varies between five and fifteen days. Through the intermediary of one of our coreligionists living in Asmara, a certain number of young people could be placed in Asmara every year and could be taught a trade, given the type of monopoly that the Falashas have of particularly highly valued and remunerative trades.

The construction of a railway between the Somali coast and Addis-Ababa and the flow of Europeans toward that town make the practice of trades more indispensable there than elsewhere. Manual work, even the roughest, is very highly paid today. Falashas who would have learned the trade of the blacksmith, weaver, mason, joiner, shoemaker, tailor, or watchmaker, would have a secure livelihood and could bring their families to live with them, families who are at present sunk in absolute isolation, and a considerable group of workers would thus gradually be formed.

Agriculture in Eritrea is experiencing considerable growth; olive growing and cotton growing are particularly widespread. It would be much in the Falashas' interest to learn to graft and grow the olive trees, which stand out like genuine little forests on a number of mountains. As for cotton, attempts by the Italians in recent years in the plains of the Setit have yielded marvelous results, and it is thought that the colony of Eritrea will one day succeed in competing with Egypt.

My proposals may not seem commensurate with the interest that the Israelite public is evincing in the Falashas today and above all with the agitation on their behalf aroused in certain quarters. But let us not lose sight of two essential points: (1) there are barely 6,000 to 7,000 Falashas, split up into groups of five to ten families over a considerable region; it is therefore difficult, if not impossible, to know them all and to collect them together in order to be able to have some sort of an effective influence on them; (2) we are dealing with a population whose mentality is still primitive and to whom we can not apply the educational methods that the Alliance has practiced in Morocco or Turkey; it is indispensable to proceed with great caution if we want to bring the Falashas morally and mentally to our level.

I think, given the political state of Ethiopia, and soberly weighing the material and economic conditions of the country, that I cannot conscientiously suggest anything else to you.

(*BAIU* 33 [1908], 107–37)

The Alliance itself pointed out the gaps in Haim Nahum's report. Nevertheless Nahum had taken his mission seriously: while away, he had even read up on the Abyssinian calendar, chronology, and hierarchy as well as on earlier missions. But his probable misunderstanding of the local language and his relatively short stay in the region prevented him from collecting sufficient data, which he supplemented by information gleaned locally from strangers. He thus allowed himself to be influenced by the Alliance's earlier reservations on the urgent need to help the Falashas. In this crucial period in his career, Nahum did not wish to contradict his patron.

As for Faitlovitch, who knew Amharic, the many local contacts made during his earlier mission, as well as the much longer duration of his stay (fifteen months) enabled him to gain a much better knowledge of the terrain.

Nahum thought that the Falashas were probably of Greek origin. He excluded the idea of initiating an educational project that in the end would only create a "category of classless people." He estimated the number of Falashas at 6,000 or 7,000. According to him, this was a population of "primitive mentality," unsuited to benefit from the educative methods that the Alliance had successfully practiced in Morocco and the Empire. In addition he appealed for great caution in view of the political situation in Abyssinia.

Jacques Faitlovitch was obviously far from sharing these views. He estimated the number of Falashas at tens of thousands. He brought back from his mission a letter in which the Falashas themselves asked their coreligionists to open schools for them and to send them books.

Nahum's conclusions were widely discussed for a long time. In reality the debate must be set in the context of the rivalries among various Jewish societies anxious to develop their own philanthropic, educational, and cultural policy in that period of Jewish solidarity.

Constantinople, 14 April 1909

Dear Monsieur Bigart,

(. . .)

Coming back to the Falashas.

It is very hard to form an exact idea of the dogmatic beliefs and the extent of the theological knowledge of the kahen. Moreover, all of these latter are sunk in absolute ignorance and engage in barely anything but the external trappings of the religion and a few attempts at exorcism. One of the kahen to whom I spoke to ask him the date of the festival of Pentecost, was able to answer me only after he had consulted the book of commandments that he carried with him! . . . You are well aware that kahen and laymen generally keep stubbornly silent. They answer only in half words and often even evasively. In view of this state of mind, it is never possible to obtain a satisfactory reply from them, particularly on matters of a purely abstract, speculative nature. On several occasions I asked them about messianism, the resurrection, and the immortality of the soul. On the first point, they firmly believe, though without the idea of the Messiah, that God will lead all the children of Israel back to Jerusalem. There is no conception of resurrection. As for the immortality of the soul, they confuse it with the idea of reward. The leading role in all these matters is played by angels and demons. Consequently their ancient theology can be understood only by analyzing their liturgical books, because today, as I said, the kahen are completely ignorant of anything concerning religious study and know nothing of Mosaism except for a few religious practices and the holy history, mingled with a host of legends also shared by all the Abyssinians.

Conversions:

There are no forced conversions. All of them are voluntary today. This is how they take place:

1. First, there are conversions that occur of their own accord, without an intermediary. Force of circumstances obliges Falasha workmen engaged in building a church or a palace for the ras to transgress the strict laws of Mosaism and the traditional practices, particularly those relating to food and to ablutions in the case of contact with a Christian or Muslim Abyssinian. Those who have been in contact with the Amharas the Falashas consider converted, and because of this, they are obliged to live outside the circle occupied by the Falashas when they return home.

2. Those who convert officially, that is to say via the intermediary of a missionary. We saw two missionaries, both living in Djenda. They customarily make regular tours of their district, that is to say, the provinces of the Dembea and the Sekelt. They stand in front of dwellings, preaching the New Testament, and eventually succeed in winning over Falashas. We were told that in this way they have succeeded in converting a large number of Falashas. These missionaries often send the young . . . Falashas to Asmara to the Swedish mission stations to which they themselves belong. Their field of action is limited in the provinces of Asmara, never in the Tigre (statements made to us by the Falashas of Addis-Shoa).

However brief, these notes will give you some idea about what you asked me. If there are any further obscure points, please let me know.

(. . .)

(AAIU, Turkey, II C 8)

POWER; OR, AMBITION ACHIEVED

There was a danger that the "Young Turk" revolution in July 1908 would upset the general situation in the country. Nahum was the progressives' candidate for the post of chief rabbi. The secretary-general of the Alliance warned the president of his regional committee in Istanbul against such a choice.

Paris, 2 August 1908

Dear Monsieur Fernandez,

You are right in thinking that we are following the unexpected events taking place in Turkey with intense interest. You were kind enough to telegraph us that elections have begun for the chief rabbi's replacement. Nahum, who left yesterday evening, received letters from his wife telling him that he was a possible successor to Monsieur Moïse Lévy.[1] I told him that in my opinion he should give way to Monsieur Abraham Danon and that this latter would be the better choice. Monsieur Danon probably has not many practical talents, but he has the prestige, the necessary qualities, and if a reaction should come about—which is very possible—it would sweep Nahum away if he held office, while Danon would be able to withstand it or rather would probably be spared by the fact that his candidature, or rather his personality, is such that even the ancien regime can come to terms with it. I am afraid that Nahum is a little too progressive—at present—for the environment of Constantinople, and I would prefer a transitional regime under his father-in-law's consulship.

Forgive me if I seem to be giving advice, but at a distance and outside the atmosphere of feverish excitement in which you are living, it is not certain that one cannot judge the situation sensibly. Certain circles here are skeptical about the survival of the new regime and fear a regression.

Cordially,
J. Bigart
(AAIU, Register of Correspondence,
S 217)

Shortly afterward, when Nahum had been elected locum tenens, the same secretary-general, Jacques Bigart, urged him to moderation.

---

[1]The reference is to the locum tenens, Moshe Halévi.

Paris, 21 August 1908

My dear Nahum,

So your dream and my prediction have been realized. I do not need to tell you how delighted we are at this happy event: happy for us, for Ottoman Jewry, and for our work. Now is the time when your savoir-faire and your energy will need to be put into practice. There will be no lack of work, but let us go slowly, not rush anything; take the questions one by one, as you might say, and try to solve them in turn. Distrust the zealous enthusiasms of friends who are too eager for innovation.

I am pleased to have seen this day of liberation for Ottoman Jewry.

Fondest good wishes to you and
Madame the chief rabbi [sic].
(AAIU, Register of Correspondence,
S 218)

Nahum served his apprenticeship for his onerous task.

Constantinople, 6 September 1908

Dear Monsieur Bigart,

First, a thousand apologies for my delay in replying to your kind letter. I am so overburdened with work that I scarcely find the time to eat lunch. I arrive at the chancellery at eight o'clock every morning and do not leave till six.

Feelings are still running very high, and I receive telegrams every day from the different communities in the Empire asking me for the immediate dismissals of their respective chief rabbis. Jerusalem, Damascus, and Saida are the towns that most complain about their spiritual leaders. I am sending Rabbi Habib of Bursa to hold new elections in these places.

As for me, I am trying to complete as quickly as possible the formalities necessary for the permanent election of the chief rabbi of Turkey, for whom I am the locum tenens.

. . . all the members of the cabinet gave me a warm welcome, particularly the grand vizier and the *seyhülislam*.[2] Last Tuesday I was received by the sultan with the Greek, Armenian, and Chaldean patriarchs. I handed him a congratulatory address on behalf of all Ottoman Israelites.

All our former revenues, notably the "gabelle,"[3] have disappeared for the moment following the proclamation of the constitution. We are looking for others and not finding them.

(. . .)
(AAIU, Turkey, XXX E)

[2]Head of the religious hierarchy.
[3]Communal tax paid by the Jews on the consumption of meat, cheese, and kosher wine.

Constantinople, 8 September 1908

Dear Monsieur Bigart,

The reproaches you made me in yesterday's post did not come as a surprise. I expected them, but there was nothing I could do to avoid them; seeing me so busy, my wife voiced her intention to inform you on current events herself, but her days are so taken up with the calls she has to receive from morning to evening that she is having to stay up this evening to act as my secretary.

My present activities are all directed toward accomplishing the task with which I have been officially charged, that is to say, the election of the chief rabbi of the Ottoman Empire. This election will require at least two months' work so that it can be carried out in accordance with archaic laws that can only be reformed after the chambers[4] have been convened. These laws require that the chief rabbi be elected by the national assembly[5] of eighty members, sixty of whom are laymen and twenty religious figures, plus forty provincial delegates. These formalities have never been fulfilled, since there has never been a haham başi, properly speaking, since the laws were made; there have only been kaymakam. I am going to give you a brief chronological account of the most important recent events and expect to be able to send you the detailed translation of what the local papers reported about them toward the end of the week. (I must tell you in passing that the paper *El Telegrafo,* my predecessor's organ, after having tried to create problems for me by proclaiming the illegality of the council that appointed me, has finally come over to my side, on pain of seeing its paper put on the index by its own readers and subscribers.)

The day after the promulgation of the constitution therefore, the old chief rabbi, in order to follow the example of other religious leaders, convened a commission charged with the preparations to be made for the convocation of the Great Assembly. It was members of this commission who, via David Fresco, editor of *El Tiempo,* sent me the dispatches that you know about. Immediately after my arrival in Constantinople, the general assembly of eighty members was convened . . . in order to proceed to the appointment of three members to occupy three vacant places on the great religious council. Those chosen were M. Danon (thirty-nine votes), Dr. Marcus (thirty-four),[6] and myself (forty-two) out of forty-five voters. A delegation was immediately sent to find us and conduct us into the hall where the assembly was taking place; as we approached it, we were greeted by an enormous crowd shouting, . . . long live the Alliance.

---

[4] The various Jewish councils.

[5] The general Jewish council.

[6] Dr. David Marcus, principal rabbi of the Ashkenazi community, connected with the Alliance's rival, the Hilfsverein der deutschen Juden, and a Zionist sympathizer.

At the same session, this same assembly appointed the consistory of nine members, all of them young, active, inspired by liberal and impartial sentiments. This is the first time a consistory has been composed of such elements.

This consistory's first task was to frustrate all the maneuvers of the chief rabbi and obtain his resignation. Then, according to the law, it joins up with the *bet din* (rabbinical tribunal), of which my father-in-law forms part, to elect a kaymakam. The result you know; I obtained a dozen of the sixteen votes. The same day as the elections, the local papers published a supplement on this subject, and a delegation visited my home in Şişli to tell me the news. A report was drawn up there and then and a copy sent to the minister of religions. The latter referred me to the grand vizier, who sent me his approval after having had it ratified by the Council of Ministers.

When this ratification had been received, I took up my position, starting with official calls on the grand vizier, the minister of religions, the şeyhülislam, and other members of the cabinet. The cordiality of the reception I was given exceeded anything I could have hoped for. The şeyhülislam was particularly charming; he escorted me to the door of his large salon, and this was the first time that the supreme leader of Islamism has honored in this way a religious leader of another faith.

As for the attitude toward my election on the part of the Jewish population throughout the Empire, I would find it easy to tell you, if it did not concern myself, that the enthusiasm is extraordinary, indescribable. Telegrams expressing enthusiastic support have reached me and are still reaching me from every commune and community in Constantinople, from every province and village in the Empire, from Salonika to the Yemen. Almost all the communities express an immediate wish to see me permanently at the head of Ottoman Jewry as soon as possible. It seems that a spirit of liberalism and unity has suddenly wafted through the oldest, the most reactionary, heads. Italians, Karaites, and the rest are all filled with the same goodwill, nay, even enthusiasm toward me and feel united for the first time in the person of a leader who seems to correspond to each individual's personal views.

I will mention, among other interesting calls, the one by Selim Sirri bey, the sultan's aide-de-camp, vice president of the Committee of Union and Progress, the one by the Comte de Camondo,[7] who was passing through Constantinople (he left me 1,000F for the poor), by all the editors of French papers in the capital, by a special correspondent from the *Matin,* Monsieur de Jouvenel, who came to interview me, by two special correspondents of two large St. Petersburg papers, etc., etc. . . .

---

[7]Isaac de Camondo (1850–1910), grandson of the great Turkish Jewish banker and philanthropist Abraham Camondo, who settled in Paris in 1870.

Among dispatches from Europe, I will draw your attention to those from the Hilfsverein, the Alliance Israélite in Vienna and from Monsieur Wolff-sohn,[8] . . . etc.

Monsieur Boppe, chargé d'affaires of the French ambassador, with whom I have had excellent relations for a long time, sent me a charming letter congratulating me.

On the occasion of the sultan's accession last Tuesday, 1 September, a solemn ceremony was organized in the Galata temple. The crowd was so large that it was difficult to make one's way through the streets near the temple; and my two speeches, in Spanish and in Turkish, were outstandingly successful. Monsieur Danon, headmaster of the École Normale,[9] who was there, will have the opportunity to tell you about them. I left the temple amid ovations and calls of "long live our chief rabbi" (one of the amusing incidents was when a little old man made his way with difficulty to my carriage and forced me to accept a few cloves intended to protect me from the evil eye). And I went to the imperial palace, where the sultan received me with all the religious leaders. The sultan's new secretary, Ali Cebab, and the second chamberlain, Emin bey, greeted me very warmly.

Today, Tuesday, 8 September, I called on Prince Sabaheddin,[10] the sultan's nephew, who returned from Paris last week with the remains of his father Mahmut pasha,[11] the sultan's brother-in-law. He was anxious to kiss my hand and said all manner of kind things. He said he would visit me the day after tomorrow. Then I went to the Ministry of War, to Pertev pasha, major general of the general staff and assistant to the minister of war. I have known him well for a long time, and he is a great friend to our work. He told me that he is in the process of drafting the ruling on the recruitment of non-Muslims into the army in order to present it to the opening of the Chambers; in the meantime, at the end of the holidays, all the military schools will be open to Israelites and Christians on the same basis as to Muslims.

I am planning to go and see the new minister of public education in the course of next week to ask him for the free admission of Israelite pupils to the boardingschools of the government *écoles supérieures*. As for the evening classes you spoke to me about when I was leaving, I find it pointless to consult the minister on this matter, in view of the freedom of assembly that we now enjoy. Just give our headmasters the necessary orders and urge them to organize them; I will take responsibility for this.

[8]David Wolffsohn (1856–1914), second president of the World Zionist Organization.
[9]École Normale Israélite Orientale (ENIO), where the Alliance's teachers were trained.
[10](1877–1948), Young Turk leader.
[11]Damat Mahmut Celaleddin pasha (1853–1903) went into exile in 1899 with his sons.

My wife has promised that she will keep you informed of everything interesting in the future.

(. . .)

(AAIU, Turkey, XXX E)

The opposition was organizing its forces. The victory of the "moderns" was still tenuous.

Constantinople, 8 October 1908

Dear Monsieur Bigart,

It was impossible for me to write to you last week. I was too occupied with other things and in particular too preoccupied! A reactionary movement has begun, insignificant, it is true, but it severely hampers the progress of business, especially as the communal coffers have run dry over the past two and a half months. My expenses have increased considerably, I borrow so as to meet them and not discourage the members of the consistory, who are already struggling with incomparable zeal.

I am not in the slightest discouraged because, when it comes down to it, there are basically two or three people behind it, one of whom is Jacques de Léon, ex-jeweller to the sultan and patron of Chief Rabbi Lévy.[12] This individual is spending money to win over a few ignorant rabbis, but the population as a whole is up in arms about it. The reaction is against all that has been done. Monsieur Fernandez and several highly placed notables have spent two days trying to establish an entente between these two or three people and the three members of the consistory against whom they harbor grievances. As you know, in the whole Orient, and in Constantinople in particular, intrigues, trickery, mean-mindedness, and pettiness prevail.

Almost the whole Israelite population is with us. I am being patient for the moment and am seeking entente and conciliation, but if this continues I will be forced to take other measures.

(. . .)

(AAIU, Turkey, XXX E)

Jewish integration would be improved if Jews held high positions in the machinery of the state.

Constantinople, 2 December 1908

Dear Monsieur Bigart,

(. . .)

We have to work very hard to set ourselves on our feet and unite. In

---

[12]The outgoing locum tenens.

respect of the government, I have been trying to advance the careers of our coreligionists for some time. In my interview with the grand vizier and the minister of the interior some ten days ago, I again asked for a place on the Senate and a ministerial portfolio for our Israelites. Perhaps we will succeed in placing Daoud effendi Molho in the Senate. As for a ministerial portfolio, the minister of the interior promised me to appoint Faradji effendi[13] (or Carasso effendi)[14] to the ministry of trade.

(. . .)

(AAIU, Turkey, XXX E)

*The day after the Young Turk revolution, Jerusalem and other Jewish commu-
nities asked, like Istanbul, for the dismissal of their chief rabbis, whom the
communities wished to have replaced by more progressive people. Groups
opposed to the Alliance and to Haim Nahum used the opportunity to declare
war on them. The opposition was prepared to accept new allies.*

Constantinople, 7 December 1908

Dear Monsieur Bigart,

I made an ordinary courtesy call on the German ambassador and arranged for my kapu-kâhya . . . and Monsieur Kaufmann, German teacher at the Hasköy schools, to accompany me.

Our conversation lasted about half an hour and had no particular significance. . . . The ambassador added a few words about the energy and intel-
ligence of the Israelites and particularly about their efforts toward progress. I added that, as far as the oriental Jews were concerned, we largely owed this to the Alliance schools.

Then the ambassador asked me if, as spiritual leader of Ottoman Jewry, I was able directly to appoint and dismiss rabbis! This was probably the purpose of the interview. Furthermore, I was aware of all the maneuvers and intrigues the orthodox[15] in Germany had engaged in on the matter of Panigel.[16] I replied that our communities were autocephalous in principle; they themselves appointed their chief rabbis, leaving confirmation to the chief rabbi of Turkey and likewise dismissals.

Official approaches on this subject had undoubtedly been made in Berlin to make the ambassador intervene because, the day after our interview, the *Osmanische Post,* the official organ of the German ambassador, inserted a short paragraph that began with the following words: "At the command of

---

13Vitali Faradji, Jewish deputy for Istanbul.
14Emmanuel Carasso, Jewish deputy for Salonika.
15The reference is to orthodox Jews.
16Eliyhu Panigel (1850–1919), locum tenens in Jerusalem from 1907.

the government of H.M. the emperor of Germany, S.S. Marshall von Bieberstein spoke with His Eminence the chief rabbi." It is also more than probable that the Zionists are acting in conjunction with the orthodox.

. . . I will tell you later the part the Hilfsverein is playing in this affair and even in the Zionist movement that is being planned for Turkey.

. . . I am extremely busy and, above all, preoccupied. For today permit me to remain silent a little longer.

(. . .)

(AAIU, Turkey, XXX E)

Constantinople, 21 December 1908

Dear Monsieur Bigart,

I have received your letter of the eleventh instant.

Thank you for the good wishes you send for my permanent appointment. The hostile movement led by two or three reactionaries quickly burned itself out, faced with the countless and impressive demonstrations of support, unique of their type, that took place in every district of the capital. The largest was a meeting of 15,000 people in the Ok-Meydan hippodrome. So do not worry about this. The moral crisis I mentioned to you is a different matter. I hope that in a few more days it will disappear completely. I think the election will take place in three weeks. Nearly all the provincial delegates have been named.

My first tasks have been very arduous. You know that I came in at a time when the communal coffers were empty. There was not a single source of revenue: the main one, the gabelle, no longer existed. This state of affairs lasted for two and a half months. Very strong approaches had to be made to the Sublime Porte and very firm words spoken to the minister of justice and religions in order to enforce the privileges of the chief rabbinate. Today, thank God, these revenues are coming in regularly and are on a much firmer basis than previously.

After that, I turned my attention to the question of an Israelite deputy for the capital.[17] The Committee of Union and Progress was kind enough to grant us this favor because, by law, we needed a male population of 50,000, and we had only half that. Fortunately, this question too has been solved to the great satisfaction of the whole community, despite a few intrigues by certain self-seeking people. The deputy of our choice, Monsieur Vitali Faradji, legal counselor to the Tobacco Board[18] (lawyer to the ICA),[19] was elected with a very large majority of votes (fourth out of ten).

---

[17]For the elections to the Chamber of Deputies that followed the Young Turk revolution.

[18]The state tobacco monopoly of the Ottoman Empire formed in 1883.

[19]Jewish Colonization Association, a Jewish philanthropic association founded in 1891 by Baron Maurice de Hirsch.

Last week I went to see the grand vizier to discuss the matter of the Israelites in the Yemen.[20] [I did so] following a letter signed by the rabbi of Sanaa and the notables of that town, complaining that our coreligionists are still somewhat harassed by a few Arabs, despite the promulgation of the constitution. I asked the grand vizier to take strong action. He will telegraph the governor general immediately, ordering him to enforce the law. The grand vizier did not know that Jews existed in the Yemen. He even added that in the case of our wanting to open schools there, the government would not fail to help us.

Moreover, the new commander of the army corps in the Yemen, Rüşdi pasha, is a good friend of mine. He has not yet left to take up his post. I will ask him to send me a detailed report on the condition of our Yemenite coreligionists.

The opening of the Chamber took place on Thursday. The Sublime Porte sent me an official letter inviting me to be present at the speech from the throne. We now have three Israelite deputies in the Chamber[21] (apart from the one who will come from Baghdad)[22] and one member of the Senate.[23] This week I will ask for two more Israelites to be added.

(. . .)

(AAIU, Turkey, XXX E)

Constantinople, 23 December 1908

Dear Monsieur Bigart,

Something new today. The rabbi members of the religious council of the capital have received registered letters from Frankfurt-am-Main at their respective addresses, signed by several rabbis, whose names I will give you.

In my opinion, they are apocryphal. The signatures are in the same writing in Rashi script, and they have been sent here at the instigation of a few German rabbis in Jerusalem in connivance with someone in Constantinople. There will certainly be an investigation to discover the source. What is significant about this letter in which the signatories speak in the name of the Torah, of Jewish interests and of Palestine, is this very clear phrase: "without consideration (favor) either of the man or the great and strong society."

This must certainly be a maneuver by the orthodox Hilfsvereinists[24] or Zionists, who already never leave off accusing me. For me, this is an honor that I attribute to the fact that I am an Alliancist.

---

[20]This country formed part of the Ottoman Empire.

[21]Apart from the two already mentioned, there was also the deputy for Smyrna, Nissim Mazliah.

[22]The reference is to David Sasson.

[23]Béhor effendi Eskénazi.

[24]Connected with the Hilfsverein der deutschen Juden.

. . . I will keep you informed of what happens.

(. . .)

(AAIU, Turkey, XXX E)

Constantinople, 11 January 1909

Dear Monsieur Bigart,

Despite all the criticism and all the maneuvers by the German orthodox, the general religious council composed of twenty rabbis, at its session on Tuesday the twelfth instant, approved the list of five candidates sent to it through my channel, the consistory.[25]

At our meeting on Wednesday we fixed Sunday, 24 January, for the election of the chief rabbi of Turkey, vacant for forty-seven years.[26] . . . We await developments.

In any case, if I am elected, it will really be a victory for the Alliance, because a very strong campaign is being conducted against our society.

(. . .)

(AAIU, Turkey, XXX E)

The secretary-general of the Alliance greeted Nahum's permanent election to the post of chief rabbi of the Empire with enthusiasm.

Paris, 25 January 1909

Dear Monsieur Nahum,

Your victory is so glorious and so complete that one begins to doubt whether it was ever in question. Everything that conservative reaction, lies, and obscurantism could muster was in league against you; your success is therefore the success of liberal ideas in the French sense of the phrase. The Alliance played its part in your victory because, almost despite its wishes, people identified it with you and wanted to regard your appointment as the triumph of its ideas. Let us accept this consequence. Thus is may well be said that the whole Turkish revolution is like the triumph of our ideas, ideas that are so moderate yet so liberal and solely inspired by love of the common good.

Now that you have won, make your peace with your father-in-law; you can make the first move; your success allows you, commands you, to do so, and you will have peace in the home. It would be a great shame if Madame Nahum's eyes were still red with weeping. Let joy reign over you and yours.

(. . .)

(AAIU, Register of Correspondence, S 219)

---

[25]These candidates included his father-in-law, Abraham Danon.

[26]The last chief rabbi was Jacob Avigdor (1860–1863). His successors were only locum tenens.

Despite Nahum's election, the opposition did not disband.

Constantinople, letter received on
24 February 1909

Dear Monsieur Bigart,

It will soon be a month since you have had a letter from me, not even a reply to your telegrams of congratulations. It is not only my manifold tasks that have prevented me from writing to you. More than anything, it is the countless worries and annoyances. Just imagine, I experienced difficulties even after the election. You know that this latter has to be approved by the Council of Ministers and ratified by imperial irade.

Well, letters and telegrams were actually sent to the grand vizier stating that illegalities had occurred in connection with this election. It seems that the grand vizier was influenced by an old friend of his, and he suggested that the Council of Ministers refer back to the minister of religions to clarify the matter. The latter protested in writing the very next day, saying that everything was in accordance with the law and that the complaint should be seen as nothing more than simply personal rancor, coming as it did from an anonymous source. By the time this protest from the minister of justice and religions had reached the grand vizier, this ministry had fallen.

We now have a new grand vizier associated with "Young Turkey." I paid an official call on him yesterday. I think that the dossier will be read at the next Council, that is to say next Sunday or at the latest Tuesday, if other difficulties do not arise.

Despite the public demonstrations in the capital and the provinces, the small number of reactionaries and schemers refuse to admit defeat. In the meantime, they are creating new obstacles for me by once again stirring up the butchers' guild,[27] which asks for nothing better than to follow bad advice, which brings it some profit. The government is still very weak to be able to act with the strength necessary to enforce the laws of the communities. I am not letting myself be discouraged so as not to discourage all those gentlemen of the consistory who are working selflessly. And we have again been totally without revenues for almost two months now, and Passover is approaching!

As for me, I am receiving nothing for the very good reason that the coffers are empty.

I have done as you asked. I went to see my father-in-law. It took a superhuman effort, but I did it, believe me, for you, I will say no more about what passed between us. Let the matter be settled and that's it.

---

[27]It constituted an important economic force because it paid over to the chief rabbinate the "gabelle" on kosher meat, one of its main revenues.

. . . I have not acknowledged the congratulations because I do not yet have the irade.

(. . .)

(AAIU, Turkey, XXX E)

Haim Nahum's election was not finally ratified until 2 March 1909, by an imperial firman that at the same time redefined the legal status of the Jewish communities in the Empire.

I, Sultan Mehmed Reşad,[28] son of the Sultan Mecid,[29] by this great and glorious firman; I declare under the imperial seal:

After the election of a new incumbent for the vacant post of the chief rabbinate has been conducted, in accordance with the law, at the invitation of the minister of religions and with the approval of the Council of Ministers,

I issue this *berat* to the honorable Haim Nahum effendi and, in the lines that follow, at the same time confirm all the ancient privileges:

I appoint Haim Nahum chief rabbi of all the Jews in the capital and its dependencies, and also of all the Jews inhabiting the Ottoman Empire. Rabbis and community leaders, as well as all Jews great and small, must recognize him as their chief rabbi. All questions relating to his duties must be addressed to him. It is expressly forbidden to act contrary to his instructions. All Israelites must obey him in everything concerning their rite.

. . . the chief rabbi and persons named by him for this purpose have the sole right to solemnize marriages, pronounce divorces, and settle any questions relating to them, and to decide, with the consent of the two parties, disputes between Jews.

The chief rabbi has the right to demand that an oath be taken in the synagogue when he examines a matter or institutes an investigation. He can also bar persons whom he considers guilty from his religious community, and he can do so without any judge's intervening in a matter of this type, or making an appeal, whatever form this may take.

. . . rabbis appointed in other towns are recognized only after having been approved by the chief rabbi. Any appointment that does not have this prior approval is null and void.

No one can require the chief rabbi to appoint a specific rabbi to a specific locality or to assign a synagogue to a specific rabbi.

When a governor or a judge requests the transfer or dismissal of a rabbi because of his conduct, his request is only granted insofar as the chief rabbi acknowledges the justification for his complaint.

. . . the chief rabbi, the rabbis, their representatives, and their staff can be judged for crimes and offenses against the state only in the

---

[28]He reigned from 1909 till 1918.
[29]Abdülmecid I (sultan, 1839–1861).

capital. If a rabbi has to be arrested by virtue of the law, the chief rabbi must have his arrest effected.

No Jew can be forcibly converted to Islam.

A Jew does not have the right to refuse or to postpone payment of the annual state taxes, the charity tax, and the "gabelle" or the taxes assignable to the chief rabbinate.

. . . when the chief rabbi requires his rabbis, his officials, or his employees to use force to bring an Israelite who is said to have broken a religious law to the chief rabbinate, the police have no right to oppose the execution of this order.

. . . the Israelites cannot be prevented from levying a tax for places of pilgrimage in either the capital or the provinces.

The Israelites can bury their dead according to their rites, read the Law as they understand it.

Any request relating to the rites, addressed to the government under the chief rabbi's seal, must be granted.

The chief rabbi cannot be forced to take anyone into his employ.

The aforementioned Chief Rabbi Haim Nahum effendi has complete freedom in the fulfillment of his duties, and no one has the right to create any obstacle to the exercise of his ministry.

(BAIU 34 [1909], 46–49)

The customary ceremonies took place.

Constantinople, 25 March 1909

Dear Monsieur Bigart,

The official receptions have just come to an end. They have been very warm, particularly on the part of the grand vizier and the president of the Chamber. This latter was anxious to keep me with him for an hour and to see me to the door of Parliament. He is going to come and call on me next week. But our conversation was very typical. Talking about the Israelites' loyalty, H. E. Ahmed Riza bey added: "We depend on you and are formally telling you that we need your help. Our Empire has always been very hospitable to the Israelites and should be so again. We will open our doors to your coreligionists from Russia and Rumania. We need them. Look at Mesopotamia, for instance, so vast, so adaptable, and yet deserted, barely six people per square kilometer. Your coreligionists are good workers, excellent craftsmen. A great deal of methodical and persevering work is needed to revive the economic situation in our country. We are asking you to intervene with the Alliance Israélite, ICA and Monsieur E. de Rothschild in Palestine so that they make our task easier. Do me the honor of calling on me from time to time so that we can discuss these important matters. I will come to see you often, etc., etc. . . ."

All the ministers have been charming, but the grand vizier outdid them all by arranging for his aide-de-camp and all his ordonnance officers to follow our procession, which was composed of three chiefs of protocol with horsemen.

. . . in your last letter you told me not to lose contact with you. I do not need this injunction, since, starting today, I am going to communicate with you as often as possible, at least once a fortnight, about all our work, which is nothing but your own.

(. . .)

(AAIU, Turkey, XXX E)

Constantinople, letter received
29 March 1909

Grand vizier's speech

Eminence,

Of all the components that form the great Ottoman nation, the noble Jewish nation is the one that has most distinguished itself by its intelligence, its abilities, and its aptitude for the study of the different branches of knowledge and has always worked to reach the front rank. It has just given obvious proof of its great intelligence by choosing a spiritual leader with enlightened ideas such as yourself. I can assure you that your appointment has given the Ottoman government great satisfaction.

The Jews have hitherto been outstanding by their attachment and their sincere friendship for the great Muslim Ottoman nation, with which they have always lived in a very good relationship, like a single body and a single soul. The loyal Jewish nation has always been an active and useful element. We hope that it will render many more services to the government and the country. I thank you most particularly for your promises to work to strengthen the feelings of friendship between the different elements and for your words of support to me. May God grant you complete success in your new office.

(AAIU, Turkey, XXX E)

The reactionary uprising of 13 April spread to Anatolia, resulting in the massacre of Armenians in Adana in southern Turkey. Nahum was afraid lest the Jews become the rebels' next target.

Constantinople, 14 April 1909

Dear Monsieur Bigart,

(. . .)

You must have heard by telegraph of what has been happening here since yesterday. For more than twenty-four hours we have been living in real anarchy. All the troops have mutinied. After tying up their officers, the soldiers besieged Parliament and the Sublime Porte. They are demanding the literal enforcement of the Law of the Sheri (religious law) and the removal of the Young Turks. Even at this very minute, they are still roaming the streets, shooting into the air. We are anxiously waiting for it to end. Will there be a reaction? For the moment, there is no sign of it. If things become serious, there is danger of revolution. In that case, I will seek refuge in the French embassy.

(. . .)

(AAIU, Turkey, XXX E)

Constantinople, 17 May 1909

Dear Monsieur Bigart,

(. . .)

You must have learned from the newspapers of the difficult times that the whole population of the capital has been living through. We have escaped a terrible massacre. The reactionary movement was going to "attack the Israelites" first. The population did not repudiate it. We are still not completely out of danger despite the state of siege and the harsh measures the present government is taking to repress any reactionary initiative. But in spite of this severity, confidence has not yet completely returned; there is general malaise, particularly in diplomatic circles. The news from the interior, although very exaggerated, is far from reassuring.

. . . Ahmed Riza bey, president of the Chamber, called on me yesterday. We talked about the present situation for more than three-quarters of an hour. He acknowledged that we are living in chaos at the moment, almost without a government, but that we need a great deal of patience and perseverance. As in our previous conversations, the president of the Chamber again talked much about the question of Jewish colonization, which he is keen on. He repeated several times that the government will be invited to support the Israelites' efforts with a view to possible immigration and to assist the immigrants. In my opinion this needs time and careful and methodical research. On the question of the community, which is in a state of pure disorganization as a result of the total absence of its revenues, he advised me to wait until a strong government is established. I am suffering terribly from this shortage of money. The meat "gabelle" does not exist, following the absence of government, and this prevents me from making any move, all the more so from initiating even the least little reform. The day will come when the Chamber will approve and implement all the laws relating to levying the "gabelle," as well as those that I must promulgate for levying a religious tax. But what do we do while we wait? The monthly budget is about 10,000F, and we have now been deprived of any sort of revenues as a result of governmental anarchy for several months. I am conscious of my duties and responsibilities; I know that I must stand firm until the end. Things cannot continue this way.

(. . .)

(AAIU, Turkey, XXX E)

The Zionist movement was gathering strength in Nahum's privileged power zone: the capital.

Constantinople, 22 November 1909

Dear Monsieur Bigart,

It is really a long time since I wrote to you. You are well aware of the reasons. I will not mention the very many occupations that absorb all my time, fourteen to sixteen hours of work a day: that was foreseen. I knew that I was pitching my tent on ruins and, most particularly, on stony ground. But what I find discouraging is my concern about the Zionist movement, which is spreading like lightning, particularly among the ignorant masses. Attempts to capture the people, especially the youth, are being made through a whole corrupt press, well-paid propagandists, and a crowd of people who fish in troubled waters. Naturally the Hilfsvereinists and Zionists begin by appealing to people's religious feelings and making them detest any movement toward progress and assimilation. They have even brought over popular lecturers from Bulgaria, and I have been obliged to close all the temples to these lectures. Propaganda is being carried out in clubs and newspapers and with the greatest possible vigor. There is already talk of overthrowing both the consistory and the chief rabbi, all accused of being Alliancists and all consequently anti-Zionists. The country's newspapers are beginning to get involved, and we have already seen a Turkish paper, edited by a deputy, declare itself anti-Zionist by publishing articles against "the Jewish shark."

Last week I invited the Israelite deputies to a joint session with members of the consistory to try and draw up guidelines for ourselves. Everyone was agreed in acknowledging the great damage caused us by the Zionist press and by the very rapid spread of this movement. As the press is free, we did not want to take coercive measures. Only Monsieur Fresco is fighting the movement in his paper, but he is attacked on all sides, here and in the provinces, insulted, publicly abused, and his paper is even boycotted. We are experiencing a severe crisis and I do not really know how to get out of it. Unfortunately, the split has already taken place and just when we were beginning to breathe again. Since July I have been able to settle the internal affairs of the community, collect revenues, and pay all the institutions regularly, while at the same time trying to establish a religious tax sufficient to provide ample support for all our projects.

What should I do? The Zionists, those very tenacious Germans, with our own people, are going to create a lot of problems for me. I also know that if we retire, everything will collapse! But it will be impossible to resist.

(. . .)

(AAIU, Turkey, XXX E)

The Alliance looked for ways to stem the spread of Zionism.

Paris, 26 November 1909

Dear Monsieur Nahum,

Your letter of 22 November, which I have just received, betrays real anxiety on your part and a discouragement that it is your duty to struggle against, both in your own interest and that of Ottoman Jewry. This is not the time to think about retirement when you have already so many achievements to your credit and when Jewry throughout the world has put its confidence in you and accorded you such high authority.

It is most urgently necessary to fight the rising tide of Zionism. But by what means? It seems to me that the most practical, the most apt to loosen the hold of Zionism and appeal to the Turkish Israelites, would be a governmental declaration, from the rostrum of the Ottoman Parliament, which I envisage along these lines:

After reaching an understanding with the grand vizier or the minister of the interior, an Ottoman deputy—not a Jew naturally—but a friend of the Jews and of the government, would address to the Chamber a question to the government as follows:

> Is the government aware that for several months active propaganda has been carried on among our Israelite cocitizens with a view to winning them over to Zionist theories? Foreign lecturers have been brought in in order to expand the Zionist program, journals have been founded that encourage the movement, and it seems that it has been sympathetically received in a certain section of the Jewish population. Does the government not think that this movement is of a nature to damage the unity of the Ottoman homeland and, in that case, what measures does it envisage taking to put a stop to it?

The minister of the interior or the president of the Council would then answer. He would speak of the loyalty of the Ottoman Israelites, which has been demonstrated in ways that are known in memorable circumstances, of the patriotism with which they welcomed the military law that now makes them the equals of their cocitizens in every respect. He would denounce the creation of a separatist nationalist movement as a very grave danger to the Israelites, which could alienate the sympathies of their cocitizens, declare that the government could not tolerate a movement of this sort provoked by outside elements that did not have the right to encroach on national unity by pernicious propaganda, and he would say that, if need be, he would ask the Chamber to furnish him with the means to stop all this oral and written agitation in the interest of the Israelite population itself, which might one day have cause to regret allowing itself to be thoughtlessly dragged into a pernicious movement.

It would be up to you to reach an understanding with the government on the matter of this question.

If you need money to fund anti-Zionist propaganda in the press, I will try very hard to obtain it for you. But forge ahead and let me know as soon as possible what you think of the idea I suggest.

(. . .)

J. Bigart

(AAIU, Register of Correspondence, S 221)

Nahum had his own program for fighting Zionism.

Constantinople, 3 January 1910

Dear Monsieur Bigart,

I am sending you by today's post the booklet published by Monsieur Fresco containing all his . . . articles.[30] These booklets were distributed this morning to all the ministers, senators, deputies, and newspaper editors. We will certainly soon hear what repercussions it has and what impressions it makes in official circles. On another count, at my request, the minister of the interior has just given the necessary orders for the literal translation of three issues of a new Zionist paper published in Judeo-Spanish by the worst type of individual. He is a very coarse man who had begun to wage a very strong campaign against me by trying to deceive the masses. I have waited until the eleventh issue in order to have serious grounds. I think that he will be summoned before a court-martial. There this matter will be more completely exposed than it could be anywhere else.

This week I was told that Riza Tevfik[31] had already given a lecture against Zionism in an Israelite club. We will have to wait a while. Do not be afraid that I am weakening. If I am being patient, it is in the interests of the cause. I will give you more details tomorrow. As for your question regarding funds, I do not need them for the moment. In a few days you will send me what

[30]The articles against Zionism by this journalist, a fervent admirer of the Alliance and supporter of Nahum (see bibliography).

[31]A Young Turk from the beginning and an influential member of the Committee of Union and Progress.

you think fit to be given to Monsieur Fresco secretly, either for his expenses so far or to continue the campaign in different ways.

(. . .)

(AAIU, Turkey, XXX E)

Constantinople, 9 January 1910

Dear Monsieur Bigart,

I have given a great deal of thought to the matter of the position of headmaster of the Talmud Torah in Salonika.

. . . there is a . . . seminarist, David Elnécavé,[32] whom you may perhaps have heard of. He has already taught at Demotica and Monastir. He is quite strong in Hebrew and French. He is very articulate and of good appearance. But necessity forced him to join the Zionist party some time ago. He publishes a small weekly magazine, *El Judio*.[33] If you want me to offer him this post, I think he would be very happy and will naturally discard all his recently adopted opinions.

The Turkish papers have begun to take an interest in Zionism. Last Friday already *Ikdam*[34] wrote a long leading article, warning Ottoman Israelites against Zionism; *Sabah*[35] did the same. In this way, the matter will come to the rostrum of Parliament of its own accord.

(. . .)

(AAIU, Turkey, XXX E)

Constantinople, 1 April 1910

Dear Monsieur Bigart,

It really is a long time since I wrote to you personally, but my tasks these days are so many and so hard that they made me ill. A nervous illness that I have never had before. I am completely alone. Alone to carry a colossal workload, especially that relating to military service.[36]

I am not complaining, but I do not know how to succeed in putting things in some sort of order and combating the new movement. The papers are no longer taking an interest in Zionism, even the word is not used; it has been replaced, however, by the term "nationalism"!

---

[32]A former pupil of Nahum's at the seminary.

[33]Istanbul/Varna/Sofia (1909–1931). This paper, subsidized by the World Zionist Organization, later waged a powerful war on Nahum and the Alliance.

[34]Turkish journal (1894–1928).

[35]An Istanbul journal (1876–1922).

[36]From 1909, non-Muslims did military service on the same basis as Muslim subjects of the empire.

I wanted to form an association here and other similar ones in all the provincial towns. Here it immediately began with schisms.

It is the Germans who are obstructing and hampering us. Helped by the apathy of our Constantinoplians, they seem to be winning. And despite this, the papers[37] (probably in the pay of I know not whom), are waging a campaign even against me, saying that I serve the interests of the Alliance rather than those of the Ottoman homeland. You can see what lengths these people's effrontery can go to; they have formed themselves into a little committee again.

The only thing I have to complain of is that I am all alone to face this gigantic task and the struggle against indifference and the movement.

It is true that I do not attach any importance to this campaign, but I still have to deal with a very ignorant and very backward population.

(. . .)

(AAIU, Turkey, XXX E)

Haim Nahum made preparations for a pastoral journey to the Jewish communities of the Empire. During this tour he also envisaged promoting his own image in the provinces, winning over the populations to his cause and putting himself forward as the right man in the right place.

Constantinople, 13 April 1910

Monsieur le Président,

It was with a strong feeling of gratitude that I read the contents of your letter of the thirtieth instant in which you were kind enough to invite me to the celebrations of the fiftieth anniversary of the Alliance.

You must have heard that I had to postpone my trip to Palestine until after Passover. But before I go there then, I plan to make a tour of Salonika, where I will spend the last two days of the festival. I will take advantage of my stay in that town to make speeches and give lectures, and I will seize the opportunity to talk about the magnificent work the Alliance has accomplished and of the sacred duty of every Israelite, particularly Ottoman Israelites, to lend their moral and material support to that institution, which is the glory of world Jewry.

From the latter town, I will go to Adrianople, where I will adopt the same program. It follows from this that I will not return to Constantinople until about 8 May, in order to preside over the fiftieth anniversary celebration organized here, which will open with a speech by me.

Consequently, I will have only some twelve days to make a decision in

---

[37]*El Relampago* (1910–?) and *El Judio* (note by Nahum).

reply to your flattering invitation. In that period I will see the grand vizier about this journey and will telegraph you the result of my interview.

(. . .)

(AAIU, Turkey, XXX E)

Constantinople, 17 May 1910

Monsieur le Président,

I have the honor to offer you my most sincere thanks for the congratulations that you were so kind as to express in your letter of the thirteenth instant. In carrying out my mission, I was only doing my most basic duty; let me add that my efforts to establish links of solidarity and friendship among the various groups and communities in the Empire did not perhaps match up to my wishes. In sermons in the Turkish language at both Salonika and Adrianople, I set out to publicize your work, its beneficent activity throughout the world and particularly in the Orient. My audience, who included members of the government, was suffused with the idea of the valuable assistance that the Alliance contributed to the homeland by spreading education, the only means of regeneration.

In my sermons in the temples and at various institutions, I strove to inspire my audience with feelings of brotherhood and unity, and encouraged the population to support the Alliance in its civilizing task, by creating societies, libraries, etc.

The state of anarchy that afflicts the community in the Holy City;[38] the civil wars between parties that are quarreling over the post of *Rishon-le-Zion*;[39] the moral and material damage that this situation causes, summon me there. I have therefore decided to make a tour to Palestine to put an end to this anarchy and establish lawfulness.

When I return, I plan to visit the towns on the coast, Beirut, Smyrna, and others, if possible. There again, I will concentrate my efforts on showing our populations the advantages of education, unity, and agreement.

(. . .)

(AAIU, Turkey, XXX E)

Constantinople, 28 July 1910

Dear Monsieur Bigart,

I have been here ten days and I have not yet had time to write to you. It is now that I am beginning to feel the fatigues of my journey through Palestine and Syria and to suffer from one or two ailments. And yet I will work night and day to settle all the business that has accumulated.

---

[38]Jerusalem.
[39]Literally "the first in Zion" (in Hebrew), chief rabbi of Palestine.

The Amicale:[40] It is going very well and gains new members every day. I will create another one for young ladies when the schools reopen. The Amicale has decided to introduce gymnastics classes into all our schools, boys and girls, to counterbalance the Maccabists' movement.[41]

(. . .)

(AAIU, Turkey, XXX E)

Constantinople, 15 November 1910

Dear Monsieur Bigart,

My illness, on the one hand, and the many occupations and preoccupations of the past days, on the other, have prevented me giving a timely reply to your letter of the twenty-eighth of last month.

I was in bed for eighteen days and had a small operation on my foot on an ingrown toenail, which had also caused a considerable infection.

I had only just recovered from my illness when I found myself in the presence of a hubbub of excitement caused by a speech against the Alliance given by the vice-president of the Maccabi society.

It would take a very long time to tell you in detail all the incidents and motives that drove me publicly in the press to express my disapproval of Maccabi's work.

. . . it is true that there was a strong upsurge against me on the part of the Zionists—"sold out to the Alliance."

. . . the Zionists are keen workers here, they pay out almost 2,000F to the papers, without counting the sums they allocate to their many propagators. The whole Jewish press in Constantinople (French, Hebrew, and Judeo-Spanish), with the sole exception of *Tiempo,* is loyal to them.

They work not openly and directly but always under the cover of "nationalism" or "the party opposed to the chief rabbinate," merely to create problems, difficulties, obstacles for me, so that nothing should succeed.

Were it not for these latest incidents and particularly the clear attitude I adopted to fight from the front this abominable campaign against the Alliance, I would have retired a long time ago, not because of the excessive work, the ingratitude, the schemes and abuse, but, more than anything else, because of the heartbreak caused me by this post, which I did not ask for and did not want.

The whole world knows it; I am working alone. I have shut myself away, at the expense of my health if the environment so requires, in order to give myself body and soul to the revival of this wretched Jewry and specifically

---

[40]Association of former pupils of the Alliance, founded in Istanbul in 1910.

[41]Members of the Maccabi gymnastics society, whose branches throughout the town of Istanbul had become bastions of Zionism.

of this unhappy Constantinople community. And in addition to all this, the happiness of the home, the only satisfaction that could give me some relief from all these ills, that happiness, I say, has been almost taken from me for reasons you know.

(. . .)

(AAIU, Turkey, XXX E)

The Alliance came to Nahum's aid when he felt overwhelmed by the spread of Zionism in Istanbul.

Paris, 22 November 1910

Dear Monsieur Nahum,

I have received your letter of 15 November, and I am very happy to learn that you have completely recovered from your indisposition.

How can you allow yourself to be depressed by the attacks directed at you; some attacks do honor to the person they are directed against. You know the Arab proverb: "the dogs bark, etc." You are rendering such great services to Ottoman Jewry that reason and good sense will necessarily triumph. What I do not understand is why you have not made use of your undisputed influence in high places to have a leading minister publicly say or write what people are thinking about Zionism and the attacks directed against you. The Ottoman Jews ask only for guidance, they must be shown the right way. Let a minister of the interior or a grand vizier arrange to be asked a question and then answer it with clarity, and you will see how everyone will rally round you.

(. . .)

J. Bigart

(AAIU, Turkey, XXX E, draft of a letter)

Constantinople, 19 December 1910

Dear Monsieur Bigart,

You must probably be aware of everything going on at the moment in both Constantinople and the provinces in connection with Zionism. The conflict gathers strength daily. It began the same day that I publicly expressed my disapproval of the Maccabi for its hostile attitude to the Alliance, an attitude that I criticized as harmful to the interests of Ottoman Jewry. The password was given, and all the Zionist papers in the capital (there are five or six papers in existence) opened the campaign.

Naturally I let them scream and shout. The group here is working night and day, and there is even another campaign going on in the Jewish press in Europe.

Here too, as everywhere else, what has sent all the paid agitators out campaigning in all the suburbs, with meetings, lectures, proclamations, and lampoons, was the communal elections. The whole intellectual class is with me, and I am carrying on till the end.

Yesterday evening, Monsieur Salem[42] came to see me, and we chatted for over three hours, and this evening our four Israelite deputies are coming for the same purpose. Salonika and principally the Cercle des Intimes[43] are joining in the struggle. Monsieur Salem is in favor of a fight, convinced that any agreement with them is impossible, and consequently he is of the opinion that we must be well organized. This is what we lack. Our people are self-respecting men and have no time to spare for anything but their own business. Their people are idlers specially paid to make propaganda for them.

They have explained my disapproval by telling a few high personages that the conflict originates from the fact that I want to Frenchify the Ottoman Jews and in this way spread French influence in the Orient. Naturally, the government attaches no importance to this. In any case, it would be a great advantage if you were kept informed of all the phases of the conflict on a day-to-day basis.

Here we have taken a small collection among a few friends to cover minor expenses. We only have *Tiempo* fighting for us, and even this it does at its own expense. We are taking a French paper and a Turkish paper in order better to defend our very just and legitimate cause.

The Israelite youth club in Balata, whose president is Monsieur Confino,[44] is giving a small soirée for the benefit of poor children. It seems that the words "Alliance Israélite Universelle," which were written on the notices stuck up in Balata streets, were obliterated during the night, probably by a few nationalist madmen.

We are opening an inquiry.

Monsieur Salem has asked me to write to you to ask if there is any way of obtaining a small amount of money to add to what we have collected here among a few friends.

(. . .)

(AAIU, Turkey, XXX E)

Will Nahum enter the Ottoman state apparatus?

---

[42]Emmanuel Salem, administrator of the Bank of Salonika.
[43]Salonikan club with close relations with the Alliance and Nahum.
[44]Albert Confino, headmaster of the Alliance school in this suburb.

Constantinople, 30 January 1911

Dear Monsieur Bigart,

I have not yet written officially to thank the central committee for the congratulations it was so kind as to send me on my appointment to the Senate, because this is not yet official. All the Turkish papers have mentioned it and a few ministers have even sent messengers to inform me. I am very perplexed to know how to reply to the letters and telegrams. Yesterday the ambassador of England called on me in person.

On yet another front, as soon as the news spread here, a few people met and immediately sent telegrams to the grand vizier, the minister of the interior, and the minister of justice and religions, asking the government to reconsider its plan so as not to create a great disturbance within Ottoman Jewry. At present I do not know what effect these telegrams had. Not satisfied with these measures, this league also wrote to provincial communities and associations, urging them to take similar action. These gentlemen are afraid that—should this appointment materialize—I will not be allowed to combine the two offices. This is the first such case to come up. Even if it should be possible, I do not think that the government, or rather part of the majority, would leave me in the post of chief rabbi, because it is an established fact that its intention is to make me enter political life, and several Young Turks even talk about the possibility of my being a candidate for the portfolio of the minister of public education.

In any case, if it is impossible for me to combine the two offices, I will work for the appointment of Monsieur Danon. I will telegraph you as soon as the news is official.

(. . .)
(AAIU, Turkey, XXX E)

A new pressure group on the communal scene: the lodges of B'nai B'rith.

Constantinople, 10 February 1911

Dear Monsieur Bigart,

I would like to consult you on quite an important matter that will come before me one day soon.

I have learned that the inspector general of the Bene Berith[45] is arriving here at the end of next week provided with a letter of introduction and recommendation to me from Monsieur C. Montefiore[46] and another of the same type for Monsieur Fernandez.

---

[45]Local pronunciation of B'nai B'rith.
[46]Claude Montefiore (1858–1938), scholar and leading figure of liberal Judaism in England.

The inspector is coming with the intention of opening and organizing similar lodges here and in some important towns in Turkey.

I think that such a project could be of great use to us here by grouping the élite of our population around a central point and will make our future a little more hopeful.

I wanted to tell you before this gentleman arrives and have your opinion on this matter.

Nothing new as far as the Senate is concerned. It is still said that I am on the second list of candidates with the grand vizier and the minister of war. We are waiting.

(. . .)

(AAIU, Turkey, XXX E)

The Ottoman Empire contained a multitude of Jewish communities scattered throughout its territory. Nahum showed an enduring interest in these, as is evident from the following three letters.

Constantinople, 27 February 1911

Monsieur le Président,

I have the honor to send you the translation of a telegram that I have just received from Diyarbakir:[47] "Community dying of cold and hunger; pressing and urgent need of help, which send via American committee." This telegram is signed by Rabbi Jacob Ibrahim; I have received confirmation of the precarious situation of our unfortunate coreligionists from Monsieur Peet, president of the committee distributing aid in Adana and Aleppo.

The financial state of the chief rabbinate does not allow it to stave off this misfortune, after our community did what it had to do to assist our own poor during the exceptionally harsh season this year. Not so long ago, I sent our brethren in Maraş[48] a certain sum, which was able to help relieve their poverty, a consequence of the latest disturbances in the *vilâyet*[49] of Adana. I am therefore turning to the Alliance and asking you to be so kind as to vote in favor of sending me urgent assistance telegraphically.

(. . .)

(AAIU, Turkey, XXX E)

---

[47]Town in southeastern Turkey.
[48]Town in southeastern Turkey.
[49]Prefecture.

Constantinople, 14 January 1913

Monsieur le Président,

I have just received a long communication from Diyarbakir, giving me the following details:

The condition of the community, which numbers four hundred and fifty souls, is very unhappy; no school, no spiritual leader; its school-age population consists of some forty children, rudimentarily clothed, barefooted, dirty, in the charge of an aged teacher, repeating prayers and a few verses of the Bible.

According to a few documents, it seems that the Alliance took an interest in this community and promised to create a school there. Sir Moses Montefiore[50] made it a gift of 100 Ltq.

In addition, this communication informs me that there is a plan to remind you of this promise and to ask you to put it into action. It is rightly thought that the school is the only means capable of reviving the population, which is vegetating in neglect and ignorance, and requests my support.

This is a town entirely isolated from any center of civilization, lost in the furthermost depths of Anatolia, without any practical means of communication, but it would still be easy for you, through the agency of one of your teachers from the frontier towns of Persia, to obtain some precise information about this poor community and bring about its moral and material revival by opening a school.

(. . .)
(AAIU, Turkey, XXX E)

Constantinople, 17 February 1914

Monsieur,

(. . .)
Yemen: I have received the anonymous letter written in Hebrew that you passed on to me, lodging a complaint against the rabbi of Sanaa. I have received three of them myself, which probably originate from the same source, given that the writing and style are identical to the first. An Israelite notable from Sanaa, passing through here, also presented me with strong complaints about this rabbi. I told him that for these complaints to be considered, the Sanaa rabbinate must send me an official letter on the matter. I sent a telegram to that effect ten days ago.

On the subject of Yemen, I informed you that the plan, which I spoke to you about in Paris, had been implemented, namely, to write to the imam

[50](1784–1885), famous English Jewish philanthropist.

Yahia asking for his protection on behalf of the Jews and that he issue strong orders to the *kadis*[51] to be fair and well disposed toward our brethren, as well as for his support for the opening of a school at Sanaa. My letter was accompanied by a warm recommendation from the minister of the interior to the governor-general of Yemen, enjoining him to give help and protection to the Israelite mission charged with bearing this letter to the imam, whose residence is three days away from Sanaa.

The rabbi of that town, to whom I sent the two letters, writes me that he has instructed two notables from the community to go to the imam Yahia. I am waiting for the result of this mission, which I will make it my duty to communicate to you.

(. . .)

(AAIU, Turkey, XXX E)

October 1912: The first Balkan war broke out. The Bulgarians headed for the Ottoman capital. The defeats, the restrictions, and failure to pay the salaries of officials and teachers provoked violent demonstrations. The populations of Macedonia and Thrace, fleeing from the occupying power, thronged to Istanbul. The second Balkan war would follow in 1913.

Constantinople, 14 November 1912

Confidential

Monsieur le Président,

I consider it my duty to inform you that for the moment the alarming reports concerning the insecurity of this town are unfounded. The French embassy keeps me informed on a day-to-day and purely confidential basis of the events taking place in our town. That was how I learned that a Russian cruiser will be stationed in front of the ecumenical patriarchate to protect the Greek orthodox and the Bulgarian church in the Fener[52] if the need arises; that an English ship will anchor in the Marmara,[53] in front of Kumkapi,[54] where the Armenian patriarchate is situated, which is mainly inhabited by Armenians. The measures taken might give the impression that the international fleet only came to safeguard the life and property of the European colony and the Christians, because people like to believe that Jews and Muslims fraternize and that we have nothing to fear. Nevertheless, despite the measures for any contingency adopted by the government, which has strengthened the patrols that move through the whole town night and day, I

---

[51]Muslim judges.
[52]District on the Golden Horn.
[53]Small sea connected to the Aegean Sea and the Black Sea by the Straits.
[54]Market town on the European shore of the Sea of Marmara.

asked Monsieur Ledoulx, first dragoman[55] to the French embassy, in confidence to request that the ambassador pass on to the admiral of the international fleet, doyen of the admirals, my wish to see a French ship anchored in the Golden Horn, between Hasköy and Balata, which are inhabited mainly by our poor coreligionists. Monsieur Ledoulx has informed me that my request has been taken into consideration.

As for me, I am staying at my post with patience and courage. My constant concern is to relieve the moral and material sufferings of the ill-fated emigrant Jews, who at present number more than 1,600.

I await events with confidence and hope not to have further misfortunes to lament.

. . . P.S. If there is any fear for public safety and if there should be a landing I will be warned twenty-four hours in advance, still by the same source, and I will then think about closing our schools temporarily.

(AAIU, Turkey, II C 8)

Constantinople, 28 November 1912

Monsieur le Président,

I have the honor to acknowledge receipt of your letters of the eighteenth and nineteenth instant and to express all my gratitude to you for the alacrity with which the central committee has been kind enough to reply so generously to my appeal on behalf of our unhappy coreligionists.

It goes without saying that the sums collected here, as well as those that reach us from abroad, are assigned to refugees from the occupied provinces.

The distribution of every sort of assistance is ensured by local commissions in the suburbs where the emigrant families are settled and are under the supervision and control of the committee over which I preside.

(AAIU, Turkey, XXX E)

Constantinople, 4 May 1914

Monsieur le Président,

I have waited till now to reply to your letter of 17 February concerning the part that our coreligionists took in the recent Balkan wars. Large numbers of our coreligionists fought in the ranks of the Ottoman army; the least little communities sent contingents; many are missing, dead, or wounded, but as for statistical data based on official documents on the Jews' numerical participation in this campaign, on their glorious deeds, etc., I much regret that I cannot satisfy you.

On one hand, the government has not yet drawn up the list; on the other,

[55]Interpreter.

the emigration, which is still continuing, has brought such disturbance to the communities that I very much doubt whether the Salonika and Adrianople communities, to whom I sent circulars on this matter, can be in a position to meet my wish for a reply.

A commission, which has just been set up for the erection of a monument to the memory of Jewish soldiers who fell in battle, might have more success, and I will make it my duty to supply you with all the information it may collect.

(. . .)

(AAIU, Turkey, XXX E)

Nahum broke off his correspondence with the Alliance during the First World War because of the overall situation. He resumed it a few months after the end of the war.

Constantinople, 27 April 1919

Confidential
Monsieur le Président,

The campaign carried on against me for six months has reached such a pitch and assumed such a character that it is no longer a struggle against me as an individual but also and primarily against the ideas that I represented and still represent today, I mean those of the Alliance. I see it as my duty to give you a summary of all the events which have taken place here recently. I had also asked Monsieur Benveniste[56] to send you a report of them.

My departure: On 21 October 1918, a few days after the Talât cabinet fell, I was summoned by his successor Izzet pasha, grand vizier of the cabinet, which concluded the armistice,[57] who made me the following speech word for word: "The Ottoman government is turning to you with a plea; knowing your interest in entente and having confidence in your tact, your savoir-faire, it would like you to help it enter into contact with the powers of the Entente; we lack an intermediary; our intermediary would be the United States of America, with whom we are not at war but have simply broken off relations. We would like you to use your acquaintances, the friendships that you were able to cultivate in America, to succeed in preparing the ground for a resumption of relations, and that you arrange to have Monsieur Elkus sent to us as the ambassador of Monsieur Wilson, whose fourteen principles we here and now accept. The government will instruct our minister at the Hague to make official approaches on this subject; your task would be to prepare the ground unofficially. We will have a diplomatic passport made

---

[56]Abraham Benveniste, headmaster of the Alliance school in Galata.
[57]The armistice of Mudros (30 October 1918).

ready for you so that you can leave as soon as possible. In order to keep the matter secret, until you have been able to cross the German-Dutch frontier, you will plead health reasons when you request leave of absence from the minister of justice and religions." On the twenty-fourth I was received in audience by the prince, heir to the throne, and by H.M. the sultan, who spoke to me in almost the same terms. According to the agreement reached, I would wait until my leave were authorized according to the rules and leave on Tuesday, 29 October. The day after, Friday the twenty-fifth at two-thirty, there was a telephone call from the Admiralty informing me that, following orders from higher authority, a small yacht was already under steam and I had to board it that same day for Constantza in order to cross the German frontier before the conclusion of the armistice. The government therefore did not leave me enough time to wait for my leave to be authorized, or to announce my locum tenens, and even less, officially to convene the meclis-i cismanî, that is to say, my secular council, to inform it of the mission entrusted to me. I left at four o'clock the same day. When I arrived at the Hague, diplomatic reasons made it impossible for me to cross the Atlantic and to talk to my friends in America, a journey rendered useless, moreover, by Monsieur Wilson's departure for Europe. I carried on a telegraphic correspondence with Monsieur Elkus and made preparations to return to Constantinople and resume my duties. My journey there and back, including my stay in the Hague, lasted four months, during which I received only one letter from my wife, on 1 February, in which she asked me to return as soon as possible, whatever the risk.

This is what happened in Constantinople during my absence. The day after my departure, Monsieur Niégo, president of the B'nai B'rith lodge, threw the first poisoned dart that would stir up the population: "The chief rabbi has left without warning the official bodies of the nation, he has done wrong, he has done very wrong." The rumor ran through the town like wildfire, reached all the associations, the whole population, with the result that there was soon no public or private society where the chief rabbi's case was not judged a hanging matter. Monsieur Niégo made himself the standard-bearer for the same group that led the famous campaign against me in 1912 and whose members, then as now, are Dr. D. Marcus, Dr. I. Auerbach, Hilfsverein representative in Constantinople, Monsieur Abramovich, president of the Maccabi society, N. Rousso (nephew of Monsieur Daoud Rousso, well known ICA lawyer), then president of the central consistory, whose resignation I had procured; today, president of the Zionist Federation and my bitter enemy. What Monsieur Niégo and his colleagues aimed to do was to foist on the central consistory (*meclis-i cismanî*), outside of any law and simply by revolution, the formation of a self-styled national council, of which he would assume the presidency. He then planned to convene a national assembly to get himself delegated as the representative of the Jews of Turkey to the Jewish Congress in London and Paris.[58] He succeeded on both counts. In addition, his title as president of the national council enabled him to gain entry, together with Monsieur Nissim Rousso, to the high commissioners of the Entente and there to let slip all the perfidious insinuations about me as an individual. This was all the more despicable in that I was too far away to be aware of them and to defend myself, the lack of postal and telegraphic communications not having allowed me to give or to receive any sign from my wife.

Here are the contents of the insinuations:

1. The chief rabbi has left a diplomatic mission, the purpose of which is unknown to us, without informing the officially constituted bodies of the nation. He has thereby scorned the nation. The result: discredit cast on me as an individual in the eyes of the Jewish population of Constantinople and the provinces.

2. The chief rabbi, who left to defend the cause of the Turks, is an anti-Ententist, since the Entente is the Turks' enemy. The consequence of this blackmail: to bring my name into disrepute with the present government, with the Armenian and Greek elements persecuted by the Turks, and with the powers of the Entente.

3. The chief rabbi is an Alliancist, consequently an anti-Zionist, and his journey can only damage the cause of Zionism. The consequence: to discredit me as an individual with England and all world Jewry. The aim was to blacken my name to such an extent that I should be destroyed and all my past and all my future with me. Every sort of means was employed to this end; the press: L'Aurore, the only Jewish organ written in French, bought up by them, made use of every type of blackmail; there were public and private lectures; the creation and proliferation of all the Zionist societies for young boys and girls in all the suburbs—these were formed into permanent tribunals to judge the "chief rabbi"; subsidized public speeches inciting the poor and ignorant masses in the Bolshevik manner, making them believe that the chief rabbi was the cause of all their poverty, that one word from him to the government, had he so wished, and their husbands, brothers, and sons would have stayed at home and would not have died like dogs in the war, that he offered his flock as a sacrifice to the country in order to make himself popular with the government; that if he had so desired, a word from him and the Jews would long since have had Palestine and Jerusalem; to the enlightened class through the most indescribable calumnies. In order to gain more strength and support among the ignorant as well as the enlightened population, they spread the rumor that England was

---

[58]At the preparatory meetings of the Jewish delegation to the peace conference (1919).

against me, and these are the circumstances in which they produced proofs to support this:

Messieurs Niégo and Rousso went to see Monsieur Howler, English minister plenipotentiary, to give him their explanation of my journey, its purpose, and the nation's alleged discontent. They reported back to a joint session of the meclis-i cismanî and the national council combined, in the following terms: "It emerges from statements made by Monsieur Howler that the Entente would view it with favor if the Jewish community would dissociate itself from the chief rabbi's mission." My wife has always kept her distance from communal affairs, but when she heard about this statement and saw the gravity of the plot hatched against my honor and career, she determined, despite herself, to go and ask for an explanation from the British high commissioner and to explain the position to him. As she was confined [to bed] for a few weeks, as a result of all these emotions, she asked the high commissioner of America, Monsieur Heck, to come and see her and instructed him to make inquiries of Monsieur Howler. The result of these inquiries was that Monsieur Howler denied having said anything at all that could have led those gentlemen to believe that he would encourage the Jewish community to dissociate itself from the chief rabbi but that he could not accede to Madame Nahum's request to repudiate it publicly because he did not want his name to be mixed up in communal affairs.

This, then, was the state in which I found the community when I returned on 4 March. I had gone away four months earlier with a prestige no previous religious leader had attained; I confess this with no false modesty. I returned a prisoner at the bar, a criminal, a traitor to the Jewish nation. A small number of jealous men, led, it shames me to say, by Monsieur Niégo, had been sufficient to effect this change.

An hour after I had returned, I had more or less understood the situation and, without wasting time cleaning house, I took a stand. My first public words and actions were not in any way to recognize the would-be national council but to declare that I did not know it. The nation was asking me for explanations of the purpose of my journey, it was to its representatives that I intended to give them and, according to the law, its representatives were the members of the meclis-i cismanî (central consistory), which I convened and to which I gave the explanations that you have read at the beginning of this report, which it found satisfactory. Then the so-called national council began its campaign of defamation, reinforcing it with the pen and the spoken word, and such virulence that it led to a demonstration in front of the chief rabbinate by a bunch of callow youths who had been taught to shout: "Down with the tyrant, down with the oppressor, down with the dictator!" The result of this demonstration was to produce an adverse effect on the enemy's plans: it finally roused the notables of the community from their apathy. Some two or three hundred of them, led by Monsieur Fernandez, Monsieur Salem, the lawyer Taranto and all the members of the Amicale, were waiting for me at the chief rabbinate on my return from Kadiköy,[59] where I had spent Saturday; and that very day they solemnly formed themselves into a defense party called Bene Israël.[60] Within a few days, their program was sketched out, the statutes drafted, summed up in the desire to work for the reawakening of Jewish national feeling, while conserving the Jews' rights and duties in the countries they inhabit, of which they wished to continue to regard themselves as citizens.

This, then, as clearly and as briefly as possible, is my position vis-à-vis the community: my adversaries are the Zionists, bitter enemies to the Alliance's work, with their paid agents, their societies, and their ramifications and branches in all the suburbs, their means of influencing young people through Maccabi. One of its lecturers today is David Niégo, son of J. Niégo, who makes indescribably defamatory speeches to a crowd of Maccabists and pupils from his school[61] . . . in his father's presence, explaining that he is following his father's policy when any of our friends tell him of their indignation. Supporting and defending me, I have all those who form the cream of a society, so to speak, lawyers, doctors, merchants, financiers, ordinary employees; all mature and distinguished men, going to work in the morning and concerning themselves with communal affairs as a relaxation, not turning them into a profession, a livelihood, in a word, and much too distinguished to use against their adversaries the latter's own vile and cowardly weapons. Between the two, I am the target and receive all the blows of the first to force me to retire and leave the field clear and the encouragement of the second who want me to stand firm to the end in the interests of the community. That is my position vis-à-vis the Jews.

I am going to try and give you the details, first of my relationships with the Ottoman government and then with the representatives of the powers of the Entente.

1. My relations with the government: The blackmail propagated in the papers has it that I must be ruined in the eyes of the present government, since I was on good terms with the preceding government. It received me with open arms, and I am on the best of terms with all the ministers, and the plot mounted against me produced such indignation among the Turks that I have never been so popular either in official circles or with the population.

2. My relations with the Entente: The same procedure, the same black-

---

[59]District on the Asiatic coast of Istanbul.

[60]"Sons of Israel" (in Hebrew). Association founded in 1919 by Nahum and his friends, with the name of a Zionist association of 1910.

[61]B'nai B'rith high school, founded in 1915 in Istanbul.

mail; I had become Germanophile and Francophobe from the fact that I
traveled through Germany twice, where I took a three-week cure at Bad-
Homburg, in order to go to Holland and Sweden. This time the lie was too
shameless by far, since the same people had denounced me to the German
embassy at the beginning of the war as Germanophobe. The German ambassador had complained about me to Talât bey, then minister of the interior, who summoned me and said: "Nahum effendi, you are accused of
Germanophobia." Without turning a hair, I replied: "Excellency, I admit
that I am Francophile, but being Francophile does not mean being Germanophobe; I respect the alliances that the government has contracted for a
purpose it judges useful to the interests of the country; it is not for me to
meddle in matters that do not concern me, but I cannot renounce my
feelings of sympathy for the country where I did my training, where I have
friends and every close emotional and intellectual bond." "I understand,"
Talât said, "and I have confidence in you, but you have to justify yourself to
the German embassy." The situation was serious, even dangerous, the explanation took place. So successfully did I retain my right to an independent
opinion that, despite the apparent courtesy of the relations that I maintained
with the German ambassadors, they never ceased to mistrust me. This
mistrust was translated into a violent report against me to the minister
of foreign affairs in Berlin from Weitz, correspondent of the *Frankfurter
Zeitung,* who was all-powerful at the German embassy and already in the
days of Abdülhamid making the rain fall and the sun shine. I was told about
this report when I passed through Berlin by Monsieur Lichtheim, Zionist
representative in Constantinople.

We were thus going through the period of pan-Germanism: French Christian schools had been closed; the teaching of French abolished in Ottoman
schools; the French language spurned in boats, trams, in the streets; so great
was the chauvinism that one avoided speaking it so as not to arouse suspicion and cause gossip; shop signs previously written in French were replaced
by German and Turkish signs; there were formal instructions to ask for
numbers on the telephone in Turkish; in a word, French was banished.
Imagine my fears for the fate in store for the Alliance schools. They were
justified. The first to receive the order to evacuate, to close, was the one in
Hasköy; I then had to fight like a lion. Everything militated against them:
the language, the syllabus, the central seat of the Alliance, everything was
French, everything contributed to spreading the French language and influence in the Orient. I maintained that they were entirely Jewish and that if
they were closed, I would close the synagogues; this was the only means of
protesting against the government. Finally, I won my case and a circular was
immediately sent to all the officials in the capital and the provinces ordering
them not to touch the Alliance schools, neither their staff, nor their syllabus.
Monsieur Côte, consul general of France in Rotterdam, whom I know, and

to whom I told the story, really appreciated how important this victory was and took care to mention it on the passport he handed me for my return to Constantinople.

The Or-Yehudah[62] farm and the one in Yakacik,[63] Messila-Hadasha,[64] were subject to the same risk and I obtained deferment after deferment to prevent their seizure. I hope that Monsieur Niégo, who has today thought it in his interest to present himself as an enemy, will have the courage not to deny this.

The representatives of France in Constantinople today give me not only proof of sympathy and friendship but also encouragement, the most effective moral support in the testing time I am living through. The general-in-chief, H.E. Franchet d'Espérey, Monsieur Defrance,[65] Admiral A. Foulcques-Duparc, Monsieur Ledoulx, Colonel Foulon, Monsieur Le Révérend, etc., are all cooperating in making my task easier. The day after he called on me on the first day of Passover, the general-in-chief told me that he had written about me to the French government, and yesterday Monsieur Defrance renewed his pledge of full support. I could not be grateful enough for their unfailing proofs of friendship.

3. My relations with the representatives of Italy: My relations are excellent. I had occasion during the war to defend the interests of the Italian community when their synagogue, cemetery, even money deposited in the banks, were in danger of being seized, and I preserved its independence. Monsieur Fernandez and Monsieur Salem heard about it when they returned, and they thanked me by letter and in public in the name of their community. They also informed Count Sforza, Italian high commissioner, who thanked me for this, as well as for the support I gave to Italian subjects, like Auguste de Médina, son of Monsieur Élie de Médina, treasurer of the Alliance's regional committee, whom I released from prison, Monsieur Isidore Gherson, member of the regional committee, whom I succeeded in keeping in Constantinople with his title of director-general of the Wiener-Bank Verein despite his Italian citizenship, etc.

4. America: My relations, as you know, have always been excellent, and when he left, Monsieur Elkus unofficially asked me to watch over the interests of the American educational institutions. I successfully intervened on behalf of these institutions on several occasions, as well as on behalf of American Israelite subjects going back to America from Palestine. That is

---

[62]Established near Smyrna by the Jewish Colonization Association at the beginning of the century for immigrant Jews from Eastern Europe.

[63]District on the Asiatic coast.

[64]Colony founded by the Jewish Colonization Association, again for immigrant Jews from Eastern Europe.

[65]Ambassador of France.

why Madame Nahum spontaneously turned to Monsieur Heck, American high commissioner, to make the inquiries I mentioned above. He took up my defense with England during my absence and has continued to do so after my return. Monsieur Heck left a fortnight ago and is at present in Paris, where he went to confer with President Wilson. If you think it necessary, you could arrange a meeting with him and ask him personally for all the details of the situation, the campaign and its ringleaders, of which he has a thorough knowledge.

5. England: I told you at the beginning of this report that England alone seems to have lent a more sympathetic ear to my enemies' despicable insinuations. Yet for no other country in the Entente did I compromise myself in the eyes of the Germans and the Germanophile unionists so deeply. Before the bombardment of the Dardanelles in February 1915, at the unofficial request of an English friend then in Salonika, who knew that I was sympathetic to the cause of entente, I made approaches for a separate peace and even succeeded in sending a Turkish delegate to Dedeağaç to talk to the English delegate. The negotiations came to nothing, as the Turkish cabinet found the English conditions too hard; this move earned me the German embassy's complaints and mistrust. As for the interests of English subjects, I have taken them to heart every time that circumstances arose, not only Jews but also Christians. For example, I succeeded in securing the return to Constantinople of the lawyer Mizzi, who, old and ill, was exiled in Konya,[66] and his transfer from here to Malta. Unfortunately, my intervention on behalf of Reverend Frew, an English chaplain, was unsuccessful. My relations with successive English ambassadors here were so well known in England that Monsieur Franklin, brother-in-law of Lord Montagu,[67] sent me a letter, with the authorization of the English government, asking me to intervene with the Ottoman government with a view to improving the conditions of English prisoners.

How is it that my adversaries have been able to convince all and every one that the whole Entente is for me except England? And yet my relations with its representatives are correct. I paid an official call on Admiral Webb, who returned it in the company of Monsieur Howler, minister plenipotentiary, despite the fact that I had not called on this latter. I conclude from this that all the malevolent insinuations that my enemies have been able to drop into their ears have collapsed of their own accord like a badly made building that is fundamentally unsound, in view of the fact that one cannot be against Germans and the Entente at the same time. But they did succeed on one

---

[66]Town on the Anatolian plateau.
[67]Edwin Samuel Montagu (1879–1924), Anglo-Jewish politician.

point: they made me appear to be anti-Zionist, and they did get the Zionist committee in London[68] to recommend them to the English embassy.

. . . despite all the explanations given to them: that it was my duty not to make myself the standard-bearer of Zionism during the war period and before, in the interests of the 400,000 Jews in the Empire for whom I bore the heavy responsibility; that I rendered greater services to Zionism in my obscurity than the most fervent of them; and that, thanks to the policy I followed, I prevented the Jews of Turkey and Palestine from sharing the fate of the Armenians and Greeks (and the Greek papers themselves have proclaimed this loud and clear); despite, as I say, all these clarifications, it seems to me that they are still accusing me of anti-Zionism. It might help me to dissipate these latter doubts if you were to approach the Anglo-Jewish Association,[69] and if the Association approached the British government. However that may be, my position is difficult, if not untenable. I am fighting desperately, not for my position, which has scarcely been enviable, but to show France that I am very grateful to it for the encouragements it has showered upon me, to the Alliance, whose work would be endangered if I retired. We have come to the same point in Constantinople today as in Bulgaria a few years ago. The new association, Bene Israël, which grew out of the Amicale, will work zealously to win as many supporters as possible to its cause in order not to hand over the community, its institutions, and its work to this handful of schemers. I am at this moment trying to obtain authorization to convene a congress of the representatives of the Jews of Turkey, a congress that the Zionists call by the pompous name of the constituent national assembly, in order to give the community new statutes. The agitators are working relentlessly to foment the same disturbances in the provinces, in order to win over the youth, so that the majority of the members of this assembly will support them. Our battle consists of thwarting their plans. Will we or won't we succeed: *Chi lo sa?*

(. . .)

(AAIU, Turkey, XXX E)

After his resignation from the post of chief rabbi, Nahum continued to work for the Alliance. He went to the United States twice to make propaganda there, and here he again came up against the Zionists.

---

[68]After 1917, the World Zionist Organization decided to move its headquarters to London.

[69]British organization founded in 1871 originally to defend Jewish rights by diplomatic means. It also undertook educational work in North African and Near Eastern Jewish communities.

New York, 24 January 1921

Dear Monsieur Bigart,

Here I am in New York since last Monday, the seventeenth, after a very rough eight-day crossing.

My first concern immediately on arrival was to find an office to work in. Monsieur Taranto, who has a very luxurious office in the center of town, where the major administrative offices, banks, and business firms are situated, has been so kind as to put a room at my disposal where I can receive visitors. The offices of Monsieur Louis Marshall,[70] Monsieur Elkus, and Monsieur Morgenthau are actually situated on Broadway. I was able to telephone them the day after I arrived. Monsieur Morgenthau returned from California on Friday the twenty-first. As for Monsieur Elkus, he has kept to his room for a week following a slight indisposition.

Informed of my presence here, Monsieur Oscar Straus immediately invited me to dinner and had the tactful idea of inviting Monsieur Louis Marshall at the same time so that I could meet him. Monsieur Marshall was very friendly at this first meeting and we thus had the chance to converse for over two hours on various Jewish matters, notably the Alliance and its schools. The conversation was very lively, particularly when it concerned the immigrant Israelites, their sufferings and their poverty, etc., which people here are convinced that Jewry, and the French Israelites, have done nothing about. . . .

On the basis of information that Chief Rabbi Israël Lévi[71] gave me on the evening before my departure, I tried to show them that they were mistaken.

. . . the big Israelite papers, such as *Morgen,* which prints 90,000 to 100,000 copies daily, *Tag,* and *America* have already devoted articles to the subject of my journey.

As I had the honor of saying at the session of the central committee, I am finding that American Jewish circles, far from being sympathetic to us, are even very hostile. I will strive to the best of my ability to dissipate certain misunderstandings or prejudices. It will be a very hard, long, and exacting task, because it takes conversations repeated on a daily basis to convince people and win them over.

This week I will start to make contact with our oriental coreligionists scattered over the different districts of New York; they are not as numerous as I thought. . . .

. . . my arrival here has coincided with that of Baron James de Rothschild,[72] who has probably come to arrange an agreement between the orga-

---

[70](1856–1929), lawyer and communal leader, an influential figure in the Republican party.
[71](1856–1939), chief rabbi of France from 1919 to 1938.
[72](1878–1957), British politician, Zionist, and philanthropist.

nizations in London and New York, and also the arrival . . . of Chief Rabbi Hajès of Vienna, who has come to beg for help for our coreligionists in Austria, and we are ceaselessly told that the financial, economic, and commercial crisis is very severe at the moment and that even the Joint Distribution Relief is going through a very difficult period. . . .

(AAIU, XI A 76)

New York, 23 November 1921

Dear Monsieur Bigart,

I spent my first week in New York nursing a mild attack of bronchitis caught during the crossing. I completely recovered from it some ten days ago and have begun to pay my first calls and to converse individually with people who have a certain degree of sympathy for our work.

. . . the present situation: All these gentlemen and still others with whom I have already talked, have shown me the great difficulties I am going to come up against, particularly as a result of the serious financial and economic crisis that prevails, especially in the east of America, the industrial and commercial center par excellence. . . . This is the same pessimism I noted last January. Then as now, my arrival here coincided with the arrival of a new Zionist commission, presided over by N. Sokolow[73] and by a warning from the Joint Distribution Relief Committee.

. . . the present crisis, aggravated by the rise in the exchange rate, lack of exports, and unemployment, has certainly already caused and is still causing great ravages in the commercial world. Several people I saw in quite satisfactory positions six months ago are totally ruined today. . . .

But everyone here is convinced that this situation must change during, or toward the end of, this winter.

All these remarks, added to my own observations and to Monsieur Elkus's advice, suggested the idea that instead of wasting my time here, I should undertake a tour of South America, from where I have already received several letters, beginning with Argentina, the most important center from the Israelite point of view, and returning via Mexico and Cuba. I even went to American Express yesterday morning to obtain all the information to do this.

I am sending you, attached, the itinerary I propose to follow in case you think it right to proceed. The main centers to visit, outside the colonies, would be Rio de Janeiro, Buenos Aires, Montevideo, Rosario, go on to Valparaiso and from there via the Pacific, Lima, Mexico, and Havana.

I am sure that we will be successful in all the Israelite circles in Latin

[73](1859–1936), Hebrew writer, pioneer of modern Hebrew journalism, and president of the World Zionist Organization after the war.

America. The journey is very tiring, I know, and above all expensive, considering the great distances to be covered.

. . . Marshal Foch: You must of course have learned from the dispatches that the marshal received a delegation of American Israelites. . . . He was very touched by this and in his short speech referred to the patriotism of the French Israelites. I was invited to the large banquet given in his honor by all the French associations in New York. . . .

As the marshal was to go to Seattle, Portland, Los Angeles, etc., I wrote to our communities in those towns, advising them to send special delegations of former pupils of the Alliance to the official receptions which will be organized.

(. . .)
(AAIU, Turkey, XXX E)

New York, 25 January 1922

Dear Monsieur Bigart,

(. . .)

On 8 January, the whole American press, including all the Israelite papers, published (in large print in the Jewish press) a dispatch from the *Exchange Telegraph* saying that "the Sublime Porte is making the necessary approaches to the government of the United States requesting the resumption of diplomatic relations and its agreement to the appointment of Chief Rabbi Nahum as Ottoman ambassador to Washington." The same day Monsieur Morgenthau invited me to lunch at his home on the following day, 9 January, and despite my statement that I had no knowledge of this news, he hastened to write a very kind letter to the secretary of state.

(. . .)
(AAIU, France, XI A 76)

In the last analysis, Haim Nahum was never able to become the state Jew that he wished to be and that, at times, people had hoped he might become. In the same year, he participated in the Lausanne Conference, but in the wings. The next step would be the chief rabbinate of Cairo.

BIBLIOGRAPHY

Archives

I consulted the Turkish press but was not able to gain access to the Ottoman Archives for the period studied.

Archives of the Alliance Israélite Universelle, Paris
    France: XI A 76, XI A 80, IV D 16, VIII D 48, I G 1–6.
    Turkey: I C 1–7, II C 8–14, I G 1, I H 1, XXVIII E–XXXI E, XL E to XLVI E.
    Greece: I C 1–10, I C 41–52, I G 1–3.
    Israel: II C 9–12, I G 1–3, IX E–XII E 26–35.
    Registers of correspondence: Secretariat, Schools (1897–1922).
Archives of the Ministry of Foreign Affairs, Paris
    Series War, 1914–1918: vols. 946–947, 960, 1197–1201.
    Series E Levant, 1918–1929: Palestine, vols. 10–17.
    Turkey, vols. 112, 283–318, 537.
    Series Y International, 1918–1940: files 688–690.
    Political and commercial correspondence: new series, Turkey, vols. 1–9, 129–135, 136–138.
Archives of the Ministry of War, Vincennes
    20 N 168, 20 N 1103.
Archives of the Navy, Vincennes
    SS Ea 199 to 201.
Public Record Office, London
    Turkey, Policy, 1917–1919: FO 371/3055, 3388, 4141, 4167–4169, 4171. Peace conference, 1919 (Paris): FO 608/99, 118.
Auswärtiges Amt Akten, Bonn
    Turkey, No. 195, 1907–1920: K 692/176, 146–180, 991.
    Turkey, No. 162: vol. 9.
Central Zionist Archives, Jerusalem
    Only the documents in these groups that have a bearing on our subject have been consulted.
    Series Z2: Central Office, Cologne, 1905–1911.
    Series Z3: Central Office, Berlin, 1911–1920.
    Series Z4: Central Office and Jewish Agency, London, 1917–1955.
    Series L5: Jewish Agency, Constantinople, 1909–1917.
Private Archives
    A 19: Victor Jacobson.
    A 51: Zadoc Kahn.
    A 56: Richard Lichtheim.
    A 107: Arthur Ruppin.
    A 220: Maurice Cohen.
Central Archives for the History of the Jewish People, Jerusalem
    Magnes Papers: P3/1062–1063.

Abraham Galanté Papers: RP 112/18–19, 21, 29–30, 68, 76, 96, 99, 110, 126. Unclassified documents relating to the history of Turkey have been consulted on a sampling basis: 20 to 707.

Periodicals

Archives Israélites, Paris, 1840–1925.
L'Aurore, Istanbul/Cairo, 1909–1925.
El Avenir, Salonika, 1902–1914.
Bulletin de la Grande Loge de District XI et de la Loge de Constantinople, Istanbul, 1911–1921.
Bulletin de "Amicale," Istanbul, 1910–1913.
The Bulletin of the Joint Distribution Committee, New York, 1916–1919.
Bulletins semestriels de l'Alliance Israélite Universelle, Paris, 1860/1865–1913.
Die Welt, Vienna/Cologne/Berlin, 1897–1914.
Excelsior, Aix-les-Bains, 1921.
Ha-Herut, Jerusalem, 1909–1917.
Hamevasser, Istanbul, 1909–1911.
Ha-Olam, Cologne/Vilna/Odessa, 1908–1914.
Ha-Or, Jerusalem, 1910–1915.
Ha-Poel Ha-Za'ir, Jaffa, 1908–1915.
Ha-Zevi, Jerusalem, 1908–1909.
Ikdam, Istanbul, 1918–1923.
Israel, Cairo, 1923, 1925, 1933.
Le Jeune Turc, Istanbul, 1911–1915.
Jewish Chronicle, London, 1908–1925, 1960.
Jewish World, London, 1908–1920.
Journal de Salonique, Salonika, 1895–1910.
Journal des Communautés, Paris, 1960.
Journal des Débats, Paris, 1919.
Journal d'Orient, Istanbul, 1918–1925.
Judaïsme Séphardi, Paris/London, 1957 and 1961.
El Judio, Istanbul, 1909–1914.
Lloyd Ottoman, Istanbul, 1908–1918.
Le Matin, Paris, 1919, 1922.
Le Moniteur Oriental, İstanbul, 1908–1915, 1919.
Le Nation, Istanbul, 1919–1922.
New York Times, New York, 1917, 1921.
Le Peuple Juif, Paris, 1919–1920.
Sabah, Istanbul, 1922.
Stamboul, Istanbul, 1908–1924.
Takvim-i Vekayi, Istanbul, 1919.
Tasvir-i Efkâr, Istanbul, 1922.
Tevhid-i Efkâr, Istanbul, 1922.
El Tiempo, Istanbul, 1897–1925.
Univers Israélite, Paris, 1844–1925.
La Vara, Cairo, 1905–1908.

Books and Dissertations

Abitbol, Michel. *Abraham Danon, 1857–1925: Sa vie et ses oeuvres.* Paris: H. Elias, 1925.

————. *Les deux terres promises: Les Juifs de France et le Sionisme.* Paris: Olivier Orban, 1989.

Ahmad, Feroz. *The Young Turks: The Committee of Union and Progress in Turkish Politics, 1908–1914.* Oxford: Clarendon Press, 1969.

Alem, Jean-Pierre. *La Déclaration Balfour: Aux sources de l'Etat d'Israël.* Paris: Editions Complexe, 1982.

Barnai, Jacob. *The Jews in Palestine in the Eighteenth Century: Under the Patronage of the Istanbul Committee of Officials for Palestine.* Translated from the Hebrew by Naomi Goldblum. Tuscaloosa: University of Alabama Press, 1992.

Bat Ye'or. *The Dhimmi: Jews and Christians under Islam.* Rutherford, N.J.: Fairleigh Dickinson University Press, 1985.

Bauer, J. *L'école rabbinique de France, 1830–1930.* Paris: Presses Universitaires de France, 1930.

Bein, Alex, ed. *Arthur Ruppin: Memoirs, Diaries, Letters.* Translated from the German by Karen Gershon. London: Weidenfeld and Nicolson, 1971.

Beinart, Haim, ed. *Sephardi Heritage.* Jerusalem: Magnes Press, 1922. (in Hebrew)

Benbassa, Esther. *Une diaspora sépharade en transition: Istanbul aux XIXe–XXe siècles.* Paris: Cerf, 1993.

————. *Haim Nahum Effendi, dernier grand rabbin de l'Empire ottoman, 1908–1920: Son rôle politique et diplomatique.* 2 vols. Thèse de doctorat d'état, University of Paris III, 1987.

Benbassa, Esther, and Aron Rodrigue. *Juifs des Balkans: Espaces judéo-ibériques aux XIVe–XXe siècles.* Paris: Editions la Découverte, 1993.

Benbassa, Esther, and Aron Rodrigue. *Une vie judéo-espagnole à l'Est: Gabriel Arié.* Paris: Cerf, 1992.

Berard, Victor. *La révolution turque.* Paris: A. Colin, 1909.

Bianchi, Robert. *Interest Groups and Political Development in Turkey.* Princeton, N.J.: Princeton University Press, 1984.

Bigart, Jacques. *L'action de l'Alliance Israélite en Turquie.* Paris: Alliance Israélite Universelle, 1913.

Biliotti, A., and Ahmed Sedad. *Législation ottomane depuis le rétablissement de la Constitution.* Vol. 1. Paris: Jouve, 1912.

Birnbaum, Pierre. *Anti-Semitism in France: A History from 1789 to the Present.* Translated from the French by Miriam Kochan. Oxford: Blackwell, 1992.

————. *Les Fous de la République: Histoire politique des Juifs d'Etat de Gambetta à Vichy.* Paris: Fayard, 1992.

Braude, Benjamin, and Bernard Lewis, eds. *Christians and Jews in the Ottoman Empire.* 2 vols. New York: Holmes and Meier, 1982.

Carmin, Itzhak J., ed., *World Jewish Register: A Biographical Compendium of Notable Jews in the Arts, Sciences, and Professions.* New York: Monde Publishers, 1955–1956.

Çavdar, Tevfik. *Talât Pacha: The Biography of a Master of Organization.* Ankara: Dost Kitabevi Yayinlari, 1984. (in Turkish)

Chouraqui, André. *Cent ans d'histoire: L'Alliance Israélite Universelle et le renaissance juive contemporaine, 1860–1960.* Paris: Presses Universitaires de France, 1965.

Cohen, Eliyahou. *L'influence intellectuelle et sociale des écoles de l'Alliance Israélite Universelle sur les Israélites du Proche-Orient.* Ph.D. diss., University of Paris, 1962.

Cohen, Israel. *The Turkish Persecution of the Jews.* London: Alabaster and Passmore, 1918.

Djemal Pasha, *Memories of a Turkish Statesman, 1913–1919.* London: Hutchinson and Paternoster Row, n.d.

Documents diplomatiques: Conférence de Lausanne. 2 vols. Paris: Imprimerie nationale, 1923.

Dumont, Paul. *Mustafa Kemal.* Paris: Editions Complexe, 1983.

Eliav, Mordechai. *David Wolffsohn: The Man and His Times.* Tel Aviv/Jerusalem: Institute for Zionist Research/Publishing House of the World Zionist Organization, 1977. (in Hebrew)

Elmaleh, Abraham. *Palestine and Syria During the World War.* Vol. 2. Jerusalem: Mizrah ve Maarav, 1929. (in Hebrew)

Encyclopaedia Judaica. New English ed. 17 vols. Jerusalem: Keter Publishing House, 1972.

Engelhardt, Ed. *La Turquie et le Tanzimat ou histoire des réformes depuis 1826 jusqu'à nos jours.* 2 vols. Paris: A. Cotillon, 1882–1884.

Ettinger, Shmuel, ed. *History of the Jews of Moslem Lands.* 3 vols. Jerusalem: Zalman Shazar Center, 1981–1986. (in Hebrew)

Faitlovitch, Jacques. *Notes d'un voyage chez les Falachas (Juifs d'Abyssinie).* Paris: E. Leroux, 1905.

———. *Gli Ebrei d'Abissinia (Falascia).* Acqui: A. Tirelli, 1907.

Fargeon, Maurice. *Les Juifs en Egypte depuis les origines jusqu'à ce jour.* Cairo: Imprimerie Paul Barbey, 1938.

Fattal, Antoine. *Le statut légal des non-Musulmans en pays d'Islam.* Beirut: Imprimerie catholique, 1958.

Findley, Carter V. *Bureaucratic Reforms in the Ottoman Empire: The Sublime Porte, 1789–1922.* Princeton, N.J.: Princeton University Press, 1980.

Franco, Moïse. *Essai sur l'histoire des Israélites de l'Empire ottoman.* Reprint. Paris: Centre d'Etudes Don Isaac Abravanel/U.I.S.F., 1980.

Fresco, David. *Le Sionisme.* Istanbul: Imprimerie "Fresco," 1909.

Friedman, Isaiah. *The Question of Palestine, 1914–1918: British-Jewish-Arab Relations.* New York: Schocken Books, 1973.

———. *Germany, Turkey, and Zionism, 1897–1918.* Oxford: Clarendon Press, 1977.

Fua, Albert. *Le Comité Union et Progrès contre la Constitution.* Paris: E. Noury, 1911.

Galanté, Abraham. *Documents officiels turcs concernant les Juifs de Turquie.* Istanbul: Haim, Rozio, 1931.

———. *Turcs et Juifs.* Istanbul: Haim, Rozio, 1932.

———. *Abdul Hamid II et le Sionisme.* Istanbul: Fratelli Haim, 1933.

———. *Histoire des Juifs d'Anatolie.* 2 vols. Istanbul: M. Babok, 1937–1939.

———. *Histoire des Juifs d'Istanbul.* 2 vols. Istanbul: Hüsnütabiat, 1941–1942.

Gaon, Moshe David. *The Oriental Jews in Palestine.* Jerusalem: Hoza'at ha-mehaber, 1938. (in Hebrew)

Gerber, Jane. *The Jews of Spain: A History of the Sephardic Experience.* New York: Free Press, 1992.

Girard, Patrick. *Les Juifs de France de 1789 à 1860: De l'émancipation à l'égalité*. Paris: Calmann-Levy, 1976.

Graetz, Michael. *Les Juifs de France au XIXe siècle: De la révolution française à l'Alliance Israélite Universelle*. Translated from the Hebrew by S. Malka. Paris: Seuil, 1989.

Gran Rabinato de Turkia. *Las eleksiones para el medjlis umumi*. Istanbul: "El Korreo," 5671/1910.

Hahamhane Nizamnamesi. Estatuto organiko de la komunidad israelita. Istanbul: Imprimeria Izak Gabai, 5673/1913.

Halévy, Joseph. *Excursion chez les Falachas en Abyssinie*. Paris: Imprimerie de E. Martinet, 1869.

Hertzberg, Arthur. *The French Enlightenment and the Jews*. New York: Schocken Books, 1968.

Israel, Jonathan I. *European Jewry in the Age of Mercantilism, 1550–1750*. 2d ed. Oxford: Clarendon Press, 1989.

Jabotinsky, Vladimir. *Speeches, 1905–1926*. Jerusalem: Hoza'at Sefarim Jabotinski, 5707/1927. (in Hebrew)

Jabotinsky, Zeev. *Correspondence, 1898–1914*. Edited by Daniel Carpi and Moshe Halevy. Jerusalem: Jabotinsky Institute in Israel, Hassifriya Haziyonit, 1992. (in Hebrew)

Juhasz, Esther, ed. *Sephardi Jews in the Ottoman Empire: Aspects of Material Culture*. Jerusalem: Israel Museum, 1990.

Kalderon, Albert E. *Abraham Galante: A Biography*. New York: Sepher-Hermon Press, 1983.

Karpat, Kemal H. *Ottoman Population, 1830–1914*. Madison: University of Wisconsin Press, 1985.

Katz, Jacob. *Out of the Ghetto: The Social Background of Jewish Emancipation, 1700–1870*. Cambridge, Mass.: Harvard University Press, 1973.

Kedourie, Elie, ed. *Spain and the Jews: The Sephardi Experience, 1492 and After*. London: Thames and Hudson, 1992.

Kolatt, Israel, ed. *History of the Jewish Community in Palestine since 1882*. Jerusalem: Israel Academy, Bialik Institute, 1989. (in Hebrew)

La konstitusion para la nasion israelita de Turkia. N.p.: Estamparia Djornal Israelit, 5625/1865.

Krämer, Gudrun. *The Jews in Modern Egypt, 1914–1952*. London: I. B. Tauris, 1989.

Landau, Jacob M. *Pan-Turkism in Turkey: A Study of Irredentism*. London: C. Hurst, 1981.

Laqueur, Walter. *A History of Zionism*. New York: Schocken Books, 1976.

Las, Nelly. *Les Juifs de France et le Sionisme: De l'affaire Dreyfus à la Seconde Guerre mondiale, 1896–1939*. Ph.D. diss., 3d cycle, University of the New Sorbonne—Paris III, 1985.

Leven, Narcisse. *Cinquante ans d'histoire: L'Alliance Israélite Universelle, 1860–1910*. 2 vols. Paris: Alcan and Guillaumin, 1911–1920.

Levy, Avigdor. *The Sephardim in the Ottoman Empire*. Princeton, N.J.: Darwin Press, 1992.

Lewis, Bernard. *The Emergence of Modern Turkey*. London: Oxford University Press, 1965.

————. *The Muslim Discovery of Europe.* London: Weidenfeld and Nicolson, 1982.

————. *The Jews of Islam.* Princeton, N.J.: Princeton University Press, 1984.

McCarthy, Justin. *The Arab World, Turkey, and the Balkans, 1878–1914: A Handbook of Historical Statistics.* Boston: G.K. Hall, 1982.

Mandel, Neville J. *The Arabs and Zionism before World War I.* Berkeley: University of California Press, 1976.

Madelstam, André. *Le sort de l'Empire ottoman.* Lausanne: Payot, 1917.

Mantran, Robert, ed. *Histoire de l'Empire ottoman.* Paris: Fayard, 1989.

Marrus, Michael R. *The Politics of Assimilation: A Study of the French Jewish Community at the Time of the Dreyfus Affair.* Oxford: Clarendon Press, 1971.

Méchoulan, Henry, ed. *Les Juifs d'Espagne: Histoire d'une diaspora, 1492–1992.* Paris: Liana Levi, 1992.

Misiroğlu, Kadir. *Lausanne: Victory or Defeat?* Istanbul: Sebil Yayinevi, 1965. (in Turkish)

Morgenthau, Henry, and French Strother. *All in a Lifetime.* Garden City, N.Y.: Doubleday, Page, 1922.

Moutsopoulos, N. K. *Thessaloniki, 1900–1917.* Greece: Molho Publications, 1981.

Néhama, Joseph. *Histoire des Israélites de Salonique.* 7 vols. Salonika: Durlacher, Molho, 1935–1978.

Nicault, Catherine. *La France et le Sionisme, 1897–1968.* Paris: Calmann-Lévy, 1992.

Nicolaïdes, N. *L'Empire ottoman: Une année de Constitution, 11/24 juillet 1908–11/24 juillet 1909.* Brussels: Th. Dewarichet, 1909.

Öke, Mim Kemal. *Abdülhamid II, the Zionists, and the Palestine Question.* Istanbul: Kervan Yayinlari, 1981. (in Turkish)

————. *Zionism and the Palestine Question.* Istanbul: Üç Dal Neşriyat, 1982. (in Turkish)

Pappenheim, Bertha. *Sisyphus - Arbeit.* Leipzig: Paul E. Linder, 1926.

Pech, Edgar. *Les Alliés et la Turquie, Oct. 1918–Av. 1925.* Paris: Presses Universitaires de France, 1925.

Pinon, René. *L'Europe et la Jeune Turquie: Les aspects nouveaux de la question d'Orient.* 3d ed. Paris: Perrin, 1913.

————. *La question juive devant la conférence de la Paix.* Paris: Alliance Israélite Universelle, 1919.

Polk, William R., and Richard L. Chambers, eds. *Beginnings of Modernization in the Middle East: The Nineteenth Century.* Chicago: University of Chicago Press, 1968.

Ramsaur, E. E. *The Young Turks: Prelude to the Revolution of 1908.* Princeton, N.J.: Princeton University Press, 1957.

Recanati, David, ed. *Memorial of Salonika.* 2 vols. Tel Aviv: Committee for the Publication of Books on the Community of Salonika, 1971–1986. (in Hebrew and French)

Report of District No. 11 to 1920 General Convention (B'nai B'rith). N.p., 1920.

Reports received by the Joint Distribution Committee of Funds for Jewish War Sufferers. New York: n.p., 1916.

Rodrigue, Aron. *French Jews, Turkish Jews: The Alliance Israélite Universelle in Turkey, 1860–1914.* Ph.D. diss., Harvard University, 1985.

————. *Images of Sephardi and Eastern Jewries in Transition. The Teachers of the Alliance Israélite Universelle, 1860–1939.* Seattle: University of Washington Press, 1993.

————. *French Jews, Turkish Jews: The Alliance Israélite Universelle and the Politics of Jewish Schooling in Turkey, 1860–1925.* Bloomington: Indiana University Press, 1990.

————, ed. *Ottoman and Turkish Jewry: Community and Leadership.* Indiana University Turkish Studies. Bloomington: Indiana University Press, 1992.

Rosanvallon, Pierre. *L'État en France de 1789 à nos jours.* Paris: Seuil, 1990.

Rozanes, Salomon A. *History of the Jews of Turkey and the Middle East.* 6 vols. Jerusalem: Rav Kook Institute, 1907–1945. (in Hebrew)

Said, Edward W. *Orientalism.* New York: Pantheon Books, 1978.

Salonika, mother-town in Israel. Tel Aviv: Research Centre on Salonika Jewry et alii, 1967. (in Hebrew)

Scheinkine, M. *Lettre ouverte aux communautés juives de Turquie.* Jaffa: Imprimerie A. Itine, 22 Adar 5671/ 22 March 1911. (in French and Hebrew)

Schneiderman, Harry, and Itzhak J. Carmin, eds. *Who's Who in World Jewry.* New York: Monde Publishers, 1955.

Schopoff, A. *Les réformes et la protection des Chrétiens en Turquie, 1673–1904.* Paris: Plon, 1904.

Shaw, Stanford J. *The Jews of the Ottoman Empire and the Turkish Republic.* New York: New York University Press, 1991.

Shaw, Stanford J., and Ezel Kural Shaw. *History of the Ottoman Empire and Modern Turkey.* Reprint. 2 vols. Cambridge: Cambridge University Press, 1978.

Sokolow, Nahum. *History of Zionism, 1600–1918.* 2 vols. London: Longmans/ Green, 1919.

Stern, Selma. *The Court Jew.* Philadelphia: Jewish Publication Society, 5710/1950.

Stillman, Norman. *The Jews of Arab Lands.* Philadelphia: Jewish Publication Society, 1979.

————. *The Jews of Arab Lands in Modern Times.* Philadelphia: Jewish Publication Society, 5751–1991.

Straus, Oscar S. *Under Four Administrations: From Cleveland to Taft.* Boston: Houghton Mifflin/Riverside Press, 1922.

Thobie, Jacques. *Intérêts et impérialisme français dans l'Empire ottoman, 1895–1914.* Paris: Publications de la Sorbonne, 1977.

Trask, R. Roger. *The United States Response to Turkish Nationalism and Reform, 1914–1939.* Minneapolis: University of Minnesota Press, 1971.

Tunaya, Tarik Zafer. *The Political Parties in Turkey.* 2 vols. Istanbul: Hürriyet Vakfi Yayinlari, 1984–1986. (in Turkish)

Vital, David. *The Origins of Zionism.* Oxford: Clarendon Press, 1980.

————. *Zionism: The Formative Years.* Oxford: Clarendon Press, 1982.

————. *Zionism: The Crucial Phase.* Oxford: Clarendon Press, 1987.

Weber, Frank G. *Eagles on the Crescent: Germany, Austria, and the Diplomacy of the Turkish Alliance, 1914–1918.* Ithaca: Cornell University Press, 1970.

Weizmann, Chaim. *The Letters and Papers.* Vols. 7, 9, 11. London: Oxford University Press, 1968.

Who's Who in Egypt and the Middle East. Cairo: Imprimerie Française, 1950–1959.

Wininger, S. *Grosse Jüdische National-Biographie.* Vol. 1. N.p.: Druck "Orient," n.d.

Young, George. *Corps de droit ottoman.* Vol. 2. Oxford: Clarendon Press, 1905.

Articles

Ahmad, Feroz. "Unionist Relations with the Greek, Armenian, and Jewish Communities of the Ottoman Empire, 1908–1914." In *Christians and Jews in the Ottoman Empire,* edited by Benjamin Braude and Bernard Lewis, vol. 1, 401–34. New York: Holmes and Meier, 1982.

Albert Cohen, Phyllis. "Ethnicité et solidarité chez les Juifs de France au XIXe siècle." *Pardès* 3 (1986): 29–53.

Attrep, Abe. "'A State of Wretchedness and Impotence': A British View of Istanbul and Turkey, 1919." *International Journal of Middle East Studies* 9 (February 1978): 1–9.

Barnai, Ya'akov. "The Status of the 'General Rabbinate' of Jerusalem in the Ottoman Period." *Cathedra* 13 (1980): 47–69. (in Hebrew)

———. "Jews in the Ottoman Empire." In *History of the Jews in Islamic Lands: Contemporary Period, Up to the Mid-Nineteenth Century,* edited by Shmuel Ettinger, vol. 1, 73–118. Jerusalem: Zalman Shazar Center, 1981. (in Hebrew)

———. "Jews in the Ottoman Empire." In *History of the Jews in Islamic Lands: From the Mid-Nineteenth to the Mid-Twentieth Century,* edited by Shmuel Ettinger, vol. 2, 183–297. Jerusalem: Zalman Shazar Center, 1986. (in Hebrew)

Benbassa, Esther. "L'Alliance Israélite Universelle et l'élection de Haim Nahum au grand rabbinat de l'Empire ottoman, 1908–1909." In *Proceedings of the Ninth World Congress of Jewish Studies,* 83–90. Jerusalem: World Union of Jewish Studies, 1986.

———. "Presse d'Istanbul et de Salonique au service du sionisme, 1908–1914: Les motifs d'une allégeance." *Revue Historique* 276/2 (560), (October–December 1986): 337–65.

———. "Israël face à lui-même: Judaïsme occidental et Judaïsme ottoman, xixe–xxe siècles." *Pardès* 7 (1988): 105–29.

———. "Zionism in the Ottoman Empire at the End of the Nineteenth and the Beginning of the Twentieth Century." *Studies in Zionism* 11 (2), (Autumn 1990): 127–40.

———. "Le procès des sonneurs de tocsin: Une accusation calomnieuse de meutre rituel à Izmir en 1901." In *Society and Community: Proceedings of the Second International Congress for Research of the Sephardi and Oriental Jewish Heritage, 1984,* edited by Abraham Haim, 35–53. Jerusalem: Misgav Yerushalayim, 1991.

———. "Education for Jewish Girls in the East: A Portrait of the Galata School in Istanbul, 1879–1912." In *Studies in Contemporary Jewry,* edited by Ezra Mendelsohn, vol. 9, 163–173. Oxford: Oxford University Press, 1993.

———. "Les 'Jeunes-Turcs' et les Juifs, 1908–1914." In *Mélanges offerts à Louis Bazin par ses disciples, collègues, et amis,* edited by Jean-Louis Bacqué-Grammont, Rémy Dor, et al., 311–19. Paris: L'Harmattan, 1992.

———. "Processus de modernisation en terre sépharade." In *La Société juive à travers l'histoire,* edited by Shmuel Trigano, vol. 1, 565–605. Paris: Fayard, 1992.

———. "Zionism and the Politics of Coalition in the Ottoman Jewish Communities in the Early Twentieth Century." In *Ottoman and Turkish Jewry, Community, and Leadership,* edited by Aron Rodrigue, 221–51. Indiana University Turkish Studies 12. Bloomington: Indiana University Press, 1992.

Benbassa, Esther, and Aron Rodrigue. "L'artisanat juif en Turquie à la fin du XIXe siècle: l'Alliance Israélite Universelle et ses oeuvres d'apprentissage." *Turcica* 17 (1985): 113–26.

Burrows, Matthew. "'Mission civilisatrice': French Cultural Policy in the Middle East, 1860–1914." *Historical Journal* 29 (1), (1986): 109–35.

Davison, Roderic H. "Turkish Attitudes Concerning Christian Muslim Equality in the Nineteenth Century." *American Historical Review* 59 (1954): 844–64.

Dumont, Paul. "La condition juive en Turquie à la fin du XIXe siècle." *Les Nouveaux Cahiers* 57 (Summer 1979): 25–38.

———. "Un communauté en quête d'avenir: Le sionisme à Istanbul au lendemain de la première guerre mondiale (d'après *La Nation,* organe de la Fédération sioniste d'Orient, 1919–1922"). In *Les Juifs dans la Méditerranée médiévale et moderne.* Proceedings of a study group at Nice on 25 and 26 May 1983, University of Nice, Centre de la Méditerranée Moderne et Contemporaine. Nice: Centre d'études médiévales, 1986.

Eliav, Mordekhai. "German Interests and the Jewish Community in Nineteenth-Century Palestine." In *Studies in Palestine during the Ottoman Period,* edited by Moshe Ma'oz, 423–41. Jerusalem: Magnes Press/Yad Izhak Ben-Zvi, 1975.

Elmaleh, Abraham. "Rabbi Haim Nahoum: Sa vie, ses oeuvres." *Le Judaisme Séphardi* 22 (August 1961): 946–48.

Farhi, David. "Documents on the Attitude of the Ottoman Government towards the Jewish Settlement in Palestine after the Revolution of the Young Turks, 1908–1909." In *Studies in Palestine during the Ottoman Period,* edited by Moshe Ma'oz, 190–210. Jerusalem: Magnes Press/Yad Izhak Ben-Zvi, 1975.

———. "The Jews of Salonika during the 'Young Turk' Revolution." *Sefunot* 15 (1971–1981): 137–52. (in Hebrew)

Frankel, Jonathan. "Crisis as a Factor in Modern Jewish Politics, 1840 and 1881–82." In *Living with Antisemitism: Modern Jewish Responses,* edited by Jehuda Reinharz, 42–58. Hanover, N.H.: University Press of New England, 1987.

Friedman, Isaiah. "German Intervention on behalf of the Yishuv, 1917." *Jewish Social Studies* 33 (1) (January 1971): 23–43.

———. "The Hilfsverein, the German Minister of Foreign Affairs, and the Polemic with the Zionists, 1908–1911." *Cathedra* 20 (July 1981): 96–122. (in Hebrew)

Hacker, Joseph R. "The Chief Rabbinate in the Ottoman Empire in the Sixteenth and Seventeenth Centuries." *Zion* 49 (3), (1984): 225–63. (in Hebrew)

Haim, Abraham. "The Chief Rabbi of Istanbul and the Rabbinical War in Jerusalem." *Pe'amim* 12 (1982): 105–13. (in Hebrew)

Hanioğlu, M. Şükrü. "Genesis of the Young Turk Revolution of 1908." *Osmanli Arastirmalari/The Journal of Ottoman Studies* 3 (1982): 277–300.

———. "Ottomanism." In *Encyclopaedia of Turkey, from the Reform to the Republic.* Vol. 5, 1389–90. Istanbul: Iletişim Yayinlari, 1985. (in Turkish)

"The Imperial Sanction for the Ratification of the Post as Chief Rabbi of Haim Nahum effendi." In *Dûstûr. Terbib II, C1. Dersaadet: Matbaa-i Osmanive,* no. 95 (1329/1911): 351–54. (in Ottoman)

Kaufman, Edy. "The French Pro-Zionist Declaration of 1917–1918." *Middle Eastern Studies* 15 (3), (May 1979): 374–407.

Kedourie, Elie. "Young Turks, Freemasons, and Jews." *Middle Eastern Studies* 7 (1), (January 1971): 89–104.

Landau, Jacob M. "The 'Young Turks' and Zionism: Some Comments." In *Studies in Honor of Raphael Patai,* edited by Victor D. Sanua, 197–205. Rutherford, N.J.: Fairleigh Dickinson University Press, 1983.

Laskier, Michael. "Abraham Antebi, Aspects of his Activity in the Period 1879–1914." *Pe'amim* 21 (1984): 50–82. (in Hebrew)

Lazare, Lucien. "L'Alliance israélite universelle en Palestine à l'époque de la révolution des 'Jeunes Turcs' et sa mission en Orient du 29 octobre 1908 au 19 janvier 1909." *Revue des Etudes Juives* 138 (July–December 1979): 307–35.

Mandel, Neville J. "Turks, Arabs, and Jewish Immigration into Palestine, 1882–1914." *St. Antony's Papers* 17 (1965): 77–108.

———. "Ottoman Policy and Restrictions on Jewish Settlement in Palestine, 1881–1908, Part I." *Middle Eastern Studies* 10 (3), (1974): 312–32.

———. "Ottoman Practice as Regards Jewish Settlement in Palestine, 1881–1908." *Middle Eastern Studies* 11 (1), (January 1975): 33–46.

Mani, M. "A la mémoire du Grand Rabbin Nahoum." *Journal des Communautés* 251, 4 December 1960, pp. 5–7. (Speech)

Mendes Flohr, Paul. *"Fin-de-siècle* Orientalism, the *Ostjuden,* and the Aesthetics of Jewish Self-Affirmation." In *Studies in Contemporary Jewry,* edited by Jonathan Frankel, vol. 1, 96–139. Bloomington: Indiana University Press, 1984.

Mevorah, Baruh. "The Role of the Damascus Affair in the Expansion of the Jewish Press, 1840–1846." *Zion* 23–24 (1958–1959): 47–65. (in Hebrew)

Molho, Rena. "The Jewish Community of Salonika and Its Incorporation into the Greek State." *Middle Eastern Studies* 24 (4), (October 1988): 391–403.

Nahoum, Haim. "Mission chez les Falachas d'Abyssinie." *Bulletin de l'Alliance Israélite Universelle* 33 (1908): 100–37.

———. "Jews." In *Modern Turkey,* edited by Eliot Grinnell Mears, 86–97. New York: Macmillan, 1924.

Öke, Mim Kemal. "The Ottoman Empire, Zionism, and the Question of Palestine, 1880–1908." *International Journal of Middle East Studies* 14 (1982): 329–41.

———. "Young Turks, Freemasons, Jews, and the Question of Zionism in the Ottoman Empire, 1908–1913." *Studies in Zionism* 7 (2), (1986): 53–73.

Rabinovitz, Ya'akov. "The New Turkey, the Jews, and Zionism." *Ha-Shiloah* 19 (1908): 280–88, 456–61, 548–57. (in Hebrew)

Rodrigue, Aron. "The Alliance Israélite Universelle and the Attempt to Reform Rabbinical and Religious Instruction in Turkey." In *L'"Alliance" et les communautés du bassin méditerranéen à la fin du XIXe siècle et son influence sur la situation sociale et culturelle,* edited by Simon Schwarzfuchs, liii–lxx. Jerusalem: Misgav Yerushalayim, 1987.

———. "Abraham de Camondo of Istanbul: The Transformation of Jewish Philanthropy." In *From East and West: Jews in a Changing Europe, 1750–1870,* edited by Frances Malino and David Sorkin, 46–56. Oxford: Basil Blackwell, 1990.

Sharaby, Rachel. "The Chief Rabbinate of Jerusalem: Conflicts and Personalities, 1906–1914." *Cathedra* 37 (September 1985): 95–121. (in Hebrew)

Shaw, Stanford J. "The Ottoman Census System and Population, 1831–1914." *International Journal of Middle Eastern Studies* 9 (1978): 325–38.

———. "The Population of Istanbul in the Nineteenth Century." *Turk Tarih Dergisi* 32 (1979): 403–14.

Shmuelevitz, Aryeh. "Two Hebrew-Language Weeklies in Turkey: An Appeal to Revive the Concept of a National Culture." In *Actes du colloque: La presse de langue étrangère en Turquie* (16, 17, 18 May 1984), 111–25. Istanbul: Istanbul Universitesi Yayinlari/Basin-Yayin Yüksekokulu Yayinlari, 1985.

Szajkowski, Zosa. "The Alliance Israélite Universelle in the United States, 1860–1949." *Publications of the American Jewish Historical Society* 29, pt. 4 (June 1950): 389–443.

———. "Conflicts in the Alliance Israélite Universelle and the Founding of the Anglo-Jewish Association, the Vienna Allianz, and the *Hilfsverein.*" *Jewish Social Studies* 19 (1–2), (January–April 1957): 29–50.

Thobie, Jacques. "La France a-t-elle une politique culturelle dans l'Empire ottoman à la veille de la première guerre mondiale?" *Relations Internationales* 25 (Spring 1981): 21–40.

Valensi, Lucette. "La tour de Babel: Groupes et relations ethniques au Moyen-Orient et en Afrique du Nord." *Annales* 4 (July–August 1986): 817–35.

Verete, Mayir. "The Balfour Declaration and Its Makers." In *Palestine and Israel in the Nineteenth and Twentieth Centuries,* edited by Elie Kedourie and Sylvia G. Haim, 60–88. London: Frank Cass, 1982.

Weill, Georges. "Charles Netter ou les oranges de Jaffa." *Les Nouveaux Cahiers* 21 (Summer 1970): 2–36.

———. "Emancipation et humanisme: Le discours idéologique de l'Alliance Israélite Universelle au XIXe siècle." *Les Nouveaux Cahiers* 52 (Spring 1978): 1–20.

———. "L'action éducative de l'Alliance Israélite Universelle de 1860 à 1914." *Les Nouveaux Cahiers* 78 (Autumn 1984): 51–58.

———. "L'Alliance Israélite Universelle et la condition sociale des communautés méditerranéennes à la fin du XIXe siècle, 1860–1914." In *L'"Alliance" dans les communautés du bassin méditerranéen à la fin du XIXe siècle et son influence sur la situation sociale et culturelle,* edited by Simon Schwarzfuchs, vii–lii. Jerusalem: Misgav Yerushalayim, 1987.

Yale, William. "Ambassador Henry Morgenthau's Special Mission of 1917." *World Politics* 1 (3) (1949): 308–20.

INDEX

Some frequently used words were not included in the index, such as Alliance Israélite Universelle, Ottoman Empire, Nahum, Haim, Turkey, and so forth.